Making the most of
Everyday Ingredients

ROBERT CARRIER'S KITCHEN

Making the most of
Everyday
Ingredients

Marshall Cavendish   London Sydney & New York

Editor	Roz Fishel
Editorial Staff	Caroline Macy
	Penny Smith
	Kate Toner
Art Editor	Ross George
Series Editor	Pepita Aris
Production Executive	Robert Paulley
Production Controller	Steve Roberts

Photography
Bryce Attwell: 9, 11, 12, 32, 38, 60
Paul Bussell: 13, 16, 34, 43, 64, 66, 67, 68, 72, 75, 78, 80, 89, 93, 94, 96, 108, 109
Alan Duns: 51
Laurie Evans: 18, 24, 55
Melvin Grey: 36
James Jackson: 15, 22, 46
Chris Knaggs: 21, 65, 84, 107
David Levin: 39, 40, 101
Vernon Morgan: 61
Peter Myers: 10, 12 (lower), 20, 27, 29, 30, 48, 56, 60 (lower), 83, 106, 110
Roger Phillips: 28, 49, 81, 82, 91, 101
Paul Webster: 35, 63, 98, 100
Andrew Whittuck: 88
Paul Williams: 14, 25, 41, 44, 52, 58, 70, 86, 87, 92, 102, 103, 104, 105
Peter Williams: 50, 74 (lower)
Cover picture: **Roger Phillips**

Weights and measures
Both metric and imperial measurements are given. As these are not exact equivalents, please work from one set of figures or the other. Use graded measuring spoons levelled across.

Time symbols
The time needed to prepare the dish is given on each recipe. The symbols are as follows:

 simple to prepare and cook

 straightforward but requires more skill or attention

 time-consuming to prepare or requires extra skill

must be started 1 day or more ahead

On the cover: a selection of everyday ingredients

This edition published 1985
© Marshall Cavendish Limited 1985

Printed in Italy by
L.E.G.O. S.p.a. Vicenza

Typeset by Quadraset Limited, Midsomer Norton, Bath, Avon

Published by Marshall Cavendish House
58 Old Compton Street London W1V 5PA
ISBN 0 86307 264 X (series)
ISBN 0 86307 403 0 (this volume)

Contents

Just how much versatility there is in food products we happily call 'everyday ingredients' can be seen in this latest volume of my new cookery series. Who would have thought there were so many unusual recipes one could make with eggs, butter, cream and yoghurt, for example? Why not try Poached eggs provençale — poached eggs on crispy croûtons covered with tangy anchovy paste — or thick Yoghurt and lemon soup?

Dairy products are not only nutritious and economical but butter and cream in particular often add that essential taste of luxury to recipes. Smoked salmon butter, for example, will make sole extra delicious. The cream in my Chicken, cream and celery recipe makes a simple dish into a special one. And, for the health conscious, why not make your own yoghurt? It's easier than you may think and I will show you how.

My section on staples — flour, rice, pulses, wheat, oats, cereals, tea, coffee and oils — tells you all you need to know about the regular stock in your kitchen cupboard. My reference guide provides accessible information on the different types of these basics: how to identify them, store them and cook them, as well as some of their fascinating historical uses. Again, I hope my recipes give you some new ideas: Rich corn bread, a semi-sweet cake bread, takes only forty minutes preparation time. Basque rice with mussels, a kind of spicy *paella*, is a colourful dish with red pepper, prawns, spicy pork sausage, mushrooms and shallot, as well as mussels. Pulses, now increasingly fashionable, can be cooked in a number of ways. Try Boston baked beans — haricot beans with salt pork and treacle — which is guaranteed to be a success with the family.

Honey, syrups and treacle offer an alternative sweetening to ordinary sugar. Try Honey-glazed carrots with coriander, or Veal cutlets with apple and port which includes clear honey. My section on sweet ingredients gives you temperatures and tests for boiling sugar so that you can make your own syrups, fudges and toffees. Chocolate recipes are also included — what about treating yourself to some Rum truffles? Also, did you know that chocolate is used in savoury dishes in the cuisine of various countries, most often with game. The amount added is tiny but it enriches the sauce in an interesting way. I've included it in a recipe for Rabbit casserole.

A good reference guide to herbs and spices is essential for any cook. Just listing the galaxy of flavourings available makes you want to experiment. Spinach and chervil soup, a rich green soup served with sour cream, or Liver with sage and Madeira sauce are both simple and quick to make and also tempting to try. So is home-made Sweet chilli tomato chutney to serve with curries. Finally, my section on nuts — almonds, peanuts, cashews, walnuts, chestnuts and others — contains such mouth-watering recipes as Beef saté with peanut sauce, Coconut salad, Stir-fried chicken with cashew nuts and Walnut and orange cake — all designed to make meal times something really special.

Happy cooking and bon appétit!

Robert Carrier

Eggs & Dairy Products

ALL ABOUT EGGS

As well as being one of the most versatile — and economical — ingredients on hand in your kitchen, eggs have the added virtue of being one of the most nutritious foods you can buy.

Eggs are one of the highest protein foods and they provide essential fats, minerals and vitamins. As they are low in carbohydrates they are ideal food for slimmers — one medium-sized uncooked egg contains only about 85 calories. Although brown-shelled eggs are often said to be better for you, their advantage is purely cosmetic — the food value being exactly the same as that of eggs with white shells.

In the recipes in this chapter I use hens' eggs (large-sized ones, unless otherwise stated), but there are several other kinds of eggs you can buy:

Duck and goose eggs can often be purchased from poulterers. They are larger — goose eggs may weigh up to 200 g /7 oz — and richer than hens' eggs and have a higher fat content. As they are more porous than hens' eggs, they are more likely to be contaminated and it is important to destroy any harmful bacteria that may have penetrated the shell by thoroughly cooking the eggs. They are therefore not suitable for any dish which is cooked briefly or at a low temperature. Boil duck eggs for at least 10 minutes, goose eggs for slightly longer.

Guinea fowl and bantam eggs are small and delicately flavoured. They can be cooked by any method suitable for hens' eggs, but cooking times should be slightly reduced.

Plover and quail eggs, which are about the size of a large cherry, are considered a delicacy and are usually served boiled or poached as an hors d'oeuvre or garnish.

Gulls' eggs, unlike the eggs of other sea birds, do not have a fishy taste. They are available from poulterers in season.

Buying and storing eggs

Eggs are graded by weight (see chart). In EEC countries, egg packs are stamped with the week in which they were packed, Week I being the first week in January. Eggs should be bought before they are two weeks old. Check the date stamp on the pack. Some people prefer to buy free-range eggs and these can be found in good health food stores. Do not buy eggs displayed in the window, as light impairs their quality.

Store eggs in a dark place pointed end down so that the air pocket remains at the broad end. As the shells are porous, keep eggs away from strong-smelling foods. Fresh, uncracked eggs will keep for several days at room temperature and for up to three weeks in the refrigerator.

Refrigerate separated eggs and left-over beaten egg in tightly closed containers. Cover unbroken yolks with a layer of water to prevent them hardening. Use yolks and beaten egg within 3 days, whites within 4.

Freeze only fresh, raw eggs out of their shells, as the shells crack when frozen. To freeze whole eggs, place small, waxed paper cases on a baking tray and break an egg into each; cover, freeze, then pack.

When freezing egg yolks add 5 ml /1 tsp salt or 10 ml /2 tsp sugar to every six yolks (depending on whether they are to be used for a savoury or sweet dish), or 1.5 ml /¼ tsp salt or sugar if freezing yolks singly, to prevent thickening. Egg whites need no addition. They freeze well and can even be whisked to stiff peaks after defrosting.

Raw eggs, whole or separated, freeze for 8–10 months. As a guide, 15 ml /1 tbls thawed yolk is equivalent to a medium-sized fresh yolk, and 30 ml /2 tbls thawed egg white to a medium-sized fresh white.

Testing eggs for freshness

If an egg is very stale it will smell bad and should be discarded. Always break eggs separately into a cup before use so that a bad one will not ruin the rest. Test an egg by placing it on its side in a bowl of cold water; a very fresh egg will remain horizontal on the bottom. A week-old egg will tilt; a 2- to 3-week-old egg will stand upright. If it floats, it is stale.

Using eggs in cooking

Eggs have many culinary uses; yolks thicken and enrich, while the effect of whisked egg whites is to lighten and increase volume. Eggs are also used raw, as a binding agent, or in drinks such as Egg flip (see recipe).

Beaten eggs act as raising agents in a variety of dishes — cakes, steamed and baked puddings and mousses. They are used to thicken sauces, soups and custards, and to bind dry mixtures (for rissoles, croquettes, fishcakes and rich pastry doughs, for instance). Food intended for deep frying is dipped in beaten egg and then in breadcrumbs to give it a protective coating. Bread, buns and pastries can be brushed with beaten egg before baking to give a rich golden glaze. Beaten egg is also used to seal pastry layers and pie trimmings.

Egg yolks will form an emulsion with oil or melted butter, providing the base for mayonnaise or hollandaise and related sauces. Egg yolks feature in some rich cake fillings and icings, and they are used to bind ground almonds and sugar for almond paste.

Eggs can be used in so many different recipes

Egg whites are used for meringues and meringue-based desserts — fruit Pavlovas and some ice creams, for instance. They are beaten with icing sugar to make Royal icing, and with sugar syrup to make American cake frostings. Whisked egg whites lighten and aerate sweet and savoury mousses and soufflés, fruit snows and iced sorbets, as well as unbaked cheesecakes, chiffon pies and other cream- and gelatine-based confections. Both whisking and folding in egg whites require care and skill.

You can give fruit such as cherries or grapes, or the rims of glasses, an attractive frosting by dipping them in lightly beaten egg white, then in caster sugar. Lightly beaten egg white and crushed egg shells are used to clarify aspics, consommés and fresh fruit jellies.

Egg garnishes: use cold, shelled hard-boiled eggs; cut them across into thin slices, either with a sharp knife or a special egg-slicer, or lengthways into wedges; arrange in a pattern on top of a dish, or round the edge of a serving platter. (Hard-boiled egg is a traditional garnish for borscht, the Russian beetroot soup.) Or finely chop hard-boiled eggs and scatter them over the surface of a fish or vegetable dish. For a mimosa garnish, sieve the yolks and finely chop the whites: this is good with an egg mayonnaise starter.

Techniques with eggs

Separating eggs: crack the egg smartly against the side of a bowl. With your thumbs, prise the shell in half, leaving the yolk in the bottom half, and let the white drip into the bowl below. Gently tip the yolk from one half shell to the other until all the white is drained off; slip the yolk into a separate container.

There is another way to separate eggs which is simpler and therefore a good method for children to use. First break the egg onto a rounded plate or saucer. Then place an egg-cup over the yolk, being careful not to break it. Tip the white into a bowl and keep the yolk in another container.

Whisking egg whites: very fresh egg whites and eggs over 2 weeks old do not whisk well. They should be at least 2–3 days old. Allow the egg whites to come to room temperature before whisking and make sure they do not contain even a speck of yolk.

Use a balloon whisk or a hand-held electric mixer. (A rotary whisk or electric table-top mixer will do, but the volume will be reduced.) An unlined copper bowl is ideal — the acidity of the metal stabilizes the egg whites and helps give maximum volume. Make sure you do not use aluminium which can impart a greyish tinge. Select a wide, shallow bowl if using a balloon whisk, or a deep narrow bowl in the case of a hand-held or rotary whisk.

Both whisk and bowl must be perfectly clean and dry — any trace of moisture or grease will prevent the whites from reaching full volume. Stand the bowl on a damp cloth so that it does not slip during whisking.

Whisk slowly until the whites begin to foam, add a pinch of salt or cream of tartar (this helps the whisked egg whites hold their maximum volume longer). Increase speed and when the whites begin to stiffen, start

testing: lift some of the egg white on the whisk — when it holds a drooping peak it has reached the 'soft peak stage'. For the 'stiff peak stage' whisk for a few minutes more until the whites stand up from the whisk in a stiff pyramid. Stop when you reach this stage as beyond this point you will be whisking air out of the whites.

Use egg whites immediately they reach the required stage — they will separate if left to stand. (You can whisk them up again, but their volume will be reduced.) This is particularly important when making mousses.

Folding in egg whites: scoop the whisked egg whites on top of the mixture into which they are to be incorporated. This prevents the air bubbles in the whisked whites from bursting. Using a spatula or large metal spoon held on its side, cut down from the centre to the bottom of the bowl. Turn the spoon and draw it towards you and up the side of the bowl. Lift the spoon out of the mixture and back over to the centre. Continue cutting and folding, using quick, light strokes, while slowly rotating the bowl until the whites are just incorporated.

If the mixture to be folded in is very stiff, stir up to a quarter of the whisked whites into it to loosen it first.

Cooking and serving eggs

Eggs can be prepared as dishes in their own right in a variety of ways. They can be scrambled (see basic recipe, with imaginative variations), boiled, as in Breakfast eggs (see recipe), fried, poached, as in stylish Poached eggs provençale (see recipe), and baked, as in smooth, delicious Baked egg custard (see recipe). Eggs can also be made into tempting main-course dishes such as my Hot curried eggs or savoury Egg mousse.

The key to success with eggs is gentle cooking. Too high a heat toughens eggs, making them rubbery. The only exception is deep-fried eggs which require very hot oil to puff and crisp the whites.

If you keep eggs in the refrigerator, allow them to come to room temperature before using; otherwise the yolk tends to beak and the white will not whisk up well.

Soft-boiled eggs: eggs should in fact never be boiled, but simmered for between 3½ and 4½ minutes. Soft-boiled egg with hot toast makes a nourishing breakfast.

Hard-boiled eggs: place the eggs in a saucepan, cover them with cold water and bring the water to the boil. Reduce the heat so that the water barely simmers and cook for 6 minutes for small, 7 minutes for medium-sized and 8 minutes for large eggs. Add 2 minutes to these times if the eggs are very fresh. (To centre the yolks in eggs which are going to be stuffed, turn the eggs over once or twice with a metal spoon at the first sign of boiling.)

When the eggs are cooked, immediately drain them and plunge them into cold water (to prevent a blue ring from forming around the yolk). Do not cut the hard yolk with a carbon steel knife because it discolours.

Shelled hard-boiled eggs make ideal food for packed meals and are excellent sliced into salads. Chopped hard-boiled egg, bound with mayonnaise, is a lovely filling for sandwiches. Wrapped in sausage-meat and deep-fried, hard-boiled eggs become Scotch eggs — another picnic favourite.

Fried and scrambled eggs: ring the changes by serving fried eggs on a bed of savoury rice or beans instead of with the usual fried potatoes. In Denmark a favourite starter is cold, lightly scrambled eggs mixed with mayonnaise.

Poached eggs: in England these are usually served plain for breakfast, on buttered toast, but for a superb lunch try my Poached eggs florentine with spinach and cheese.

Baked eggs: baking is one of the oldest methods of cooking eggs. Today eggs are usually baked in individual ramekins or cocottes, with a topping of cream or melted butter. They are also very attractive baked in hollowed out tomatoes or baked potatoes.

Breakfast eggs

🍴 15 minutes

Serves 4
8 medium-sized eggs
25 g /1 oz soft butter
salt and freshly ground black pepper
fingers of hot toast, to serve

1 Soft-boil the eggs by cooking them in barely bubbling water for 3½ minutes, or 4–4½ minutes if they are very fresh.
2 As soon as the time is up, lift the eggs out of the water with a slotted spoon and slice off the top of each egg with a knife. Use a spoon to scoop 2 eggs into each of 4 glasses, keeping the yolks whole, if possible.
3 Top each serving with a quarter of the butter and season with a pinch of salt and pepper. Serve with fingers of hot toast.

Hot curried eggs

🍴🍴 hard-boiling the eggs, then 1 hour

Serves 4
6 eggs, hard-boiled, plunged in cold water and left until cold
25 g /1 oz butter
1½ medium-sized onions, finely chopped
23 ml /1½ tbls flour
10 ml /2 tsp curry powder
600 ml /1 pt hot chicken stock, home-made or from a cube
60 ml /4 tbls thick cream
5 ml /1 tsp mango chutney (avoiding the pieces of mango)
a few drops of lemon juice
boiled rice, to serve
salt and freshly ground black pepper
7.5–15 ml /½–1 tbls finely chopped fresh parsley, to garnish

1 Shell the hard-boiled eggs and cut them in half lengthways.
2 Melt the butter in a heavy-based sauce-pan and sauté the finely chopped onion for about 10 minutes, until soft and golden. Stir

Egg mousse

in the flour and curry powder and cook for a further 2–3 minutes.
3 Gradually add the chicken stock, stirring vigorously to prevent lumps forming. Bring to the boil, stirring continuously, then simmer gently, uncovered, for 30 minutes.
4 Remove the pan from the heat, beat in the thick cream, mango chutney and lemon juice. Season to taste with salt and freshly ground black pepper.
5 Carefully place the halved hard-boiled eggs in the sauce and spoon the sauce over them. Return the pan to the heat and heat through gently for 3–4 minutes.
6 Serve the curried eggs on a bed of boiled rice, sprinkled with finely chopped parsley.

Egg mousse

🍴🍴 30 minutes draining for the cucumber, then 30–40 minutes, plus chilling

Serves 6 as a starter, 4 as a main course
225 g /8 oz cucumber, peeled, seeded and finely chopped
salt
3 hard-boiled eggs, finely chopped
2 spring onions (including the green tops), finely chopped
45 ml /3 tbls finely chopped fresh parsley
175 ml /6 fl oz well-seasoned mayonnaise
50 ml /2 fl oz natural yoghurt
10 ml /2 tsp powdered gelatine
freshly ground black pepper
1 medium-sized egg white
For the garnish
6–8 anchovy fillets, soaked in milk for 10 minutes, drained and split lengthways
2 hard-boiled eggs, sliced
slivers of spring onion tops
fresh parsley leaves

1 Sprinkle the cucumber lightly with salt and toss well; turn into a colander, weighted down with a plate, and leave to drain for at least 30 minutes. Remove the plate and press the cucumber gently to extract any remaining liquid from it.
2 Turn the cucumber into a bowl, add the chopped eggs, spring onions and parsley and

mix well. In a large bowl, blend the mayonnaise and yoghurt.
3 Sprinkle the gelatine over 45 ml /3 tbls water in a small, heavy-based saucepan and leave to soak for 5 minutes; set the pan over a very low heat for 2–3 minutes until the gelatine is completely dissolved. Remove it from the heat.
4 Stir a few spoonfuls of the mayonnaise mixture into the dissolved gelatine, then pour onto the bulk of the mixture in the bowl, stirring continuously. Stir in the egg and cucumber mixture and season to taste with black pepper. Chill until it is just beginning to thicken.
5 In a clean, dry bowl whisk the egg white until soft peaks form, and fold it into the egg mousse. Turn the mousse into a serving bowl and chill for 2–3 hours until set. Just before serving, arrange the split anchovies, lattice fashion, over the top of the mousse and place slices of hard-boiled egg around the edge. Garnish with spring onion and parsley, then serve chilled.

Scrambled eggs

🍴 10 minutes

Serves 4
9 eggs
salt and freshly ground white pepper
60 ml /4 tbls thick cream or water
50 g /2 oz butter

1 Break the eggs into a bowl. Add salt and freshly ground white pepper to taste and mix well with a fork to combine the yolks and whites. Stir in the thick cream or water.
2 Select a heavy pan in which to cook the eggs — either a wide saucepan or a deep frying-pan. Reserve a little less than 15 g /½ oz butter. Place the rest of the butter in a pan and heat until the butter is sizzling but not

How to poach eggs

Break an egg into a cup, then slip it into the water. Repeat, quickly and carefully, with 1 or 2 more eggs. Make a mental note of the order in which you put them in the pan.

coloured. Swirl the butter around so that it coats the base and sides of the pan.

3 Quickly pour in the egg mixture, set the pan over a low heat and immediately start stirring with a wooden spoon. Keep stirring, making sure the spoon reaches the corners of the pan, and keeping all of the egg mixture on the move for the whole of the cooking time. Continue to stir over a gentle heat until the egg mixture is thick and creamy and almost set.

4 Remove the pan from the heat and stir for a few seconds until the egg is lightly set. Next, quickly flake the reserved butter onto the egg and fold it in. Add a little more salt and freshly ground white pepper, if necessary, and serve immediately.

● You can serve plain scrambled eggs, or any of the following variations:
● Cut 175 g /6 oz smoked salmon into strips. Gently toss the strips in the butter for a few seconds before adding the stirred eggs. Cook the eggs in the normal way, then, just before serving, stir in a few drops of lemon juice and 45 ml /3 tbls finely snipped chives or spring onion tops.
● Thinly slice 6 white button mushrooms and sauté them in 25–40 g /1–1½ oz butter for 5 minutes. Keep them hot while scrambling the eggs, then add the sautéed mushrooms and their butter just before serving. Omit the flakes of cold butter.
● When the eggs are thick and almost setting, remove the pan from the heat and stir in 50 g /2 oz freshly grated Parmesan cheese, 50 g /2 oz grated Gruyère or 100 g / 4 oz grated mature Cheddar.

Poached eggs provençale

🔪 25 minutes

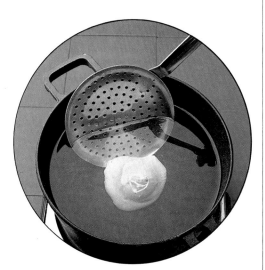

Raise the heat so that the water bubbles up. Use a slotted spoon to draw the white around the yolk of each egg. Reduce the heat and barely simmer for 3–4 minutes.

Serves 4
50 g /1¾ oz canned anchovy fillets, drained
25–40 g /1–1½ oz unsalted butter, softened
2.5–5 ml /½–1 tsp lemon juice
a pinch of cayenne pepper
freshly ground black pepper
2 slices white bread, crusts removed
15 ml /1 tbls olive oil
15 g /½ oz butter
4 eggs
8 tomato wedges, to garnish
4 watercress sprigs, to garnish

1 First prepare the anchovy paste. Cut 4 of the anchovy fillets in half lengthways and reserve for decoration. Mash the remaining anchovy fillets to a smooth paste with the unsalted butter and the lemon juice. Add the cayenne pepper, and season to taste with freshly ground black pepper. (The mixture will be salty enough already.)

2 Prepare the croûtons: cut each slice of bread into 2 triangles. Heat the olive oil and butter in a frying-pan and sauté the triangles of bread until they are crisp and golden brown. Drain well on absorbent paper.

3 Spread the croûtons with the anchovy paste and keep them warm in a low oven.

4 Poach the eggs (see introduction). Place an anchovy-spread croûton on each of 4 plates and place a poached egg on top. Make a cross on top of each egg with 2 of the reserved anchovy strips and garnish with tomato wedges and watercress.

Poached eggs provençale

Poached eggs florentine

40 minutes

Serves 4

250 g /9 oz made-weight shortcrust pastry,
 defrosted if frozen
225 g /8 oz frozen spinach
50 g /2 oz butter
30 ml /2 tbls freshly grated Parmesan cheese
30–45 ml /2–3 tbls thin cream
about 1.5 ml /¼ tsp lemon juice
a pinch of freshly grated nutmeg
salt and freshly ground black pepper
4 eggs

For the white sauce

15 g /½ oz butter
15 g /½ oz flour
150 ml /5 fl oz milk
salt and freshy ground black pepper
30 ml /2 tbls freshly grated Parmesan cheese

1   Heat the oven to 200C /400F /gas 6. Roll
out the pastry to 3 mm /⅛ in thickness and
use it to line 4 × 10 cm /4 in individual fluted
tartlet tins. Lightly prick the base of each all
over with a fork. Line each one with greaseproof paper or aluminium foil and fill with
dried beans.

2   Place the tins on a baking sheet and bake
in the oven for 8–10 minutes. Remove from
the oven and reduce the oven temperature to
180C /350F /gas 4. Carefully lift out the
paper (or foil) and beans. Return the pastry-
lined tins, on the baking sheet, to the oven
and bake for a further 8–10 minutes, until
the pastry is set and golden. Once cooked,
remove the pastry cases from their tins and
keep them warm in a low oven.

3   Meanwhile, make the spinach filling:
place the frozen spinach in a heavy pan with
the butter. Using a wooden spoon, stir and
mash the mixture over a gentle heat, until
the spinach has defrosted. Simmer for 5–7
minutes, stirring, to evaporate off any excess
moisture. Beat in the freshly grated Parmesan
cheese, the thin cream, the lemon juice and
the freshly grated nutmeg. Season to taste
with salt and freshly ground black pepper.

4   For the white sauce: melt the butter over
a low heat and then stir in the flour. Cook for
2 minutes, stirring constantly. Add the milk,
a little at a time, and bring to the boil.

5   Poach the eggs in hot water for a few

Poached eggs florentine

minutes until the whites are firm and the
yolks are still runny (see introduction).

6   Divide the spinach mixture among the
pastry cases. Place a poached egg on top of
the spinach and spoon a little of the white
sauce over each egg. Sprinkle the freshly
grated Parmesan cheese on top, then slip the
pastry cases under a hot grill for a few
minutes, until the tops are bubbling and
golden. Serve immediately either as a starter
or as a light lunch.

Egg and watercress sauce

25 minutes

Makes 250 ml /9 fl oz

2 medium-sized eggs, hard-boiled
a pinch of salt
1 medium-sized egg yolk, lightly beaten
finely grated zest and juice of ½ lemon
25 g /1 oz watercress sprigs, finely chopped
150 ml /5 fl oz thin cream
freshly ground black pepper

1   Shell the eggs and cut them in half
lengthways. Scoop out the yolks (reserving
the whites), and mash them thoroughly. Add
the salt and gradually work in the raw egg
yolk to make a thick, smooth paste.

2   Add the lemon zest and slowly beat in
the lemon juice. Stir in the watercress and
then the cream, a little at a time. Finely chop
the white of 1 hard-boiled egg and stir it into
the sauce. (Reserve the remaining egg white
for another use.) Season to taste and then
cover and refrigerate the sauce until required
(it will keep in the refrigerator for about
3 days); stir it before using. Serve it
with fish, or as a dressing for rice salads.

Oeufs moulés with a herb sauce

Oeufs moulés

🕐 making the sauce and base,
then 20 minutes

Serves 4
butter, for greasing
4 eggs, at room temperature
4 baked pastry cases or fried bread rounds,
7.5 cm /3 in diameter

1 Heat the oven to 180C /350F /gas 4. Butter 4 dariole moulds. Pour boiling water into a small roasting tin to a depth of 25 mm /1 in. Stand the moulds in the tin.
2 Break an egg into each buttered mould. Bake for 15 minutes, until the whites are just set but the yolks are still runny.
3 Remove the tin from the oven and take out the moulds. Slip a small knife around between the eggs and the moulds, then turn the eggs out onto the pastry cases or the rounds of fried bread. Serve immediately, with one of the following sauces:
● purée of skinned, seeded and chopped tomatoes softened in butter, flavoured with a hint of finely chopped shallot and thyme.
● purée of poached artichoke hearts, asparagus tips or another vegetable of your choice enriched with cream.
● white sauce with chopped herbs, particularly parsley, seasoned with salt.

Baked egg custard

🕐 30 minutes,
then 1 hour baking

Serves 4
butter, for greasing
600 ml /1 pt milk
3 strips orange zest
2 eggs and 2 egg yolks
60 ml /4 tbls caster sugar
2.5 ml /½ tsp vanilla essence
2.5 ml /½ tsp freshly grated nutmeg

1 Heat the oven to 170C /325F /gas 3, and generously butter an 850 ml /1½ pt soufflé dish. In a medium-sized, heavy-based saucepan, scald the milk with the orange zest over a low heat.
2 Remove the pan from the heat, cover it and leave it to infuse for 10–15 minutes. (The longer the infusion, the stronger the orange flavour will be.)
3 In a large bowl, place the whole eggs, the egg yolks, caster sugar, vanilla essence and 1.5 ml /¼ tsp of the freshly grated nutmeg. Beat them together lightly with a wooden spoon.
4 Pour the milk in a thin stream onto the beaten egg and sugar mixture, stirring constantly with a wooden spoon. Strain the mixture into the soufflé dish and sprinkle with the remaining grated nutmeg.
5 Place the dish in a fairly deep baking tin and pour in enough hot water to come halfway up the sides of the dish. Bake for about 1 hour, or until the custard is set and golden brown on top. To test that the custard is cooked, insert the point of a sharp knife into the centre: the knife should leave a visible mark. If the custard flows together again, bake it for a little longer. Serve the custard when it is set.

Egg flip

Here's a delicious, nourishing drink which is also a very effective pick-me-up.

🕐 1–2 minutes

Serves 1
1 medium-sized egg
5 ml /1 tsp icing sugar
150 ml /5 fl oz medium sherry
ground cinnamon or nutmeg, to taste

1 Combine the egg, the icing sugar and the sherry in a blender and blend at maximum speed for 20–30 seconds.
2 Pour the egg flip into a chilled glass and sprinkle it with cinnamon or nutmeg. Serve immediately.

● If a blender is not available, whisk the egg and sugar, then gradually add the sherry.
● For a non-alcoholic orange flip, substitute 150 ml /5 fl oz chilled, unsweetened orange juice for the medium sherry.

Egg flip

MAKING THE MOST OF MILK

A glass of cool fresh milk is a most thirst-quenching and nourishing beverage. As well as being the basis for many flavoured hot and cold drinks, milk can be used for making cakes, batters, sauces and puddings.

Buttermilk pancakes

Milk is one of the most useful foods in terms of food value and economy available on the market today. The proteins in milk are of a very high quality because they contain all the essential amino-acids. It contains carbohydrate and calcium and almost all of the mineral elements and salts which the body requires, as well as appreciable quantities of vitamin A, the B vitamins and also vitamin C.

As well as being invaluable in cooking generally, it forms the basis of many other dairy products such as cream, butter and yoghurt (see separate chapters in this book), and cheese.

Fresh milk
All milk sold must be safe to drink. In most cases, milk undergoes heat treatment — it is heated to a high enough temperature to destroy any harmful bacteria.

Untreated cows' milk is not heat treated but comes instead from Brucellosis tested herds of cows. However, it is not usually available commercially.

Homogenized milk is heated and processed to break up the tiny globules of fat and distribute them evenly throughout the milk, making it more consistently creamy. It is then pasteurized to kill dangerous bacteria.

Pasteurized milk is heated, then cooled rapidly. The cream separates from the milk, floating on top and forming a distinct line in the container — the 'top of the milk'.

Sterilized milk: sterilization kills bacteria but the process causes slight caramelization and the milk has a 'cooked flavour'. It is sold in hermetically sealed containers.

Skimmed milk is milk from which the cream has been skimmed or separated. It contains the valuable proteins, minerals and vitamins of ordinary milk, but is not suitable for feeding babies because it lacks fat. Skimmed milk with added vegetable fat to replace the removed butterfat is now commercially available.

High cream content milk: milk from breeds of cows such as Guernsey and Jersey have a 4% butterfat content, compared to the 3% of other types of milk.

Soured milk: the chilled storage conditions of modern milk discourage the growth of beneficial bacteria. When a recipe calls for soured milk do not use milk that has turned sour: instead, add 15 ml /1 tbls lemon juice to 600 ml /1 pt warm milk, or use yoghurt or buttermilk.

Buttermilk is the liquid by-product left when the fats are removed to make butter. Nowadays it is made by adding a culture to skimmed milk.

Sheep's milk is creamier than cows' and is used for making yoghurt and cheese. Cheeses made from sheep's milk include French Roquefort and Greek Feta.

Goats' milk is thicker and richer than cows' milk but has smaller fat globules, which makes it easier to digest, so is recommended for people who cannot tolerate cows' milk. It makes strong-flavoured cheese.

Buffaloes' milk is clarified to make ghee in India. It was at one time used to make Italian Mozzarella cheese.

Preserved milk
Ultra heat treated milk: UHT or long-life milk is heated to a very high temperature. It keeps for several months without refrigeration in an unopened container, which usually carries a 'sell by' date.

Evaporated milk is rapidly heated to check bacteria, then concentrated by the evaporation of 70% of the water content at a lower temperature. It is homogenized to break up the fat globules and distribute them evenly, then it is sterilized and canned. The final concentration of the milk is about twice that of the original milk.

Condensed milk is similar to evaporated milk, but it is sweetened with sugar. The final concentration is about 2½ times that of the original milk.

Dried milk powder is produced by the evaporation of water from homogenized, pre-concentrated milk by heat or spray-drying. Dried whole milk contains all the nutrients of fresh milk (except thiamin, vitamin B_{12} and vitamin C), in a concentrated form. Dried skimmed milk contains virtually no fat, hence its popularity with slimmers. Dried milk and products based on it can be used for feeding babies, but it does not replace humans' milk and doctor's instructions must always be followed very carefully.

Buying and storing milk

Milk is sold by dairies and supermarkets: Britain is one of the few countries where milk is delivered to the door. Goats' and sheep's milk is obtainable from specialist dairies, health food shops or direct from some farms.

Milk should never be left in direct sunlight as this affects its flavour and destroys part of its vitamin content. It should be refrigerated or kept in the coolest place available, in the container in which it was bought. Bottled milk keeps best as the bottle is sterilized before being filled, but milk is highly perishable and has a short storage life. It also taints easily so it should be covered to prevent it from absorbing flavour from other foods.

Dried milk packed in an airtight container will keep for 6 months if unopened. Once opened, it will keep for up to 3 months in the refrigerator. Canned milk will keep almost indefinitely unopened.

Using milk in cooking

Milk is an invaluable ingredient in all kinds of dishes, savoury and sweet: sauces, cream soups, soufflés, pancakes and cakes. A variety of puddings are milk-based, in particular those made with rice, semolina (see recipe) and pasta. Milk can be used in a number of ways to give extra nourishment to a dish: certain vegetables, such as potatoes and Jerusalem artichokes, may be cooked in milk. It is also simple to make your own yoghurt using milk, and not difficult to make fresh cottage or curd cheese.

Infusing milk: this is a useful way of adding flavour to milk for making sauces. The flavouring, which can be savoury or sweet, should be strong: onion, herbs, a vanilla pod or other spices, and lemon or orange zest are suitable. Add the flavouring to the milk in a saucepan and scald the milk by bringing it just to boiling point — watch the pan carefully as milk boils very quickly. Leave the milk to cool for 20 minutes, to allow the flavour to infuse.

Using rennet with milk: rennet is an important adjunct to milk in the making of junket and cheese. It is a substance from a calf's stomach which curdles milk and is available in liquid essence or tablet form. (There is also a vegetarian rennet.)

Milk and rennet are used with a culture to make cheese, and milk and rennet together make junket.

● To make a traditional junket, warm 600 ml /1 pt milk until it is 'blood heat' and feels neither hot nor cold to your finger. Then add 5 ml /1 tsp rennet, 20 ml /4 tsp brandy and 10 ml /2 tsp sugar to the milk. Chill it for 4–5 hours until it is set, then spread thick cream and a little grated nutmeg on the top.

Milk drinks: hot milk is thought to aid good sleep and is added to cocoa, drinking chocolate or malted milk powder which is made from malt extract, dried milk and whey. A mixture of hot milk, egg yolk, honey and brandy is an old Polish remedy for colds, or just hot milk with a tot of brandy or whisky will serve much the same purpose!

Cold milk drinks with coffee or chocolate flavouring are popular. Milk shakes can be made with added ice cream and a selection of flavourings.

Buttermilk contains an acid created in the fermenting process which acts as a raising agent. It is used in baking breads and scones. Buttermilk can also be used in similar ways to yoghurt — in sauces, dressings and drinks.

Evaporated milk can be used diluted (follow the manufacturer's instructions) for drinking or cooking in the same way as fresh milk. Partially diluted, evaporated milk provides a rich, creamy liquid for desserts or savoury and sweet sauces. Undiluted, it can be used instead of cream and for icings and ice cream: if well chilled in the refrigerator, it can be successfully whipped.

Condensed milk is used mainly in the preparation of sweets such as fudge, or for Coconut candy (see recipe) and in desserts and chiffon-type pies. Its uses are limited because it is so sweet.

Fish and prawn pie

Buttermilk pancakes

 30–40 minutes

Serves 4–6
225 g /8 oz flour
5 ml /1 tsp baking powder
5 ml /1 tsp bicarbonate of soda
5 ml /1 tsp salt
2 medium-sized eggs
450 ml /16 fl oz buttermilk
60 ml /4 tbls melted butter
butter or oil, for greasing

1 Sift the dry ingredients into a large mixing bowl. In a separate bowl whisk the eggs until they are light and fluffy.
2 Stir the buttermilk into the beaten eggs. Fold this mixture into the dry ingredients and mix until smooth. Add the melted butter and stir well.
3 Heat a small, heavy frying-pan (preferably one kept specially for pancakes) until it is very hot. Add a little butter or oil to the pan and pour off any excess.
4 Pour approximately 125 ml /4 fl oz of the mixture, depending on the size of the pan, into the pan, and cook until bubbles start to appear on the surface. Turn the pancake over and cook until it is golden on both sides.
5 Stack the pancakes between sheets of greaseproof paper as you cook them, and keep them warm in a low oven.

Fish and prawn pie

You can make this fish filling ahead of time and then reheat it when you are baking the pastry topping.

 defrosting the pastry, then 1 hour

Serves 4–6
600 ml /1 pt milk
2 slices of onion
1 large bay leaf
12 black peppercorns
300 ml /10 fl oz white wine
1 medium-sized carrot, sliced
450 g /1 lb haddock fillet
225 g /8 oz smoked haddock fillet
40 g /1½ oz butter
40 g /1½ oz flour
4 anchovy fillets, chopped (optional)
100 g /4 oz peeled prawns
2 large tomatoes, blanched, skinned, seeded and roughly chopped
salt and white pepper
275 g /10 oz made-weight frozen puff pastry, defrosted
butter, for greasing
milk, for glazing

1 In a pan bring the milk to the boil with the onion, the bay leaf and the peppercorns. Remove from the heat and leave for 20 minutes to infuse. Strain the milk into a jug.

2 Heat the wine with 275 ml /10 fl oz water in a large, shallow pan. Add the carrot and fish fillets. Cover the pan and poach the contents over a medium heat for about 10 minutes, until the fish is cooked.
3 Make the sauce: melt the butter, then stir in the flour off the heat. Mix to make a smooth paste. Slowly pour on the strained milk, stirring all the time. Stir over a very low heat until the sauce thickens. Cook it gently for 2 minutes. Add the chopped anchovy fillets, if using.
4 Remove the fish from the poaching liquid (reserve the liquid for use in a fish soup) and remove the skin and any stray bones. Flake the fish into fairly large pieces and put it into a bowl.
5 Add the prawns and tomatoes to the flaked fish. Pour the sauce over the fish mixture and very gently mix together. Season with salt and pepper to taste.
6 Heat the oven to 190C /375F /gas 5. Butter a 20–23 cm /8–9 in pie dish and put the fish mixture into it.
7 Roll the pastry out to fit the top. Dampen the edge of the dish and cover the fish with the pastry lid. Brush the pastry lid with a little milk, decorate with pastry trimmings and glaze again.
8 Bake for 20 minutes, until the pastry is golden.

● This pie can also be served with a creamy mashed potato topping, forked up and lightly browned under the grill.

Semolina mould with raspberry sauce

Potato gratin with cheese

To make this dish use firm, waxy potatoes, like the red-skinned Desirée, sliced thinly. Add extra flavour with a pinch of freshly grated nutmeg, if wished.

 1¼ hours

Serves 4-6
1 kg /2¼ lb large, waxy potatoes
300 ml /11 fl oz milk
1 garlic clove, chopped
50 g /2 oz butter, plus extra for greasing
1 large onion, sliced
50 g /2 oz Gruyère or Cheddar cheese, grated
salt and freshly ground black pepper

1 Heat the oven to 190C /375F /gas 5. Peel and slice the potatoes as thinly as possible and leave them to soak in cold water for a few minutes.
2 Meanwhile, heat the milk with the garlic and the butter until the butter melts. Strain into a jug.
3 Generously butter a shallow, ovenproof dish. Drain the potatoes and dry them on absorbent paper.

4 Arrange half the sliced potatoes overlapping to form a layer on the bottom of the dish. Cover with the sliced onion and the grated cheese. Pour in half the strained milk. Season well.
5 Cover with the rest of the potatoes. Pour the remaining milk over them and season.
6 Bake for about 45 minutes, until the top is golden and the potatoes feel tender when tested with a knife. If necessary, cover the top with foil to prevent burning.

Butterscotch meringue pie

Evaporated milk gives a creamy finish to this delicious pie.

 1 hour, plus cooling

Serves 6
150 g /5 oz soft dark brown sugar
25 g /1 oz flour
25 g /1 oz butter
a pinch of salt
275 ml /10 fl oz evaporated milk
2 medium-sized eggs, separated
2.5 ml /½ tsp vanilla essence
20 cm /8 in pastry case, half-baked
60 ml /4 tbls caster sugar
2.5 ml /½ tsp cream of tartar

1 Heat the oven to 150C /300F /gas 2. Combine the brown sugar, flour, butter and salt in the top pan of a double boiler over simmering water. Stir to blend the mixture and cook for 5 minutes.
2 Add the evaporated milk and stir constantly until dissolved.
3 Lightly beat the egg yolks and add the hot mixture a little at a time, beating all the while. Return the mixture to the pan and cook it until thickened, still stirring constantly. Do not boil. Stir in the vanilla essence. Spoon the mixture into the pastry case.
4 Whisk the egg whites until stiff peaks form. Slowly add the caster sugar and cream of tartar, whisking continually.
5 Pile the meringue on top of the butterscotch filling, spreading it to the edge of the pastry case. Bake for 15–20 minutes, until the meringue is lightly browned. Serve cold.

Coconut candy

Made with condensed milk, this is a rich version of the old favourite, coconut ice. Add a little food colouring if wished.

45 minutes

Makes about 100 squares
450 g /1 lb sugar
30 ml /2 tbls milk
75 ml /3 fl oz golden syrup
200 ml /7 fl oz condensed milk
100 g /4 oz unsweetened desiccated coconut
5 ml /1 tsp vanilla essence
butter, for greasing

1 Melt the sugar, milk and golden syrup in a pan over a very low heat, stirring from time to time. Do not allow the mixture to boil.
2 When the sugar has dissolved, add the condensed milk. Increase the heat, stir well and bring to the boil. Cook until the temperature on a sugar thermometer reads 120C /240F or until a little of the mixture dropped into a cup of cold water forms a soft ball.
3 Remove the pan from the heat and let the bubbles subside. Stir in the coconut and vanilla essence.
4 Turn the mixture into a greased shallow tin, about 19 cm /7½ in square. Leave until it is quite cold, then mark the coconut candy into 2 cm /¾ in squares. Carefully remove it from the tin; it can be stored in an airtight container for up to 1 month.

Semolina mould with raspberry sauce

This sophisticated version of a school pudding looks attractive when it is made in a decorative mould and served with a brightly coloured sauce.

35 minutes, plus at least 2 hours chilling

Serves 6
850 ml /1½ pt creamy milk
a large piece of lemon zest or cinnamon stick
50 g /2 oz sugar
75 g /3 oz semolina
3 medium-sized egg yolks
225 g /8 oz raspberries
sifted icing sugar, to taste
30 ml /2 tbls kirsch

1 Bring 600 ml /1 pt of milk to the boil in a saucepan with the lemon zest or cinnamon and the sugar. Remove from the heat and leave for 20 minutes for the flavours to infuse.
2 Put the semolina in a bowl and add the remaining milk. Mix together well to dissolve the semolina. Add the egg yolks and beat well with a wire whisk.
3 Strain the infused milk onto the semolina and egg mixture, beating well. Return the mixture to the pan and cook over a very low heat, stirring constantly with a wooden spoon, until the mixture thickens and just begins to bubble.
4 Remove from the heat, stir well and turn the mixture into a moistened 1.1 L /2 pt mould. Leave until cold and then refrigerate, covered, until required.
5 For the sauce, purée the raspberries in a blender, then sieve. Stir in just enough icing sugar to give a slightly tart flavour. Add the kirsch and mix thoroughly.
6 Carefully turn the semolina mould out onto a serving plate. Spoon some of the sauce over the top and allow it to run down the sides of the dessert. Serve the remainder of the sauce separately.

● You can make this dessert in a ring mould, then turn it out and fill the centre with a mixture of fresh fruits. Serve this version with or without the raspberry sauce.

BUTTER

Toasted crumpets dripping with golden butter, piquant garnishes for fish, meat and fowl or melt-in-the-mouth pastry and biscuits — these all rely on butter for their special appeal.

Butter is almost indispensable in the kitchen — in my opinion few things can equal it for flavour and certain pastries and sauces just wouldn't be the same without it.

It is made by shaking or churning cream until globules of fat form a mass. This mass is then pressed to extract excess liquid.

There are two types of butter — sweet cream and lactic, and both may have salt added. Sweet cream butter, the type generally made and sold in Britain, Australia, the United States and New Zealand, is produced from the cream of fresh cows' milk. It is delicately flavoured, with a golden yellow colour and a firm, waxy, smooth texture that is particularly good for pastry and biscuits.

Lactic butter, usually made and sold in France, Germany and Holland, is made from cream which is slightly soured by the introduction of bacteria. This enhances the eventual flavour of the butter, which is full flavoured, soft and fine in texture, and pale cream in colour. It creams easily and so is good for cake making.

Buying and storing: to enjoy butter at its best, buy it weekly, although it can be kept refrigerated for up to 3 weeks. Keep it well covered in the refrigerator as its surface loses its gloss and darkens when exposed to the air, and light reduces its vitamin D content. Butter can be frozen, if it is wrapped in foil. Unsalted butter will keep in the freezer for 6 months, salted for 3 months.

Using butter: butter is used for sautéing and shallow frying. Clarified butter (made by melting butter, very gently, until it foams; when the foam falls to the bottom of the pan it leaves behind the clarified butter which can be poured off) or butter used with a flavourless oil is less likely to burn.

Butter improves the flavour and keeping quality of cakes, and gives a fine, even crumb. It makes a rich, crisp, short pastry and gives puff pastry an excellent flavour and texture. Use salted butter for making savoury pastries, and unsalted for sweet pastries, cakes, biscuits, icings and butter cream.

Butter is essential for making certain classic sauces such as bechamel and hollandaise. Add it to soups, too, for enrichment and flavour. Incorporate it just before serving and do not let the sauce or soup boil afterwards, or it will 'oil' and lose its flavour.

Butter and flour are cooked together to make a roux, which is used as the basis for many sauces and soups. Sauces, soups and stews can also be thickened by *beurre manié*, which is butter and flour worked together into a paste. The advantage of this method is that small pieces can be added to a boiling liquid, without lumps forming. Thus you can go on thickening a sauce or soup after it has been prepared (unlike a roux) until the required degree of thickness is reached.

Why not use a simple butter sauce over boiled vegetables, poached fish or eggs:

beurre fondu is made by melting butter and adding salt, white pepper and lemon juice.

For *beurre noisette* (nut butter), melt butter, cook it until it is a light hazelnut colour, and then add a few drops of lemon juice, salt and black pepper to taste.

For *beurre noir* (black butter), cook butter to a dark brown — it is not actually black — and add a few drops of wine vinegar, a little chopped parsley, salt and pepper. You can add some chopped capers if you wish.

Savoury butters, made by combining softened butter with flavourings, are used to garnish plainly cooked meat, fish or vegetables: mock caviar butter is made from 100 g /4 oz unsalted butter creamed with 20 ml /4 tsp red lumpfish roe and seasoned with freshly ground black pepper and lemon juice.

Tomato butter uses 50 g /2 oz unsalted butter, 10 ml /2 tsp tomato puree, 15 ml / 1 tbls chopped fresh parsley, basil, thyme or marjoram and a pinch of cayenne pepper. The variations on this recipe are many — for serving with lamb, add 10 ml /2 tsp Worcestershire sauce; for veal, add the grated rind of one lemon and 10 ml /2 tsp lemon juice; for steaks, add 2 stoned, chopped black olives; for fish, replace the cayenne pepper with black pepper and add 4 anchovy fillets which have been soaked in milk for 15 minutes, then pounded to a paste.

To serve with bread at the table, make curls or decorative pats of butter which you can keep in a bowl of cold water in the refrigerator and drain before serving.

Mushrooms with garlic butter

 30 minutes

Serves 4
225 g /8 oz open mushrooms
100 g /4 oz butter, at room temperature
45 ml /3 tbls finely chopped fresh parsley
1 shallot, finely chopped
2 garlic cloves, crushed
salt and freshly ground black pepper
French bread, to serve

1 Heat the oven to 190C /375F /gas 5. Wipe the mushrooms and trim the stems level with the caps.
2 Arrange the mushrooms, tightly packed, in an ovenproof dish, and pack the trimmings among them.
3 Beat the butter until it is soft and creamy, then gradually work in the parsley, shallot, garlic, and salt and pepper to taste. Dot the butter mixture evenly over the mushrooms and bake them for 15 minutes.
4 Serve piping hot with lots of crusty French bread to mop up the buttery juices.

Crisp-fried butter balls

 1½ hours, including chilling

Makes 24 croustade cases
225 g /8 oz butter, chilled
flour
3 eggs, beaten
100 g /4 oz fresh white breadcrumbs
oil, for deep frying

1 Cut the butter into 24 equal-sized cubes. Squeeze the cubes gently to round off their corners, without making them complete ball shapes. Place the butter balls on a baking tray and chill in the refrigerator for 1 hour.
2 Roll the butter balls to rounded shapes and return them to the refrigerator to firm.
3 Coat the butter balls lightly with flour. Roll them in the beaten egg and then in the breadcrumbs, then return them to the refrigerator to chill.
4 Roll them in egg again and then in breadcrumbs, pressing the crumbs on with a palette knife, then chill once more.
5 Heat the oil to 190C /375F. If you do not have a cooking thermometer, test that the oil is hot enough by dropping a 25 mm /1 in cube of bread into the oil. It should become golden brown in 50 seconds.
6 Deep fry the breadcrumbed balls, a few at a time, until they are golden brown. Remove them from the oil with a slotted spoon, then make a little hole to release the melted butter from inside the crust. (Reserve this melted butter for another recipe.)
7 Place the fried butter balls on absorbent

Garlic bread

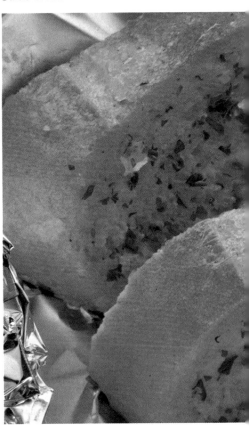

Croustades from crisp-fried butter balls

Coat chilled butter balls lightly with flour, then roll them in beaten egg and fresh white breadcrumbs. Chill until firm, then roll in egg and crumbs and chill again.

Deep fry the breadcrumbed balls in hot oil until they are golden brown. Remove them with a slotted spoon, and pierce each with the point of a knife to release the melted butter.

Just before serving, fill a greaseproof paper piping bag with the filling of your choice and pipe it carefully into the cooled crisp-fried butter balls.

paper, hole side down, and leave to get cold.
8 Shortly before serving, fill a greaseproof paper piping bag with your chosen filling — taramasalata, avocado purée or smooth liver pâte — and pipe it into the balls.

Garlic bread

25 minutes

Serves 6
1 loaf of French bread

For the garlic butter
175 g /6 oz softened butter
3 garlic cloves, crushed
45 ml /3 tbls finely chopped fresh parsley
freshly ground black pepper

1 Heat the oven to 190C /375F /gas 5.
2 Using a wooden spoon, beat the softened butter with the garlic, chopped parsley and freshly ground black pepper to taste, until it is all well blended.
3 Cut the French loaf into 15 mm /½ in diagonal slices, without cutting through the crust on the bottom, so that the loaf is still in one piece.
4 With a palette knife, generously spread both sides of the cut bread slices with the garlic butter.
5 Wrap the loaf tightly in a width of foil and place it on a baking sheet. Bake for 10–12 minutes, or until the bread is crisp and the garlic butter has melted.
6 Unwrap the bread and finish cutting the slices. Leave it in the foil or arrange the slices on a serving dish or in a basket. Serve hot.

● For a milder flavour, use only 2 garlic cloves.

Roquefort butter papillotes

45 minutes

Serves 4
450 g /1 lb rump or sirloin steak, 25 mm /1 in thick
melted butter, for brushing
salt and freshly ground black pepper
50 g /2 oz butter
½ Spanish onion, finely chopped
225 g /8 oz button mushrooms, thinly sliced
sprigs of watercress, to garnish

For the Roquefort butter
50 g /2 oz butter
5 ml /1 tsp flour
25 g /1 oz Roquefort cheese, crumbled
30 ml /2 tbls finely chopped fresh parsley
lemon juice

1 Heat the oven to 190C /375F /gas 5. Make the Roquefort butter: using a wooden spoon, mash the butter and flour in a small bowl, until it is smooth. Add the crumbled Roquefort cheese and the finely chopped parsley and mash again. Add lemon juice to taste, then place the mixture on a piece of greaseproof paper. Pat the mixture into an oblong, wrap it in the paper and chill in the refrigerator until ready to use.
2 Brush the steak on both sides with the melted butter and sprinkle with freshly ground black pepper. Heat a frying-pan and fry the steak for 2–3 minutes, turning once, until it is browned on both sides. Remove the steak from the pan and cut it, across the grain, into 16–20 thin strips. Season the steak strips with salt and freshly ground black pepper to taste.
3 Melt 25 g /1 oz of the butter in a frying pan and sauté the finely chopped onion until transparent. Add the rest of the butter and when it has melted, add the sliced mushrooms. Sauté for 2–3 minutes, then season to taste with salt and black pepper.
4 Cut 4 × 28 cm /11 in squares of double thickness foil. Place one-eighth of the onion and mushroom mixture in the centre of each square of foil. Arrange 4 or 5 steak strips on each square of foil and cover with the remaining onion and mushroom mixture. Top each packet with a quarter of the chilled Roquefort butter.
5 Seal the foil packets so that no juices can escape during cooking. Arrange the parcels on a baking tray, join upwards, and cook in the oven for 15 minutes.
6 Undo the foil wrappings and garnish the steak with sprigs of watercress to serve.

Buttered fettucine with cheese

 30 minutes

Serves 4
500 g /1 lb fettucine (ribbon noodles)
salt
freshly ground black pepper
freshly grated Parmesan cheese, for serving
For the sauce
100 g /4 oz softened butter
90 ml /6 tbls thick cream
100 g /4 oz grated Parmesan cheese

1 Bring a large 3.5–4.5 L /6–8 pt capacity saucepan of salted water to the boil. Add the noodles and simmer for about 10 minutes until tender but still firm — test a small piece first to check it is done. Stir occasionally with a fork to keep the strands separate.
2 Meanwhile prepare the sauce. Place the softened butter in a heated serving bowl and cream it with a wooden spoon.
3 Gradually beat in the thick cream, followed by the grated Parmesan cheese.
4 As soon as the noodles are cooked, drain them thoroughly in a colander. Turn them into the serving bowl, pour the sauce over them and season with freshly ground black pepper. Toss vigorously with a serving fork and spoon until the noodles are thoroughly coated with the sauce.
5 Sprinkle the noodles with more grated Parmesan cheese and serve immediately.

Sole with smoked salmon butter

 1–1¼ hours

Serves 4
8 good-sized fillets of sole
salt and freshly ground black pepper
125 ml /4 fl oz dry Vouvray or other dry
* white wine*
1 egg yolk
30 ml /2 tbls thick cream
strips of smoked salmon to decorate (optional)
For the duxelles
250 g /9 oz mushroom stalks or whole
* mushrooms, finely chopped*
1 shallot, finely chopped
25 g /1 oz butter
a dash of lemon juice
30 ml /2 tbls thick cream
salt and freshly ground black pepper
For the smoked salmon butter
75 g /3 oz smoked salmon, or salmon scraps
25 g /1 oz unsalted butter, at room temperature
a dash of lemon juice
freshly ground black pepper

1 To make the duxelles, gently fry the mushrooms and the shallot, covered, in melted butter for about 5 minutes over a low heat. Remove the pan from the heat, stir in the lemon juice and cream and season to taste. Keep warm.

Sole with smoked salmon butter

2 Heat the oven to 350F /180C /gas 4. To make the smoked salmon butter, finely chop the salmon. If using salmon scraps, remove any bits of skin first. Pound the salmon in a bowl with the softened butter until it is smooth, adding lemon juice and black pepper to taste at the last moment.
3 Spread each fillet of sole with a lengthwise strip of the smoked salmon butter about 20 mm /¾ in wide. Roll up the fillets into paupiettes. Arrange them seam-side down and close together in a shallow, flameproof pan, season lightly and pour the wine over them. Cover the pan loosely with foil, bring almost to simmering point over a low heat, and transfer the pan to the oven. Cook the paupiettes for about 8–10 minutes.
4 Spread a bed of duxelles over the bottom of an ovenproof serving dish. Reduce the oven to 130C /250F /gas ½. Remove the paupiettes from their cooking-liquid with a slotted spoon and, when well drained, arrange them on the duxelles. Reserve the liquid. Cover the dish with the same foil and keep it warm in the oven.
5 Boil the reserved liquid to reduce it by about half. Meantime, whisk the egg yolk and cream together. Strain the reduced liquid into the egg and cream mixture, whisking all the while. If it does not seem thick enough, pour it back into the pan and return the pan to a low heat for a minute or two to allow it to thicken. Do not boil the sauce or it will curdle. Season to taste and pour the thickened sauce over the paupiettes.
6 Garnish the dish with little strips of smoked salmon, if you wish. You may cover the dish and keep it warm in the oven for 15–20 minutes if necessary.

Roasted quails with orange wine butter

½ hour, 2 hours standing, 15–20 minutes spit-roasting

Serves 2–4
4 × 100 g /4 oz quails, dressed weight
freshly ground black pepper
For the orange wine butter
275 ml /10 fl oz red wine
75 g /3 oz butter
3 anchovy fillets, finely chopped
finely grated zest of 1 orange
5 ml /1 tsp orange juice
freshly ground black pepper

1 First make the orange wine butter. Boil the wine in a small pan until it has reduced to about 45 ml /3 tbls. Leave it to cool.
2 In a small bowl, beat the butter until creamy. Add the finely chopped anchovy fillets and the grated orange zest, and beat until well blended. Gradually beat in the reduced wine and orange juice, and season to taste with freshly ground black pepper. You probably will not need to add any salt to this recipe because of the saltiness of the anchovies.
3 Place one-third of the flavoured butter on a butter wrapping paper or square of greaseproof paper. Use the paper to roll the butter into a roll 25 mm /1 in across and 8–10 cm

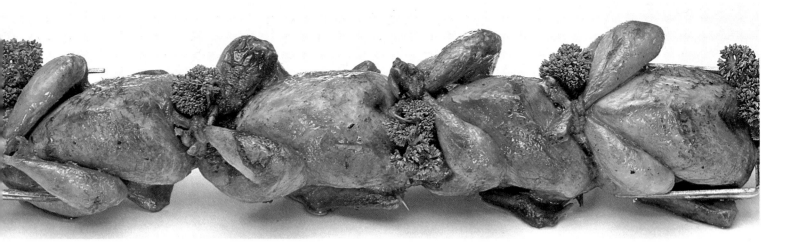

Roasted quails with orange wine butter

3–4 in long. Make sure the butter is covered with the greaseproof paper, then refrigerate it until required.

4 Rub the quails inside and out with black pepper. Divide the remaining flavoured butter among the body cavities. Next place the quails on a plate and leave them to stand at room temperature for about 2 hours, to absorb the flavour of the butter.

5 If you are using an oven rôtisserie, heat the oven to 220C /425F /gas 7. Using a double thickness of aluminium foil, make a long, narrow trough to place under the spit to catch the juices that drip from the quails as they roast. (Do not use a large tin, as any juice dripping into this will burn.)

6 Thread the quails, lengthways, onto a spit, and spit-roast them for 15–20 minutes, basting halfway through the cooking time. To test that the quails are cooked, insert a skewer into the thickest part of the inside leg; the juices should run clear.

7 Transfer the cooked quails onto a heated serving dish and tip the collected dripped juices over them. Cut the chilled butter into 4 pieces, lay one piece at the open end of each quail and serve immediately.

Sausage rolls

1 hour,
plus 30 minutes chilling

Makes 20 small rolls
375 g /12 oz pork sausage-meat
1 small egg, beaten with 5 ml /1 tsp cold water,
*   for glazing*
For easy rough puff pastry
175 g /6 oz flour
a large pinch of salt
40 g /1½ oz lard, chilled
65 g /2½ oz firm butter

1 To make the pastry, mix the flour and salt in a mixing bowl. Cut the lard and butter into small pieces and add to the bowl. Add 100 ml /3½ fl oz cold water and, using a palette knife, combine the ingredients without breaking up the fats too much. The dough should be fairly firm.

2 Put the pastry on a floured board and shape it roughly into a rectangular block. Roll out to measure about 40×15 cm /16×6 in.

3 Fold the narrow pastry ends into the centre so that they overlap each other, making 3 layers. Roll out the pastry to its original length. Next, flouring the board and rolling pin as needed, repeat the folding and rolling process 3 more times. Wrap in cling film and refrigerate for 30 minutes to allow the pastry to become cool and firm.

4 Divide the sausage-meat in half and shape each into a roll 50 cm /20 in long. Set aside.

5 Heat the oven to 220C /425F /gas 7. Roll out the pastry to measure 50×20 cm /20×8 in. Cut in half lengthways and place a sausage-meat roll along each strip.

6 Brush one long side of each pastry strip with beaten egg. Roll the pastry neatly over the sausage-meat and seal the edges underneath. Cut into 5 cm /2 in rolls and make 3 diagonal cuts on the top of each roll.

7 Arrange the rolls on a baking sheet with a 25 mm /1 in space between each. Brush with the beaten egg.

8 Bake at the top of the oven for 20–25 minutes until well browned. Lift them onto absorbent paper on a wire rack to cool.

9 When they are completely cold, store in a container and refrigerate; or seal in a container and freeze for up to 1 month.

Butter biscuits

50 minutes,
plus chilling

Makes about 30 biscuits
175 g /6 oz butter, softened, plus extra for
*   greasing*
40 g /1½ oz icing sugar, sieved
finely grated zest of 1 large lemon
100 g /4 oz flour
For the glaze
25 g /1 oz icing sugar, sieved
15 ml /1 tbls lemon juice

1 Grease 2 large baking sheets. Beat the butter until creamy, then add the icing sugar and continue beating until fluffy. Stir in the lemon zest and flour to give a soft dough.

2 Spoon half the mixture into a piping bag fitted with a medium-sized star éclair nozzle and pipe 15 large stars, spacing them out on one of the baking sheets. Pipe the remaining mixture onto the other baking sheet, and refrigerate for 30 minutes.

3 Arrange an oven shelf just above the

centre and another just below and heat the oven to 160C /325F /gas 3.

4 Bake the biscuits for 25 minutes, reversing the position of the trays halfway through the cooking time.

5 To make the glaze: combine the icing sugar with sufficient lemon juice to give a coating consistency. Remove the biscuits from the oven, brush with the glaze and return them to the oven for a further 5 minutes. Transfer to a wire rack to cool.

Pitcaithly bannock

1 hour 10 minutes,
plus 2 hours chilling

Makes 8 wedges
25 g /1 oz rice flour, plus extra for dusting
100 g /4 oz butter, slightly softened, plus
*   extra for greasing*
50 g /2 oz caster sugar, plus extra for
*   sprinkling*
175 g /6 oz flour
25 g /1 oz blanched flaked almonds, crushed
25 g /1 oz candied citron or orange peel,
*   finely chopped*

1 Dust a wooden pastry board with a little rice flour, then flour your hands. Knead the butter and sugar on the board until they are blended. Shape into a large flattish round.

2 Sift together the flour and rice flour. Work a small portion at a time into the butter mixture by putting a little flour on top and folding it in, until it is completely incorporated. Work in the almonds and candied peel, distributing them evenly. Wrap the dough in greaseproof paper and chill in the refrigerator for 2 hours.

3 Heat the oven to 170C /325F /gas 3. Shape the dough into a round slightly more than 20 cm /8 in in diameter and about 20 mm /¾ in thick. Flatten it evenly with a rolling pin. Push in and pinch up the edge all around to make the bannock 20 cm /8 in diameter with a slightly raised rim 15 cm /½ in wide. With a knife, make diagonal notches in the rim all around the bannock.

4 Cover a baking sheet with greaseproof paper lightly greased with butter. Place the bannock on the paper and bake for 45–50 minutes, until lightly browned.

5 While still warm, sprinkle with sugar. Cool it and cut into 8 wedges for serving.

CREAM & ITS USES

Cream adds a special touch to any dish, whether as a main ingredient or a decoration. Fortunately there is a wide variety of cream readily available, and my recipes here use them in imaginative, tempting ways.

Cream is, actually, just milk containing more than the normal quantity of fat. Milk contains on average about 3.8% butterfat, but cream must contain at least 12%.

All commercially sold cream is heat treated, either by pasteurization or some other method, to make it safe to use. Some creams are homogenized, that is, forced through a small valve under pressure to break up the fat globules and distribute them evenly in the milk. Homogenized cream cannot be whipped.

Types of fresh cream

Raw cream of various thicknesses is available from some dairy farms. It has a more definite flavour than commercially processed cream as it comes from cows of one breed fed on the same pasture.

Half cream must contain at least 12% butterfat. It is pasteurized and homogenized so that it becomes a thin pouring cream used on cereals or fruit, or in coffee.

Thin or single cream contains at least 18% fat. It is homogenized and pasteurized. It cannot be whipped but is delicious poured on desserts, or used in coffee or soups.

Whipping cream has a fat content of 35–42% and is pasteurized but not homogenized. It gives you a lighter, fluffier whipped cream than if you use thick cream. It is also cheaper. If a recipe specifies whipping cream you can use a mixture of half thin and half thick cream as an alternative.

Thick or double cream is a very rich cream with a 48–60% fat content, which has been slightly homogenized and pasteurized. It is thick enough to float on coffee, although it can be poured as well. It is best for desserts such as Strawberry liqueur-cream delight (see recipe) or for gateaux.

Thick double cream has the same fat content as ordinary thick cream but it is heavily homogenized. As a rule it is almost solid and is delicious when spooned generously over special desserts, but it will not whip: it turns to butter.

Clotted cream is also known in Britain as Devonshire, Cornish or scalded cream. It is richer than most thick cream, with a fat content of about 60%. Rich milk is poured into pans and left to stand for 10–12 hours. The milk is then heated to scald the cream so that a skin of cream forms on top. It is cooled slowly, then the cream is skimmed off.

Its grainy texture and scalded flavour are distinctive and too good to be used for cooking, so keep it for filling tea-cakes (see recipe) and for topping fruit pies.

Soured or cultured cream is made from fresh, homogenized thin cream, warmed and inoculated with bacteria which thicken it and give it a sharp flavour. Try Creamy onion flan (see recipe), with a tasty filling of soured cream, onion, cheese and bacon. Flageolets in soured cream (see recipe) is a delicious and rather unusual vegetable dish that is easy to prepare.

● To make your own soured cream, add 15 ml /1 tbls lemon juice to 150 ml /5 fl oz thick cream.

Soured cream has several merits: firstly, although commercial soured cream has the fat content of thin cream, it can be whipped successfully, although it will stiffen enough for piping. Secondly, its sharper flavour gives life to a lot of desserts and, more especially, to savoury, spicy dishes. It can also be boiled gently without curdling.

Smetana is used in Russian cookery: it is a combination of thick cream and soured cream. There is also a smetana sold in Britain which is like a thick buttermilk.

Crème fraîche, the everyday cream of France, is a slightly sharp fresh cream.

● To make a close substitute, mix 2 parts thick cream with 1 part soured cream and leave at room temperature for 5–6 hours until thickened. Stir, cover, then refrigerate.

Top of the milk is an ingredient old recipes sometimes call for, referring to the cream that rises to the top of non-homogenized milk. If you haven't any, use half cream or two-thirds thin cream and one-third milk.

Home-made or mock cream can be a very good stand-by if you run out of fresh cream. The simplest method is to melt 100 g /4 oz unsalted butter with 125 ml /4 fl oz milk, then process them together in a blender. Chill for several hours or overnight, to thicken. These quantities will give you about 225 ml /8 fl oz thin cream; for thicker cream, use 25 g /1 oz extra butter. You will get thicker cream and more of it (275 ml /10 fl oz) if you add 2.5 ml /½ tsp gelatine which has been dissolved in 30 ml /2 tbls water before blending.

Types of preserved cream

Long life creams: thin, whipping and thick creams are available in cartons. They have been ultra heat treated and have a shelf life of up to three months as long as they are unopened. These creams tend to separate in their cartons and, as they have a slight caramel flavour due to the heating process, they are best used in well-flavoured dishes.

Canned creams: sterilized half cream (12% fat) and full cream (23% fat) are homogenized, poured into cans, then heated; they will keep for up to two years unopened. They also have a caramelized flavour and are best used in strongly flavoured dishes, although they can be used for pouring.

Ready-whipped cream: this is available in tubs, or in aerosols with nozzles. It has been stabilized to hold the air, and heat treated.

Buying and storing cream

The standard fresh and preserved creams are widely available from most shops, although only the largest supermarkets keep a full

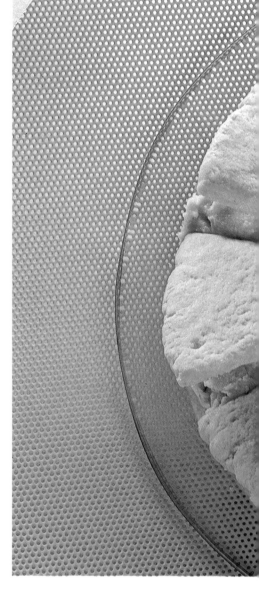

range. Raw cream can only be bought from a farm. Crème fraîche can generally only be bought in French-speaking countries.

Refrigerate and use raw cream as soon as possible. Pasteurized fresh creams will keep in the refrigerator for two to three days in summer, three to four in winter. Preserved cream should be treated like fresh cream after opening. Keep all creams covered.

The richer the cream, the better it freezes. Do not try to freeze cream with less than 35% fat. If you find that the cream is grainy when thawed, beat it lightly; it will smooth out and be quite usable in cold dishes. Its fat will, however, rise to the surface as droplets in hot drinks, and it will separate out more readily than usual in cooking.

You can freeze sweetened whipped cream in cartons, or pipe it into rosettes, open freeze, then pack loosely in boxes.

Cream can be frozen for up to six months.

Cooking with cream

Whipping cream: whipped cream can be used as a major ingredient, in a mousse for example, or as a decoration. It makes simple dishes look and taste luxurious, and adds glamour to rich ones.

The bowl, whisk and cream itself should be cold — a temperature of 5C /40F is best.

For the filling and topping

15 ml /1 tbls chive mustard
75 g /3 oz softened butter
175 g /6 oz Danish Blue cheese,
  grated or mashed
15 ml /1 tbls brandy
50 ml /2 fl oz thick double cream

1 Rub the chilled butter into the flour. Add the salt, mayonnaise and milk and mix to a soft dough. Chill for 20 minutes.
2 Heat the oven to 200C /400C /gas 6. Grease and flour 2 baking sheets.
3 Divide the dough into 2 equal portions. Shape each into a ball and place 1 on each baking sheet. Either roll or pat them out into 22 cm /8½ in rounds. Cut 1 round into 8 triangular wedges. Bake for 15 minutes and cool on the sheets.
4 While the pastry is cooling, mix the chive mustard thoroughly into the softened butter. Pound the cheese with the brandy, adding the cream gradually.
5 Spread half the mustard butter over the complete pastry round. Cover it with the creamed cheese and arrange the triangles on the top. Pipe rosettes with the remaining mustard butter as a garnish, then serve.

● The pastry, mustard butter and creamed cheese can be frozen separately and then assembled after thawing. Thaw the butter and the cheese for 6 hours at cool room temperature, and the pastry for 1½ hours.

Chicken, cream and celery

  50 minutes

Serves 4

25 g /1 oz butter
75 g /3 oz cooked ham, pork shoulder or
  boiled bacon, in very small pieces
3 celery sticks, in 5 cm /2 in pieces
25 g /1 oz flour
425 ml /15 fl oz half cream or 150 ml /5 fl oz
  thin cream, plus 275 ml /10 fl oz milk
5 ml /1 tsp freshly chopped mixed herbs
350 g /12 oz cooked chicken meat, chopped
salt and freshly ground black pepper
4 or 8 thin slices cooked ham, pork shoulder
  or bacon, to garnish
watercress sprigs, to garnish
boiled rice or pasta, to serve

1 Melt the butter in a pan. Add the ham, pork or bacon and the celery and sauté gently for 5 minutes. Add the flour and cook for 1 minute, stirring.
2 Still stirring constantly, gradually add the half cream or milk and cream. Stir it until the sauce thickens, then add the herbs and chicken. Heat the grill.
3 Reduce the heat under the sauce and simmer gently for 12–15 minutes, until it is heated through. Season to taste. Meanwhile, lightly grill the slices of meat for the garnish.
4 Arrange the grilled meat around the edge of a warmed serving platter. Pour the sauce into the centre and garnish with sprigs of watercress. Serve with boiled rice or pasta.

Whip quickly at first, by hand or using an electric whisk or food processor, until the cream takes on a matt finish, then, if you want it stiffly whipped, continue slowly until it stands in peaks. The soft peak stage is best when combining the cream with a purée or when making a soufflé, or when piping — the pressure of squeezing the cream through the bag will stiffen it further. If you overwhip cream, it will separate.

Whipping cream will easily whip to double its volume. Whipped thick cream is rich and firm, but does not have the volume of whipping cream. To obtain really fluffy cream, add an egg white to 150 ml /5 fl oz whipping cream or thick cream before you whip it.

Canned cream can be whipped if you refrigerate it for two hours, then open the can without shaking it and carefully pour off all the thin liquid — just whip the solid cream, and whip carefully because it turns grainy. Home-made cream whips well if made with 150 g /5 oz butter to 125 ml /4 fl oz milk, and it has a greater volume and lighter texture than whipped canned cream which is always rather solid.

The more stiffly you whip cream, and the richer the cream is, the longer it can wait before you use it (up to 24 hours); however,

Savoury galette

the longer you keep it the more solid it will become. Always keep the cream cool or it will separate.

Heating cream: the thinner the cream, the easier it is to heat. Half, thin or soured cream can be boiled gently. You can make a cream sauce by stirring thick cream gradually into a roux and bringing it gently to the boil; the flour acts as a stabilizer.

Thick cream can be boiled with care, even with the addition of an acid such as white wine. If it contains egg yolks, heat it in the top of a double boiler or the yolks will curdle.

Savoury galette

  1 hour 20 minutes

Serves 8

75 g /3 oz chilled unsalted butter, plus
  extra for greasing
225 g /8 oz self-raising flour, plus extra
  for dusting
a pinch of salt
30 ml /2 tbls mayonnaise
45 ml /3 tbls milk

Creamy onion flan

The crust in this flan is unusual as it does not get soggy. This tart will keep for several days in a refrigerator. Great for lunch or just a snack, it is delicious and satisfying.

 1 hour

Serves 4
200 g /7 oz bacon slices
175 g /6 oz small cheese crackers (about 48), finely crushed
90 g /3½ oz butter, melted
1 medium-sized onion, finely chopped
175 g /6 oz Jarlsberg, Gruyère or Emmenthal cheese, grated
200 ml /7 fl oz soured cream or natural thick yoghurt, or a combination of both
5 eggs, slightly beaten
salt and freshly ground black pepper
a pinch of dillweed
50 g /2 oz Cheddar cheese, grated

1 Fry the bacon in a frying-pan until it is crisp, then remove it from the pan, reserving 30 ml /2 tbls of the fat in the pan. Drain the bacon, on absorbent paper, then crumble and reserve. Heat the oven to 190C /375F / gas 5.
2 Combine the cracker crumbs with the melted butter. Press this into the bottom and sides of a 23–25 cm /9–10 in flan dish. Sprinkle in the crumbled bacon.
3 Add the onion to the reserved bacon fat in the frying-pan and sauté until it is cooked. Combine the sautéed onion with the cheese, soured cream or yoghurt, and the beaten eggs. Season with salt, pepper and dillweed.
4 Spoon the mixture into the flan case. Bake for 30 minutes or until cooked.
5 Remove the tart from the oven, sprinkle with Cheddar cheese and bake for 2–3 minutes more.
6 Eat cold or reheat gently in a moderate oven before eating.

Vegetable circlet salad

Colourful vegetables in aspic encircle a creamy purée. You can use canned asparagus, carrots and petits pois to make this delightful and unusual recipe.

 1 hour,
plus 6½–7 hours setting

Serves 6
30 ml /2 tbls gelatine
275 ml /10 fl oz boiling water
175 ml /6 fl oz chicken consommé, home-made or canned, hot
175 ml /6 fl oz dry white wine
salt (optional)
10–12 thick asparagus spears, cooked
12–14 equal-sized slices of carrot, cut into flower shapes and cooked
225 g /8 oz petits pois, cooked
100 g /4 oz diced cooked carrot
For the purée
225 g /8 oz petits pois, cooked
15 ml /1 tbls softened butter
45 ml /3 tbls whipping cream
salt and freshly ground black pepper

For the garnish
50 ml /2 fl oz whipping cream
a few drops of Worcestershire sauce

1 Rinse out a 1.1 L /2 pt ring mould. In a large bowl, soften the gelatine with 125 ml / 4 fl oz cold water. Stir in the boiling water, hot consommé and dry white wine, and add salt if needed. Stir it until the gelatine dissolves.
2 Pour 50 ml /2 fl oz of the liquid into the mould. Chill until it is lightly set, leaving the remaining liquid to cool to the consistency of unbeaten egg white.
3 Cut off any hard ends from the asparagus spears. Lay 6 spears flat in a ring on the set aspic in the mould. Spoon a little of the reserved jelly over these and then chill for 10 minutes.
4 Dip the carrot shapes in the reserved aspic and stick them around the outer edge of the mould.
5 Cut the remaining asparagus spears into 25 mm /1 in pieces, mix them with the petits pois and the diced carrot, then mix in the remaining aspic. Spoon it gently into the mould and chill for 6 hours or until it is completely set.
6 Make the purée while the aspic sets. Put the petit pois and butter in a blender and blend them until smooth. Alternatively press the peas through a vegetable mill and stir in the butter. Turn the mixture into a bowl. Whip the cream lightly and fold it in; season with salt and freshly ground black pepper.
7 Lightly whip the cream for the garnish, add Worcestershire sauce, mix thoroughly,

Vegetable circlet salad

and spoon it into a piping bag fitted with a small star nozzle.

8 Unmould the vegetable aspic circlet onto a round serving dish. Fill the centre of the ring with purée and pipe the flavoured cream around the circlet to garnish.

Flageolets in soured cream

15 minutes

Serves 4
450 g /1 lb canned flageolets, drained
white parts of 2 small leeks, thinly sliced
50 g /2 oz softened butter
60 ml /4 tbls chicken stock, home-made or
   from a cube
salt
freshly ground black pepper
90 ml /6 tbls soured cream
15 ml /1 tbls mayonnaise
freshly chopped parsley, to garnish

1 Bring the flageolets, leeks, butter and chicken stock slowly to the boil and cook gently, stirring occasionally, until the leeks are soft, about 7 minutes. Season.
2 Stir 60 ml /4 tbls soured cream and the mayonnaise into the vegetables. Reheat them gently without boiling.
3 Turn into a warmed serving dish. Spoon the remaining soured cream over the top, sprinkle with parsley and serve at once.

● If wished, substitute for the canned beans 175 g /6oz dried flageolets, soaked overnight and then cooked for 1–1¼ hours.

Strawberry liqueur-cream delight

This luscious dessert makes the best use of strawberries when they are in season.

1¼ hours draining and marinating, then 15 minutes

Serves 6–8
1 kg /2¼ lb strawberries
30–45 ml /2–3 tbls icing sugar
100 ml /3½ fl oz kirsch
50 ml /2 fl oz anisette
250 ml /9 fl oz thick cream
100 g /4 oz vanilla-flavoured icing sugar

1 Wash the strawberries in a colander and leave them to drain for about 15 minutes.
2 Hull the berries and put them in a large bowl, then dust them with the plain icing sugar. Pour the kirsch and anisette over the fruit, cover and leave the bowl in a cool place for about 1 hour.
3 Whip the cream until stiff and then fold in the vanilla-flavoured icing sugar, which is made by leaving a piece of vanilla pod in an airtight container of icing sugar for a couple of weeks. Arrange the strawberries with some of their juice in individual glass dishes, top them with the cream and serve.

Strawberry liqueur-cream delight

Bath tea-cakes

Bath tea-cakes used to be dunked into tea and coffee when these drinks became so popular during the 17th century.

 1¾ hours

Makes 12
20 ml /4 tsp fresh yeast
30 ml /2 tbls caster sugar
50 ml /2 fl oz fresh or long-life thin cream,
   plus a little extra
225 g /8 oz flour, plus extra for dusting
a pinch of salt
100 g /4 oz butter
oil, for greasing
5 ml /1 tsp caraway seeds
butter or clotted cream, to serve

1 Cream the yeast with 15 ml /1 tbls sugar in a small bowl. Mix in the cream and 15 ml / 1 tbls warm water. Put aside for 10 minutes.
2 Sift the flour and salt into a large bowl.

Rub in the butter with your fingertips until the mixture resembles fine crumbs. Add the yeast mixture to the centre.
3 Mix thoroughly, first with a wooden spoon, then by hand, to make a soft dough. Add 15 ml /1 tbls extra cream if needed. Knead the dough in the bowl until it is smooth and elastic.
4 Dust a baking sheet lightly with flour. Shape the dough into 12 equal-sized balls and place them 7.5 cm /3 in apart on the baking sheet. Flatten them slightly and place the sheet in a large, oiled polythene bag.
5 Leave the tea-cakes in a warm place for 40 minutes or until they are puffy. Meanwhile, heat the oven to 190C /375F /gas 5.
6 Brush the tops of the risen cakes with cream and sprinkle them with the caraway seeds and remaining sugar. Bake the cakes for 18 minutes, or until they are a light fawn colour.
7 Serve the tea-cakes while they are still warm, split and filled with butter or clotted cream.

● For a special tea-time treat, serve the cream-filled Bath tea cakes with home-made preserves, such as raspberry or blackcurrant.

WAYS WITH YOGHURT

Yoghurt can be used in many delicious ways, and the recipes here show just how adaptable it is — from a chilled soup to an exotic marinade to a luscious dessert. Try making your own, it's easy and nutritious.

Yoghurt is very versatile: you can eat it on its own as a tasty, nourishing snack; or you can use it in soups, sauces, casseroles and desserts — see the recipes on the following pages — for a delicious, creamy texture and taste.

Yoghurt is basically milk, preserved or solidified. Natural yoghurt has most of the food values of the milk from which it is made, and it is also the most easily digested form of milk. It is therefore especially suitable for children and the elderly. It's ideal for slimmers, too, because it is usually made from low-fat milk (although if you make or buy yoghurt with full-fat milk it will be appetizing but not slimming).

To turn milk into yoghurt, two special types of 'friendly' bacteria (minute, invisible living organisms in the air) are necessary, plus a gentle warmth to promote their growth. As the bacteria breed and feed, they make the milk more acid so that the solid milk particles stick together in a soft mass like a thick custard — what we call yoghurt. Once you have made your first batch of yoghurt, reserve some as a 'starter culture' for your next batch.

Yoghurt is called a 'live' food because it contains these living bacteria, which also help to keep the stomach free of other harmful bacteria.

In hot countries, it is one of the safest ways to take milk, so it is especially popular in the East. It is also the ancient traditional way of consuming milk in the Slav countries and Bulgaria, Greece, Turkey and Hungary, and it is still very widely used there, both as a straight drink and as an ingredient in savoury meat dishes and sweet desserts.

Buying and storing yoghurt

There was a time when yoghurt sales were confined mainly to health food shops, but increasingly in recent years it has become big business, with many varieties competing with each other. Each brand has a slightly different consistency and taste — some are thicker, some sweeter, and so on. Choose the one you enjoy most, or which best suits your recipe.

There is a vast range of flavoured yoghurts available. Some have pieces of fresh or preserved fruit stirred in, some are mixed with fruit syrup and some have flavouring which contains artificial colours and preservatives.

Yoghurt does not freeze successfully. Commercial and stabilized home-made yoghurt can be frozen, but they lose some of their smooth texture on thawing.

Making your own yoghurt

At home you can use any type of milk or combination of types: homogenized or pasteurized milk; canned evaporated milk, mixed (usually half-and-half) with water for a caramelly flavour; skimmed milk powder reconstituted with water for low-fat yoghurt;

ultra-heat-treated milk, or any sterilized kind.

To each 600 ml /1 pt milk use about 15 ml /1 tbls natural, unflavoured yoghurt. Buy a small carton for your first batch, making sure it is new stock; yoghurt that is several days old can give acid-tasting results. Or use a dried Bulgarian-type culture, available from most health food shops.

Bring the milk to boiling point and simmer it for 1–2 minutes. Next, let it cool to 46C / 115F. If you have a cooking thermometer, you can determine this accurately. If not, dip in a scrupulously clean finger and count to ten. Your finger should feel slightly hot by then. If you are using already sterilized milk, do not boil it, just heat it to the required temperature.

While the milk is cooling, sterilize the equipment you will need in boiling water. Dry it with an absolutely clean cloth and keep it covered until ready to use. The introduction of any unwanted bacteria from washing up can inhibit the setting process.

You can easily make yoghurt without any special equipment, but if you intend to make it on a regular basis, buy an electric yoghurt maker. It keeps the milk at the right temperature for incubation and is easy to use.

A wide-necked vacuum flask is perfect for keeping the incubating culture at a steady temperature. Or use a heatproof casserole or bowl, or small pots (commercial yoghurt pots or margarine tubs are good). Choose containers with wide necks so you do not break up the yoghurt too much when you spoon it out.

The yoghurt culture should be at room temperature when you put it into the sterilized flask or bowl. Slowly pour on the warm milk, stirring or whisking vigorously to mix it thoroughly, then if you are using small pots pour the mixture into them. Cover each container with its lid or with cling film. Put a vacuum flask on a surface where it can be left undisturbed.

Containers other than a vacuum flask will need to be kept warm — wrapped in a towel in an airing cupboard, on top of a warm radiator or in the warming drawer of an oven. A temperature of 18C /65F is best.

The length of time you leave the yoghurt affects its flavour. It will usually start to set after 3 hours. If you refrigerate it straight away the yoghurt will have a faintly sweet taste. The sweetness disappears and then the yoghurt becomes increasingly sharp the longer you leave it. Eight hours should be the maximum for incubation.

In Middle Eastern countries yoghurt is served warm, straight from its incubation period, with a little sugar or honey spooned on top. If you prefer it chilled, transfer the container straight to the refrigerator (it will thicken a little more as it chills) and store it there for up to one week, reserving enough to start your next batch. Make yoghurt in small

quantities on a 'little and often' basis, when the starter culture can be fresh.

Flavouring plain yoghurt

Most flavourings are best added to the yoghurt after it has set, but you can infuse the milk with a subtle flavour during the incubation period. Suspend a bunch of mint, basil, thyme, bay leaves or rosemary from the rim of the container with string, or immerse a spring onion or a garlic clove in it. Sink a cinnamon stick, a vanilla pod or thinly pared citrus zest in the milk for a delicate flavour.

Try stirring snipped chives, chopped spring onions and/or green or red peppers into unflavoured yoghurt and spicing it with a small pinch of cayenne pepper or paprika. Stir in a little chopped mango chutney and a large pinch of curry powder, or add a good squeeze of tomato purée, a few drops of Worcestershire sauce and chopped prawns.

You can make lovely dips with plain yoghurt: try stirring in a mixture of grated cheese, chopped olives and hard-boiled egg; or finely grated carrot, diced cucumber and smoked mackerel; or diced ham, drained canned sweetcorn and mashed banana.

Make an avocado-yoghurt dip by blending together the flesh of one avocado, 50 g /2 oz cream cheese at room temperature, 150 ml / 5 fl oz plain yoghurt, and lemon juice, salt and freshly ground black pepper to taste. Chill before serving with raw vegetable sticks.

Easy-to-make desserts can be made quickly by adding a whole range of ingredients including fresh, canned, dried or candied fruit; nuts; crushed nut brittle or praline; desiccated coconut; grated chocolate; muesli; toasted porridge oats; toasted marshmallows; or lightly crushed meringues or biscuits.

Thickening yoghurt

Thickened yoghurt is easy to make at home. It makes a less rich, less expensive — and less fattening — alternative to cream, and has the great advantage over store-bought yoghurt in that it looks like cream, too. It can be used in many recipes that call for cream.

Thickened yoghurt can be made with normal pasteurized or homogenized milk. It can also be made with cartons of skimmed milk available from supermarkets — the results will be a little thinner and lighter.

The process for making thickened yoghurt is almost the same as for making plain yoghurt. The main difference is that dried skimmed milk powder is added to the milk before you start to give a thicker end result (see recipe).

You can make thick yoghurt (not to be confused with thickened yoghurt) by reducing the milk by one-third before adding the starter. This yoghurt, though thicker than normal, will not be stabilized.

Stabilizing yoghurt

Home-made yoghurt should be thickened or stabilized before being used in cooking. Otherwise when it is cooked or stirred into hot dishes it is likely to separate or give the appearance of curdling.

To stabilize yoghurt, tip 600 ml /1 pt set yoghurt into a small pan and heat it gently

Yoghurt and lemon soup

until it becomes runny. Mix together 7.5 ml / 1½ tsp cornflour with 15 ml /1 tbls cold milk; or lightly beat a small egg white. When the yoghurt is runny, gradually stir in the cornflour paste or the egg white, very slowly. Bring it gently to the boil, slowly stirring in one direction only, so that the yoghurt is just moving but not swishing about in the pan. Simmer uncovered for ten minutes. Remove the pan from the heat, pour the yoghurt into a container and leave it to cool. Cover and store it in the refrigerator for up to one week.

Cooking with yoghurt

Yoghurt features prominently in Eastern cuisines. In India it is spiced and coloured with cayenne pepper and garam masala and then used as a marinade to tenderize meat before cooking; and heavily spiced yoghurt is often brushed onto tandoori-cooked meats. Chopped mint and/or diced cucumber added to yoghurt is perfect with curries.

In Turkey, minced meat balls or lamb kebabs are often served in a herby yoghurt sauce. Yoghurt is used in soups from the Hungarian black cherry soup to the Lebanese yoghurt and almond soup. Chilled Yoghurt and lemon soup (see recipe) is unusual, and has a wonderfully refreshing taste.

For a really light dressing for fruit salads, try stirring unsweetened orange juice or pineapple juice into yoghurt. Add lemon juice if the mixture includes apples, pears or bananas.

Make mayonnaise lighter by stirring in an equal quantity of plain yoghurt, mix a spoonful into a vinaigrette dressing or combine it with unsweetened fruit juice as a dressing for cole slaw or raw vegetable salads.

Orange and almond cheesecake (see recipe) made with yoghurt has an air of luxury, yet it's very quick to make. Yoghurt can also be used in soda bread, scones and other baked goods instead of soured milk. It is a delicious and lower-caloried substitute for cream in Ginger and honey ice cream and Mango and yoghurt mousse (see recipes). To convert your own favourite recipes, as a rule substitute standard yoghurt for thin cream and thickened yoghurt for thick cream.

Yoghurt and lemon soup

🥄 10 minutes,
plus chilling

Serves 4–6
600 ml /1 pt yoghurt, chilled
600 ml /1 pt tomato juice, chilled
5 ml /1 tsp tomato purée
½ small cucumber, peeled and finely diced
1 medium-sized green pepper, finely chopped
2 spring onions, thinly sliced
juice and grated zest of 1 large lemon
salt and freshly ground black pepper
a large pinch of cayenne pepper
2.5 ml /½ tsp paprika
15 ml /1 tbls freshly chopped chives
thin lemon slices, to garnish
lemon wedges, to serve

1 Tip the yoghurt into a bowl. Gradually beat in the tomato juice and purée until the mixture is smooth and well blended.
2 Stir in the cucumber, green pepper, spring onions, lemon juice and zest. Season to taste with salt and black pepper and stir in the cayenne pepper and paprika.
3 Cover and chill until needed. Just before serving, stir in the chopped chives. Pour the soup into chilled bowls, garnish them with lemon slices and serve very cold, with a lemon wedge for each person.

Aubergine and macaroni bake

🍴🍴 1½–1¾ hours

Serves 4
500 g /1 lb aubergines, trimmed and cubed
salt
50 ml /3½ tbls olive oil
1 medium-sized onion, chopped
1 garlic clove, chopped
50 g /2 oz red pepper, seeded and chopped
2.5 ml /½ tsp dried mixed herbs
1.5 ml /¼ tsp ground cinnamon
400 g /14 oz canned tomatoes, drained
freshly ground black pepper
175 g /6 oz macaroni
2 medium-sized eggs
275 ml /10 fl oz plain yoghurt
50 g /2 oz mature Cheddar cheese, grated

1 Layer the aubergine cubes in a colander, sprinkling generously with salt in between. Leave to drain for 20–30 minutes, then rinse them well in cold water and pat them dry with absorbent paper.
2 Heat 30 ml /2 tbls olive oil in a heavy-based saucepan. Add the onion, garlic and red pepper. Cover the pan and cook gently for 5 minutes, stirring occasionally, until the vegetables are softened.
3 Add the aubergine cubes, herbs and cinnamon to the pan and cook, stirring, for 2 minutes. Add the tomatoes and season to taste with salt and black pepper. Stir well and bring it to simmering point. Cover the pan, reduce the heat and simmer gently for 20–25 minutes until the aubergines are very soft. Taste and adjust the seasoning.
4 Meanwhile, cook the macaroni in 1.7 L / 3 pt salted, boiling water with the remaining oil for 8–10 minutes until it is *al dente* (still slightly firm). Drain and reserve. Heat the oven to 200C /400F /gas 6.
5 Spoon half the aubergine mixture over the base of an oiled, 1.7 L /3 pt ovenproof dish. Arrange the drained macaroni on top and season lightly. Cover with the remaining aubergine mixture.
6 Beat together the eggs, yoghurt and cheese, and season. Pour this over the top layer of aubergine. Bake for 20–25 minutes until the topping is set and lightly coloured.

Spiced yoghurt kebabs

Home-made thickened yoghurt

 8 hours, plus chilling

Makes 600 ml /1 pt
600 ml /1 pt milk
30 ml /2 tbls natural yoghurt
45 ml /3 tbls dried skimmed milk powder

1 Warm the milk until it is almost boiling. Turn off the heat and leave it to cool to 40–43C /105–110F (hold your clean little finger in the milk to the count of 10; if it still feels hot to the touch then the temperature is right).
2 Mix the yoghurt and the milk powder together to a thick paste. Gradually beat in the milk until it is thoroughly combined and free from lumps.
3 Pour the mixture into a vacuum flask which has been rinsed out with hot water and insert the stopper immediately. Leave the mixture undisturbed for 8 hours or until it is thick. Transfer it to a covered container and chill it for about 1 hour before using.

Spiced yoghurt kebabs

 overnight marinating, then 40 minutes

Serves 4
500 g /1 lb lean lamb, cut into 25 mm /1 in cubes
50 g /2 oz button mushrooms
4–8 small onions, blanched in boiling water for 3 minutes, then drained
1 medium-sized green pepper, cut into squares
8 small or 4 halved medium-sized tomatoes
oil, for brushing skewers
8 bay leaves
boiled rice, to serve
flat-leafed parsley, to garnish
For the marinade
275 ml /10 fl oz stabilized yoghurt (see introduction), or thickened yoghurt (see recipe)
5 ml /1 tsp garam masala
2.5 ml /½ tsp ground coriander
1.5 ml /¼ tsp ground turmeric
2.5 ml /½ tsp ground cumin
2.5 ml /½ tsp salt
1.5 ml /¼ tsp chilli powder (optional)
grated zest and juice of 1 lemon

1 First make the marinade. Beat all the ingredients together and pour them into a thick polythene bag. Add the lamb cubes and tie the top of the bag firmly. Shake it so that the meat is well covered with the sauce. Put the bag on a plate and leave it in the refrigerator overnight. Turn the bag over now and again if it is convenient.
2 Prepare the vegetables.
3 Remove the cubes of lamb from the marinade using a slotted spoon. Pour the marinade into a small pan and set it aside.
4 Brush 4 kebab skewers with oil and then

thread them with the lamb, mushrooms, onions, pepper, tomatoes and bay leaves.
5 Heat the grill to high and line the grill pan with foil. Brush the kebabs with oil and grill them for about 15 minutes, turning them once, so that the lamb is just cooked through.
6 While the kebabs are cooking, gently heat the marinade, stirring it occasionally.
7 Serve the kebabs on a bed of rice and garnish the dish with flat-leaved parsley. Pour the hot sauce into a heated sauce-boat and serve immediately.

Lamb with yoghurt and paprika sauce

 2 hours 20 minutes

Serves 4
700 g /1½ lb lean lamb, in 25 mm /1 in cubes
salt
freshly ground black pepper
10 ml /2 tsp paprika
40 g /1½ oz butter
1 medium-sized onion, sliced
1 medium-sized red pepper, thinly sliced
400 g /14 oz canned tomatoes
15 ml /1 tbls tomato purée
1 bay leaf
2.5 ml /½ tsp dried oregano
150 ml /5 fl oz stabilized yoghurt (see introduction)
15 ml /1 tbls chopped fresh parsley, to garnish

Lamb with yoghurt and paprika sauce

1 Put the cubes of meat into a polythene bag with the salt, pepper and paprika and shake until the meat is well coated and tinted pink.
2 Melt the butter in a frying-pan over a moderate heat and, when it is hot, fry the cubes of meat for about 6 minutes, turning them frequently so that they are sealed on all sides. Using a slotted spoon, transfer the meat to an ovenproof casserole. Heat the oven to 180C /350F /gas 4.
3 Add the onion and red pepper to the fat remaining in the pan and stir well. Fry over a moderate heat for about 3 minutes. Do not allow the onion to brown. Add the tomatoes with their juice, stir in the tomato purée and add the bay leaf and oregano. Bring the sauce gently to the boil, season it with salt and freshly ground black pepper and pour it over the meat in the casserole. Stir well to blend.
4 Cover the casserole and then cook it for 1½–1¾ hours, or until the meat is tender in texture.
5 Remove the casserole from the oven. Discard the bay leaf and stir in the yoghurt thoroughly until the sauce is smooth and the colour is even. Return the casserole to the oven for about 5 minutes, just to heat it through. Sprinkle with the chopped parsley and serve the casserole hot.

● Using stabilized yoghurt here ensures that the yoghurt will not separate or curdle when it is added to the hot casserole.

Ginger and honey ice cream

In this recipe, lower-priced, lower-caloried yoghurt is substituted for cream — with mouthwatering results.

 1 hour, 4 hours freezing, plus 1 hour thawing

Serves 6–8
275 ml /10 fl oz milk
2 eggs, separated
45 ml /3 tbls clear honey
60 ml /4 tbls syrup from a jar of preserved ginger
275 ml /10 fl oz yoghurt
50 g /2 oz preserved ginger, thinly sliced
For the sauce
75 ml /5 tbls syrup from a jar of preserved ginger
30 ml /2 tbls clear honey
5 ml /1 tsp cornflour
2.5 ml /½ tsp ground ginger
30 ml /2 tbls lemon juice
5 ml /1 tsp grated lemon zest

1   If using the freezing compartment of your refrigerator, turn it down to its lowest temperature an hour before you start.
2   Put the milk and egg yolks into the upper pan of a double boiler, or a bowl that fits over a pan. Pour hot water into the lower pan and set it over a low heat. Do not allow the water to boil. Stir the milk and egg mixture constantly until it starts to thicken and coats the back of the spoon — this will take about 15 minutes.
3   Remove the pan from the heat, remove the upper pan or bowl and leave the custard to cool, stirring it occasionally. Stir in the honey and the ginger syrup. Pour the mixture into a metal ice-cube tray, cover it with foil and freeze it in the freezer compartment

Orange and almond cheesecake

of the refrigerator. Place a large bowl in the refrigerator to chill.
4   After 1 hour, turn the partly frozen mixture into the chilled bowl and beat until it is smooth. Whisk the egg whites until they form stiff peaks. Fold the yoghurt and egg whites into the custard mixture. Gently stir in the chopped ginger. Return the mixture to the ice-cube tray and freeze it, covered, for a further 3 hours.
5   Before serving the ice cream, transfer the container to the refrigerator for 1 hour to soften the ice cream.
6   To make the sauce, put 75 ml /5 tbls water into a small pan with the ginger syrup and honey and heat gently. Put the cornflour into a small bowl with the ground ginger, mix well and gradually mix in the lemon juice. Add a little water if necessary to make a smooth paste. Pour the paste into the mixture in the pan and stir in the lemon zest. Stir for about 3 minutes, until the sauce thickens.
7   Serve the ice cream in scoops, decorated with the thinly sliced ginger. Serve the sauce separately, hot or cold.

Orange and almond cheesecake

From the base of crushed macaroons to the toasted almond topping, this delicious cheesecake has an air of luxury, yet it's very quick to make.

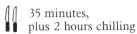 35 minutes, plus 2 hours chilling

Serves 6
butter, for greasing
75 g /3 oz butter, melted
225 g /8 oz almond macaroons, crushed

For the filling
225 g /8 oz curd cheese
150 ml /5 fl oz yoghurt
2 medium-sized eggs, lightly beaten
30 ml /2 tbls clear honey
15 g /½ oz powdered gelatine
grated zest and juice of 1 orange
50 g /2 oz almond macaroons, crushed
25 g /1 oz blanched almonds, toasted

1   Butter a 20 cm /8 in flan ring and stand it on a flat plate or dish.
2   Combine the melted butter and the crushed macaroons and mix them well. Tip the mixture into the flan ring, press it down smoothly to cover the base and form the sides of the flan. Chill it in the refrigerator while you make the filling.
3   Beat together the cheese and the yoghurt until they are completely smooth. Beat in the eggs and honey.
4   Put the gelatine into a cup with the orange juice. Stand it in a pan of hot water and stir occasionally until the gelatine has completely dissolved.
5   Remove the gelatine mixture from the heat and allow it to cool. Pour it steadily into the cheese mixture, blending well. Stir in the orange zest and crushed macaroons.
6   Pour the mixture into the flan case and chill for about 2 hours, or until the mixture is set. Decorate the top with the toasted almonds. Remove the flan ring to serve.

Mango and yoghurt mousse

20 minutes, plus chilling

Serves 6
250 g /9 oz canned mangoes in syrup
15 g /½ oz powdered gelatine
50 g /2 oz caster sugar
300 ml /10 fl oz thickened yoghurt (see recipe)
2 medium-sized egg whites

1   Drain the mangoes, reserving the syrup. Measure 60 ml /4 tbls syrup into a small heat-proof bowl and sprinkle the gelatine over it. Leave it to stand until it is spongy.
2   Meanwhile put the mango flesh and the sugar in an electric blender and blend them to a smooth purée.
3   Stand the bowl of gelatine in a pan of hot water and heat it gently until the gelatine is dissolved. Stir it into the mango purée, then leave it in a cool place until it is just beginning to set.
4   Beat the mango purée and the yoghurt together. Whisk the egg whites until they are stiff, then fold them into the purée until it is evenly blended.
5   Pour the mixture into a rinsed 600 ml / 1 pt mould and chill it in the refrigerator overnight until it is set. Turn it out to serve.

● Use any 250 g /9 oz can of fruit instead of mangoes.
● Fresh mangoes can be used in this recipe, if wished. Peel and stone 2, about 225 g /8 oz each, then use water and lemon juice to taste as a substitute for the syrup.

Staples

FACTS ABOUT FLOUR

From time immemorial, wherever cereals have been grown, man has ground them into flour. This flour remains the basis of staple food throughout much of the world.

The best-known flours are obtained from grain, which must first be ground and then winnowed to separate the outer husk from the inner kernel. The earliest method of milling flour consisted of crushing the grain between two large stones. Later the Romans invented the quern, made with two conical stones, the top one revolving on a peg set in the lower one; the quern was turned by hand. The first water-powered mills were invented about 2,000 years ago. Today most wheat flour is milled by electrically-driven steel rollers, although both querns and water-mills are still used.

The word flour normally refers to the product made from wheat, but other cereals, such as rye, buckwheat, oats, barley, rice and millet, and certain pulses such as chick-peas, and even vegetables, are used for making flour in different parts of the world. The advantage of wheat flour over other types of flour is that it can be used with yeast to make a light-textured risen loaf. The main use for flour is in baking — pastry, cakes, scones, biscuits, puddings and pancakes — and bread-making.

Flours are also used to thicken sauces, soups and casseroles. The French distinguish between flour (*farine*) and *farina*, which are particularly fine flours made from starchy materials such as potatoes and chestnuts, and which are used mainly for thickening. Best known of these are cornflour and arrowroot, both of which can also be used for sweet glazes for fruit flans and gateaux. If the flour is manufactured by washing out the starch with water, it is called *fecula*.

Wheat flour

In Western countries this is the flour most commonly used for bread-making and baking. There are 3 main types of wheat from which the flours are made. Bread wheat (*Triticum aestivum*) is the most important and the most widely grown. The oldest variety (*Triticum monococcum*), which was cultivated by the prehistoric lake-dwellers in Switzerland, is still grown in Yugoslavia, North Africa and parts of Asia. Durum wheat (*Triticum durum*), an essential ingredient for many types of pasta, is also grown.

Why wheat flour is special: wheat contains gluten, a mixture of proteins, which absorbs water and then forms elastic strands. These become stronger and more flexible when the mixture is handled and this is why bread dough is kneaded. Yeast raises the bread internally and the gluten structure readily stretches to enclose the air pockets. It will then hold the shape of the bread until it is cooked and set. The gluten content of wheat flour varies according to the type of wheat used and the place where it was grown. The more gluten in the flour, the more it is able to rise, and for this reason a little wheat flour is included in the making of

almost all breads whatever the main type of flour.

White flour: during the milling process the outer layers of the wheat grain — the bran — and the centre — the germ — are removed, leaving the starchy white endosperm, which is then passed mechanically through wire, silk or nylon sieves. After the removal of the bran and wheatgerm, 70–75% of the original wheat remains, and this percentage is known as the extraction rate. The advantage of removing the wheatgerm, which contains vitamin E, is that it goes rancid very quickly, and any flour with an extraction rate of over 85% should not be kept for longer than 4 weeks. Without wheatgerm the flour has a much longer storage life.

Flour becomes whiter and improves in quality if kept in a dry place for several months. Normally the bleaching and maturing process is achieved chemically by adding various substances such as chlorine dioxide. In many countries, Britain for instance, white flour has to meet legal requirements, which means that it needs to be fortified with certain nutrients lost during the milling — thiamine, nicotinic acid, calcium and iron.

Strong flour: different varieties of wheat produce different types of flour. The wheats of America and Canada, for example, are hard wheats with a high percentage of gluten. High gluten flour is labelled 'strong flour' or 'bread flour' and it produces a light, springy, well-risen loaf. It is most commonly used by commercial bakers and is the best flour for flaky and puff pastry as well as bread.

Plain flour: this all-purpose flour is suitable for sauces and most cooking. Always use plain flour unless another type is specified.

Soft flour: this has a low gluten content and is produced in countries such as France. It makes very light cakes and crisp biscuits.

Self-raising flour: this contains chemical raising agents — a mixture of cream of tartar and bicarbonate of soda — usually added at the mill. It is a convenient flour for the cook to use in most cakes and general baking, apart from bread and pastry.

Wholewheat (or wholemeal) flour: this contains the whole of the wheat grain, not just the ground inner kernel, and therefore it has a 100% extraction rate. It contains the vitamin E from the wheatgerm which is removed from white flour and so wholewheat flour is more nutritious. Many experts now think that the fibre (bran) contained in wholewheat flour is an important element in a healthy diet.

Wholewheat flour can be milled by modern methods or by the old-fashioned stone-grinding, in which case the packet will be labelled 'stone-ground'. It is generally believed that since the wheat is kept cooler during the stone-grinding process, more of the valuable nutrients are preserved.

Wheatmeal flour: this consists of 80–90% of the grain, without the coarsest bran.

Brown flour: this contains 80–85% of the wheat, with the bran removed but the germ still present.

Special flours: these, such as scofa, are made up by the miller and consist of brown or white wheat flour with other ingredients such as wheatgerm, bran, malt, rye, barley or soya flour added. These flours can usually be bought at health food shops.

Semolina or cream of wheat: this is made from durum wheat, the cereal mainly grown to make pasta. Semolina is a coarse-grade flour used in thickening soups, as well as in the traditional English milk pudding.

Other cereal flours

Barley flour: at one time the main bread flour in Britain was barley flour. It has a low gluten content and so makes hard, flat loaves. In the 15th century these were used as plates to soak up gravy and juice, which could then be eaten at the end of the meal. Barley flour is best mixed with wheat flour. It has a pleasant, nutty flavour and is good added to scones and savoury biscuits. In Scotland it is still used in the making of the traditional bannocks and porridge.

Buckwheat flour: this is dark brown in colour and has a pleasantly rich flavour and

also used for thicken[n]g delicate dishes as it does not need to be boiled to be effective. In China rice flour is used to make a type of noodle.

Rye flour: dark grey-brown in colour, rye flour gives black bread and pumpernickel their dark colour and rich, almost malted flavour. Rye flour is popular in Northern and Eastern Europe, but its gluten content is much lower than that of wheat so it needs to be mixed with wheat flour to make a well-risen loaf.

Vegetable flours

Arrowroot: traditionally made from the dried tubers of a tropical perennial plant, this starch is a fine, tasteless white powder. It can be obtained from chemists and, as it is easy to digest, arrowroot is sometimes made into a gruel for invalids. Its chief use to the cook, however, is as a thickening agent. It is finer than cornflour and is used when a particularly clear sauce is required. It sets to a clear, jelly-like glaze when mixed with fruit juice or syrup. If you are substituting arrowroot for cornflour use half the weight of arrowroot given for cornflour.

Chestnut flour: is made from dried and ground sweet chestnuts. This kind of flour is often used in parts of Italy and Corsica to make dishes such as sweet porridge and a special cake which is unusually flavoured with rosemary.

Chick-pea flour: this is sometimes called *besan*, and can be bought at most good Indian shops. It is pale yellow in colour, high in protein, and is used for baking poppadums and *nan*, the leavened flat bread which is served in Indian restaurants, or it is used for thickening soups.

Potato flour: made from dried and ground cooked potatoes, potato flour is a gluten-free, white powder which can be used to thicken soups and casseroles where a delicate result is required. You may be surprised to know that it is also contained in some desserts. It is used because, unlike many other flours, it thickens without needing to be brought to boiling point, which can cause other ingredients in the mixture — egg yolks and cream, for example — to curdle.

Soya flour: made from soya beans, this is a soft, smooth, creamy yellow powder. It is low in starch and high in protein and will increase the nutritional value of any dish in which it is included. In China it is used to make a kind of vegetable 'cheese', *tofu*, and in Europe and the United States of America it is sometimes used as a cheap substitute for ground almonds.

Storing flour

Plain white flour, cornflour and arrowroot keep well for at least 6 months if they are stored in a cool, dry, airy place. They are best left in their packets, although you may prefer to place them inside an airtight container for extra protection. If you plan to buy it in bulk, make sure that you have sufficient containers of this kind for storage and that they are clean and dry. Never put new flour on top of old. Other types of flour should be bought from shops where there is a quick stock turnover, and kept for no longer than 2 months.

slightly gritty texture. It is best known mixed with yeast to make blinis, the famous Russian pancakes. It is used for pancakes in the United States of America and in France for the crêpes and galettes of Brittany. Buckwheat flour is also used to make crisp, thin, unleavened breads and some types of pasta.

Cornmeal: made from maize, cornmeal is white or pale yellow in colour with a coarser texture than wheat flour. It is gluten-free, so can only be made into flat breads like the Mexican tortillas. In the United States of America it is used with baking powder for muffins and semi-sweet cake-breads.

Cornmeal is not as nourishing as wheat flour as it lacks one of the important B vitamins, niacin. Polenta is another type of cornmeal flour, coarser in texture, which is a staple food in Northern Italy where it is made into a kind of very thick porridge, which is often eaten instead of bread or pasta; it can be baked or fried.

Cornflour: this is a fine powder, softer and whiter than flour, which is also made from maize. It is tasteless and generally used for thickening sauces, soups and stews. For the finest and lightest quality cakes and biscuits, make up the weight of wheat flour with a little cornflour; this lowers the gluten content still further. Cornflour is also made into milk puddings and blancmanges.

Rich corn bread, Oatcakes and Rye bread with cumin and raisins

Millet flour: millet was once the principal cereal of Europe and is still important in some European areas and in Russia, Egypt and India. The flour is not as good as wheat flour for baking but can be made into flat, unleavened breads and griddle cakes. It is used with fine semolina grains to make couscous which is eaten throughout the Mediterranean countries of North Africa.

Oatmeal: this is made from oats, and can be bought in fine, medium or coarse (pinhead) grades, the fine one being the most generally useful. A little oatmeal can be an excellent addition to wholewheat (or wheatmeal) flour. Oats are hardier than other cereals, with a higher protein content, hence their popularity in cooler places such as Scotland, where oats are used in haggis, bannocks and Atholl brose, a drink which is traditionally made from oatmeal, Scotch whisky and heather honey.

Rice flour (which should not be confused with ground rice) is made from both polished and brown rice, although brown rice flour is quite difficult to find. It is very fine and is used for dusting dough in the bakery trade. Used with wheat flour it gives cakes a closer texture and helps to make biscuits crisp. It is

Rye bread with cumin and raisins

🔪🔪 2 hours 40 minutes, including rising time, then cooking

Makes 3 small loaves
butter, for greasing
15 ml /1 tbls dried yeast
2.5 ml /½ tsp sugar
250 g /9 oz rye flour
500 g /18 oz strong white flour
10 ml /2 tsp salt
30 ml /2 tbls oil
15 ml /1 tbls black treacle
15 ml /1 tbls clear honey
15 ml /1 tbls cumin seeds
100 g /4 oz raisins

1 Butter 3 loaf tins of 800 ml /1½ pt capacity each.
2 Put the yeast and sugar into a bowl and add 225 ml /8 fl oz hand-hot water. Mix it lightly with a fork, then leave for 10 minutes until the yeast has frothed up like the head on a glass of beer.
3 Sift the flours into a large bowl, then add the salt, oil, treacle, honey, cumin seeds and raisins. Make a well in the centre and pour in the frothy yeast mixture and a further 225 ml /8 fl oz warm water. Mix the ingredients thoroughly, adding a little more flour or water if necessary to get a soft but manageable dough.
4 Knead the dough on a lightly floured surface for 10 minutes, until smooth. Put it into a large, lightly greased bowl. Cover the bowl with a piece of greased cling film and leave in a warm place for 1 hour, until the dough has risen by about one-third again (it

Shortbread

will not rise as much as all-white flour dough).
5 Knead the dough again for 2 minutes. Heat the oven to 220C /425F / gas 7.
6 Divide the dough into 3 equal pieces, form each piece into a loaf shape and place one in each of the prepared tins. Cover the tins with oiled cling film and leave in a warm place for 30 minutes, until the dough has risen and almost reached the top of the tins.
7 Bake the loaves for 10 minutes at 220C / 425F /gas 7, then turn the heat down to 200C /400F /gas 6 and bake for a further 20 minutes, until the loaves are deep brown in colour and sound hollow when they are removed from the tins and rapped on the base. Cool them on a wire rack.

● This bread freezes well.
● It makes an excellent base for open sandwiches and goes well with cream cheese.

Rich corn bread

🔪 40 minutes, then cooling

Makes 20 cm /8 in square loaf
butter, for greasing
100 g /4 oz cornmeal
100 g /4 oz self-raising flour
5 ml /1 tsp bicarbonate of soda
50 g /2 oz caster sugar
2 medium-sized eggs
150 ml /5 fl oz milk
50 g /2 oz butter, melted

1 Grease a 20 cm /8 in square baking tin. Heat the oven to 200C /400F /gas 6.

2 Put the cornmeal into a large bowl and sift the self-raising flour and the bicarbonate of soda on top of it. Add the sugar and mix thoroughly.
3 Whisk the eggs with the milk and gradually stir into the flour mixture to make a smooth batter; finally add the melted butter and mix again.
4 Pour the batter into the prepared tin, levelling the surface. Bake for about 25 minutes, until risen and golden brown. Cool the corn bread in the tin, then cut it into squares before serving.

Shortbread

🔪 50 minutes, plus cooling

Makes 8 large or 16–20 small pieces
150 g /5 oz butter, at room temperature,
  plus extra for greasing
flour, for dusting
75 g /3 oz caster sugar
200 g /7 oz flour
50 g /2 oz rice flour
a little extra caster sugar

1 Heat the oven to 170C /325F /gas 3. Lightly grease and flour a 30 × 20 cm /12 × 8 in Swiss roll tin or a 25 cm /10 in flan tin which has a loose base and fluted sides.
2 Cream the butter and sugar together in a bowl. Sift the flours into the butter and sugar and mix them well to form a dough.
3 Press the dough evenly into the tin, levelling the surface. Prick the top of the shortbread using a fork. Bake it in the oven for about 40 minutes, until golden brown.
4 Mark the shortbread into sections while hot, then leave it to cool in the tin. Sprinkle the shortbread with a little caster sugar just before serving.

Buckwheat cheese straws

🔪 25–30 minutes

Makes about 2 dozen
50 g /2 oz flour
50 g /2 oz buckwheat flour
50 g /2 oz butter, in pieces
75–100 g /3–4 oz hard, strongly flavoured
  cheese such as Cheshire or Lancashire,
  finely grated

1 Heat the oven to 220C /425F /gas 7. Sift the flours into a bowl and rub in the butter with your fingertips. When the mixture is like fine breadcrumbs, add the cheese and 15 ml /1 tbls water. Mix to a dough.
2 On a lightly floured board, roll out the dough to a thickness of 5 mm /¼ in, then cut it into strips about 10 mm /½ in wide by 5 cm /2 in long. Place the strips on a baking sheet and bake for about 10 minutes, when they should look 'set' and golden brown. Cool the cheese straws on the sheet.

● These straws can be served warm or cold.

Oatcakes

⏱ 30 minutes,
then cooling

Makes about 2 dozen
*250 g /9 oz fine or medium oatmeal, plus extra
   for rolling out*
2.5 ml /½ tsp baking powder
2.5 ml /½ tsp salt
25 g /1 oz butter
butter, for greasing

1   Heat the oven to 200C /400F /gas 6. Put the oatmeal into a bowl with the baking powder, salt and butter. Mix together lightly, using a fork, then add enough hot water (about 45–60 ml /3–4 tbls) to make a firm dough.
2   Sprinkle some oatmeal on a board and turn the dough onto this, kneading lightly. Roll out to a thickness of 3 mm /⅛ in and cut into circles with a pastry cutter. Transfer the oatcakes to a greased baking sheet and bake for about 15 minutes, until firm and lightly coloured. Cool on the sheet for a few minutes, before transferring to a wire rack to become completely cold.

Wholewheat honey and walnut flan

The wholewheat pastry adds to the flavour of this chewy flan.

⏱ 50 minutes

Serves 6
150 g /5 oz wholewheat flour
75 g /3 oz butter, cut into pieces
20 ml /4 tsp ice-cold water
For the filling
2 eggs
150 g /5 oz clear honey
15 ml /1 tbls lemon juice
50 g /2 oz walnuts, chopped

1   Heat the oven to 200C /400F /gas 6. Sift the flour into a bowl to aerate it, then add the bran from the sieve to the bowl. Rub the butter into the flour with your fingertips, until the mixture looks like fine breadcrumbs. Add water and mix to a dough.
2   Roll out the pastry on a lightly floured surface and use it to line the base and sides of a 20 cm /8 in greased flan tin. Prick the base, line it with foil and beans and bake blind for 15–20 minutes, until it is well set and lightly browned. Remove the pastry case from the oven, and remove the foil and beans.
3   Reduce the oven heat to 180C /350F /gas 4. To make the filling, whisk the eggs, honey and lemon juice together in a bowl until they are well blended and slightly foamy.
4   Sprinkle the chopped walnuts over the base of the flan, then pour the honey mixture over the walnuts in an even layer. Bake the flan for about 30 minutes, until the filling is piping hot.

Raspberry buns

Raspberry buns

⏱ 45 minutes,
plus cooling

Makes 8 buns
butter, for greasing
200 g /7 oz flour
25 g /1 oz ground rice
10 ml /2 tsp baking powder
a pinch of salt
75 g /3 oz butter
75 g /3 oz sugar
1 medium-sized egg, lightly beaten
30 ml /2 tbls milk
about 30 ml /2 tbls raspberry jam
caster sugar, to dredge (optional)

1   Heat the oven to 200C /400F /gas 6. Grease and line a large baking tray with greased greaseproof paper.
2   Sift the flour with the ground rice, baking powder and salt into a large mixing bowl. Rub in the butter with your fingertips until the mixture resembles fine breadcrumbs. Stir in the sugar. Make a well in the centre. Add the egg and milk and mix to a soft dough.
3   Cut the dough into 8 equal pieces. With lightly floured hands, shape each piece into a ball. Make a hollow in the centre of each bun with your finger, taking care not to press right through. Spoon a little jam into each hollow and pinch the edges of the dough together to seal.
4   Place the buns, sealed side down, on the prepared baking tray. Bake just above the centre of the oven for about 20 minutes, until the buns are risen, golden and firm.
5   Let the buns cool slightly on the tray for 15 minutes before transferring them to a wire rack. Dredge them with caster sugar for a crunchy finish, if wished, and leave them to cool completely.

Apple crumble tart

⏱⏱ 1 hour 10 minutes

Serves 6–8
100 g /4 oz vegetable margarine
200 g /7 oz wholemeal flour
a pinch of sea salt
For the filling
700 g /1½ lb cooking apples
30 ml /2 tbls clear honey
50 g /2 oz sultanas
5 ml /1 tsp ground cinnamon
For the topping
75 g /3 oz wholemeal flour
50 g /2 oz Barbados sugar
75 g /3 oz vegetable margarine

1   Heat the oven to 200C /400F /gas 6. To make the pastry, rub the margarine into the flour and salt, and mix to a dough with about 60 ml /4 tbls cold water. Chill.
2   Peel, core and thinly slice the apples. Mix them with the honey, sultanas and cinnamon.
3   Roll out the chilled pastry and use it to line a 20 cm /8 in flan ring. Fill the pastry with the apple mixture.
4   For the topping, put the flour into a bowl with the sugar and rub in the margarine until the mixture resembles fine breadcrumbs. Sprinkle this mixture in an even layer over the apples.
5   Bake the crumble tart for 30 minutes, until the top is golden brown and crunchy. Serve hot, with natural yoghurt.

RICE, SWEET & SAVOURY

Rice is economical and easy to prepare. It can be used for thickening soups and as a substitute for potatoes, but it can also make an elegant dessert, with cream and liqueur, suitable for the most formal occasion.

Rice is one of the oldest cultivated crops — the earliest record of it occurs in 2,800 BC, when a Chinese emperor established a ceremonial rite for rice planting. Rice is also mentioned in the ancient literature of Japan and Indo-China. In the Middle Ages, rice was brought to southern Europe by the invading Saracens. It was first introduced to America in 1694 when a ship's captain gave some seed to the Governor of Charleston, South Carolina, in return for help in repairing his ship.

The many legends in which rice appears — as well as its association with fertility, still evident today in the tradition of throwing rice at weddings — indicates the importance of this crop to ancient civilizations. Today it is equally important, being the staple diet of nearly three-quarters of the world's population. Although not generally considered to be protein food, it does contain 7–8%, protein and it is rich in minerals and vitamins. It is bland, easily digested, filling and has only 31 calories per 25 g/ 1 oz.

From the cook's point of view, rice is cheap, always available and will keep practically for ever. It has the additional advantage of requiring virtually no preparation and being simple to cook. Having no strong flavour of its own, rice forms the basis of many quite different dishes, both sweet and savoury.

Types of rice
When the outer, inedible husks have been removed, a brown rice grain remains. This grain can be cooked and eaten, but most rice is processed further. It is polished to rub away the outer bran layer.

Long-grain rice has clear, translucent grains, 4–5 times longer than they are wide. Patna is the best-known variety and although the rice no longer comes from Patna in North India, the name is often used to describe the type. Long-grain rice is the first choice for general-purpose rice for savoury dishes as the grains remain separate when cooked. You will learn by experience which brands need washing and draining after cooking to remove excess starch and which ones do not. American long-grain rice tends to stick less than other types and it is usually the best choice for cold salads.

Basmati rice also originated in India. It is a thinner, more pointed grain than Patna, so it cooks more quickly. It needs very thorough washing before cooking. Use Basmati to give authenticity to curries, pilaus and other Indian dishes.

Medium-grain rice has shorter grains: about 3 times longer than wide. Rice from Piedmont in Italy comes into this category — the two names to look for are Arborio and Avorio. This is the correct type to buy for a really creamy risotto and most other Italian dishes.

Short-grain rice looks almost round and is white and chalky in appearance. As it is the easiest type of rice to grow, it is also the cheapest type to buy. Carolina rice from America is a famous short-grain rice, although it is no longer grown in Carolina. Short-grain and pudding rice are used as synonyms because the starch in the stubby grains thickens the cooking liquid and helps the grains to cling together. Short-grain rice is the ideal choice for milk puddings, fruit condés (see recipe idea) and creamy moulds. However, short-grain rice can be used for savoury dishes; Valencia rice grown in Spain, and used for *paella*, is a short-grain.

Brown rice, or unpolished rice, is more nourishing than processed rice because it retains the outer bran layers which provide valuable fibre and B_1 vitamins (thiamine). Both long and short-grain brown rice are sold, the latter usually in health food shops. Its chewy texture and nutty flavour make it a popular ingredient in wholefood dishes. The colour lightens during cooking and it does take longer to cook than other rices.

Wild rice is not really a rice at all, but the seed of an aquatic plant growing in Canada and the United States of America. Its dark, thin grains have a distinctive flavour, but it is difficult to harvest and therefore expensive. It is usually cooked 1 part wild rice to 7 parts brown rice.

Parboiled or easy-cook rice is also sold as pre-fluffed or separate-grain rice. This is a long-grain rice that has been soaked and then steamed or boiled before husking. Surprisingly, this is more nutritious than plain milled rice because the process drives the B vitamins into the grain where they are less likely to be lost during milling. Parboiled rice is less likely to stick together so it is ideal for salads, and it can save a hostess's reputation if the rice has to be kept warm for some time after cooking!

Precooked or instant rice has been cooked then dehydrated. It is very quick to prepare because it needs only to have the water content returned and then be reheated.

Flaked rice is rice fragments; it cooks very quickly and is convenient for puddings.

Ground rice and rice flour are two grades of rice powder. Ground rice is used for making creamy milk puddings and as a thickening agent for both sweet and savoury

sauces. Rice flour, which is finer, is used for cakes and biscuits.

Rice paper, an edible paper used to line baking sheets, has nothing to do with rice, but is made from the pith of an Oriental tree.

Cooking rice

Allow 50 g /2 oz of uncooked rice for each serving; this will treble in quantity once it is cooked. Although most recipes give the quantity of rice by weight, it is actually more convenient to measure rice by volume because it is then easier to judge the quantity of water required for cooking.

Cooking on top of the stove: put the rice into a measuring jug and then use double the volume of water for cooking. Put the water, rice and 5 ml /1 tsp salt in a heavy-based saucepan. Bring the water to the boil and stir once, then lower the heat to simmer. Cover the saucepan and leave the rice to cook for 15 minutes without removing the lid. Test the rice by biting a few grains — they should be tender but not soggy and all the water should have been absorbed. Whether you need to rinse it or not will depend on the type of rice used and the dish being prepared. Finally, turn the rice into a warm dish and fluff it lightly with a fork.

Cooking in an oven: put the rice in an ovenproof casserole, bring the measured water to the boil and pour it into the casserole. Cover it with a close-fitting lid or foil and cook it at 180C /350F /gas 4 for about 40 minutes. Test the rice, and if it is not tender or if all the water has not been absorbed, cook for a few more minutes. Fluff and serve.

Exceptions to the rule: brown rice takes a little longer to cook, 40–50 minutes on top of the stove, 50–60 minutes in the oven. When cooking parboiled or easy-cook rice, allow extra water: 2½ cups of water to 1 cup of rice. Parboiled rice also needs a longer cooking time: 20–25 minutes on top of the stove, and 40–45 minutes in the oven.

Because instant rice has already been cooked, it only needs rehydrating and heating through. Follow the packet directions; as a rule instant rice may take up to 10 minutes simmering in boiling water.

Cold, cooked rice: reheat cooked rice by putting it into a large saucepan with very little water and setting it over a gentle heat. Turn the rice frequently with a fork but be careful not to break the grains. Alternatively, the rice can be reheated in an oven at 180C / 350F /gas 4; put it in a lightly greased ovenproof dish, covered with foil, for 15–20 minutes. A third method is to place the rice in a metal colander, covered with foil. Place the colander over a saucepan of simmering water.

Planning for 'left-over' rice: since this appears frequently in recipes, it is convenient to cook rice in rather larger quantities than you will eat immediately. Allow 100 g /4 oz uncooked rice to get 350 g /12 oz cold cooked rice.

Storing rice

Once a sealed packet of raw rice has been opened, keep the rice in an airtight jar. Since rice will keep almost indefinitely, it is a convenient commodity to buy in bulk. Cooked rice can be kept in the refrigerator for 1 week.

Cooked rice keeps well in the freezer: spread it out and open freeze it, then break up the lumps to make sure the grains are free running before bagging it. Dishes containing rice but little liquid, such as stuffings and croquettes, can be frozen successfully. Freeze rice for about 2 months. Rice which has been frozen in liquid invariably becomes mushy and over-cooked during reheating so plan to add raw rice to a frozen dish during reheating. It is hardly worth freezing rice to eat plain because it can be so quickly cooked.

Using rice

Rice is the basis of many dishes throughout the world, notably the Far East and India. Stir-fried rice is a Chinese speciality. Cold cooked rice is tossed in hot oil to heat and flavour it. Delicious extras such as sliced vegetables, pieces of shredded meat and fish are added. An Indonesian version of this dish is Nasi goreng, which is decorated with a lattice of omelette strips.

Pilaff is a spicy Middle Eastern dish in which vegetables, meat and rice are cooked, one after another, in the same pan. They are then combined with stock to make a tasty one-pot meal (see recipe). In India there are several ways of making a pilaff. Pilau or pulao rice is made by frying soaked and drained rice, while a biriani contains twice as much meat and butter as it does rice. Polo is another version, where rice, meat and vegetables are layered.

A celebrated recipe from Northern Italy is risotto. The rice is fried in butter and then slowly cooked in stock and white wine or vermouth which blend together in a creamy mass, then it is flavoured with Parmesan cheese.

Spanish paella is a very attractive dish, coloured with saffron, containing an exciting mixture of shellfish and often pork or chicken. Jambalaya (see recipe) is an American version of paella, which is based on cold, cooked rice and prawns.

Milk and rice are used together to make porridge in Scandinavia and nourishing, filling puddings in Britain. Cold rice pudding, flavoured with lemon, is eaten in Spain. A condé, named after an aristocratic French family, is a cold rice pudding with fresh or canned fruit on the top. Most magnificent of all condés is the French Riz à l'impératrice (see recipe), which contains cream and liqueur and is quite irresistible.

From left to right: Patna rice, available in white or brown; wild rice, the seeds of an aquatic grass; Basmati rice; pre-fluffed or easy-cook rice; minute rice; frozen or boil-in-the-bag rice; rice with added flavourings, meat or vegetables; Italian rice

For the French tomato sauce
1 kg /2 lb ripe tomatoes, cut into chunks
25 g /1 oz butter
1 carrot, diced
1 Spanish onion, diced
15 ml /1 tbls flour
½ garlic clove, finely chopped
½ bay leaf
1.5 ml /¼ tsp dried thyme
1 clove
salt and freshly ground black pepper

1 Heat the oven to 170C /325F /gas 3.
2 Prepare the sauce. Drain the excess liquid from the tomatoes. Next, melt the butter in a flameproof casserole, add the diced carrot and onion and cook gently, stirring frequently, for about 20 minutes.
3 Sprinkle in the flour and cook, stirring, for 3–4 minutes. Add the finely chopped garlic, bay leaf, dried thyme, clove and drained tomato chunks and season to taste with salt and freshly ground black pepper. Cook over a medium heat, stirring occasionally, for 5 minutes, or until the tomatoes soften and the sauce begins to blend together.
4 Bring the sauce to the boil, cover and cook in the oven for 45 minutes.
5 Cut a thin slice from the top of each tomato. Scoop out the pulp and seeds.
6 Combine the onion, garlic, parsley and mint in a bowl. Stir in the rice and 120 ml / 8 tbls of the sauce. Season to taste.
7 Season the tomato cases inside with salt and pepper, then fill them with the rice mixture. Top each with 2.5 ml /½ tsp grated Parmesan cheese and 5 ml /1 tsp olive oil. Place the stuffed tomatoes in a buttered gratin dish.
8 When the sauce is cooked, remove it and turn up the oven to 180C /350F /gas 4. Bake the tomatoes for 15 minutes.
9 While the tomatoes are cooking, press the sauce through a sieve into a clean pan and then reheat the sauce.
10 Serve the rice-stuffed tomatoes hot, on a bed of tomato sauce.

Chicken pilaff

 1 hour

Serves 4
4 large chicken pieces
salt and freshly ground black pepper
15 ml /1 tbls vegetable oil
50 g /2 oz butter
1 large onion, chopped
1 garlic clove, crushed
2.5 ml /½ tsp ground cumin
5 cm /2 in piece cinnamon stick, crushed
6 cardamoms, crushed
6 cloves
250 g /9 oz long-grain rice
600 ml /1 pt chicken stock, home-made or from a cube
2.5 ml /½ tsp saffron powder or turmeric
2 bay leaves
50 g /2 oz raisins
50 g /2 oz flaked almonds

1 Wipe the chicken and cut each joint into two pieces. Sprinkle lightly with salt and

Rice-stuffed tomatoes

These rice-stuffed tomatoes are unusual since they are served with a French tomato sauce which is cooked in the oven while you prepare the tomatoes. Try them as a rather different starter for a dinner party.

2 hours

Rice-stuffed tomatoes

Serves 3–4
6–8 large ripe tomatoes
1 large Spanish onion, finely chopped
2 garlic cloves, finely chopped
90 ml /6 tbls finely chopped fresh parsley
15 ml /1 tbls finely chopped fresh mint
90–120 ml /6–8 tbls cooked long-grain rice
salt and freshly ground black pepper
20 ml /4 tsp freshly grated Parmesan cheese
40 ml /8 tsp olive oil
butter, for greasing

pepper. Heat the oil and half the butter in a large saucepan and fry the chicken until it is browned. Remove the chicken.

2 Fry the onion in the same saucepan for 10 minutes, then add the garlic, the ground cumin, the cinnamon, the cardamoms and the cloves, and fry for a further 2–3 minutes, stirring gently.

3 Return the chicken pieces to the saucepan, cover and cook over a gentle heat for 15 minutes, stirring from time to time so that the chicken is well coated.

4 Add the rice, stock, saffron powder or turmeric and bay leaves to the chicken; bring to the boil. Cover and cook gently for 10 minutes.

5 Stir in the raisins and cook for a further 5–10 minutes until the rice is tender. Put the rice and chicken onto a warm serving dish and keep warm until ready to serve.

6 Quickly fry the almonds in the remaining butter for 2–3 minutes, until golden, then sprinkle them over the pilaff.

Rice and cheese balls

 2 hours

Serves 4–5 as a first course
225 g /8 oz Italian or long-grain rice
salt
50 g /2 oz melted butter
100 g /4 oz ham, thinly sliced
2 medium-sized eggs, lightly beaten
freshly ground black pepper
100 g /4 oz Mozzarella cheese in 10 mm /½ in cubes
oil, for frying
75 g /3 oz fresh white breadcrumbs

1 Cook the rice in boiling salted water for 15 minutes. Drain, rinse and fluff. Stir in the melted butter and leave the rice to become completely cold.

2 Cut the ham into 20 mm /¾ in squares. Mix the beaten eggs into the rice, with salt and pepper to taste.

3 Place 15 ml /1 tbls of the rice mixture in the palm of your hand and flatten it into a small circle. Lay a square of ham on top and then a cube of cheese. Top with another 15 ml /1 tbls rice. Gently roll the mixture between your hands to make a neat ball. Make about 20 balls in the same way, using up all the ingredients.

4 Heat the oil for deep frying until it reaches 180C /350F, or until a small cube of stale bread dropped into the oil turns golden in 50 seconds.

5 Meanwhile, roll each ball in breadcrumbs on a plate, to coat it all over. Shake off any excess crumbs.

6 Deep fry the balls, a few at a time, for 5 minutes or until they are golden brown. Remove them from the oil and drain them on absorbent paper. Keep the balls hot while you fry the others. Drain and serve at once.

Risotto bianco

 35–45 minutes

Serves 4–6
50 g /2 oz butter
1 onion, chopped
250 g /9 oz Italian rice
150 ml /5 fl oz dry white wine or dry white vermouth
900 ml /1¾ pt chicken stock, home-made or from cubes, heated
salt and freshly ground black pepper
60 ml /4 tbls finely grated Parmesan cheese

1 Melt two-thirds of the butter in a heavy-based saucepan. Fry the onion over a medium heat for about 5 minutes, until it is golden, but not brown. Add the rice and stir over the heat for a further 2–3 minutes.

2 Pour in the wine and cook until it has been absorbed, then add one-third of the hot stock. Cook until the stock has been absorbed, stirring often, then add another one-third of the stock. Continue until all the liquid has been absorbed and the rice is tender: 15–20 minutes.

3 Season with salt and pepper and fork in the remaining butter and the Parmesan cheese. Serve the rice in a warmed serving dish.

Basque rice with mussels

 40 minutes

Basque rice with mussels

Serves 4
250 g /9 oz Valencia or long-grain rice
450 ml /16 fl oz chicken stock, home-made or from a cube
50 ml /2 fl oz olive oil, plus extra
100 g /4 oz chorizo or any other rough spicy pork sausage, diced
1 large red or green pepper, seeded
50 g /2 oz mushrooms, chopped
1 small shallot or onion, chopped
5 ml /1 tsp paprika
1 kg /2 pt or 2 lb fresh mussels in their shells (or 250 g /8 oz frozen mussels, defrosted, plus 15 ml /1 tbls lemon juice)
100 g /4 oz boiled peeled prawns
fresh parsley and lemon slices, to garnish

1 Boil the rice for 7 minutes in unsalted water. Drain and wash under running water. Heat the oven to 180C /350F /gas 4.

2 Put the rice into an earthenware oven-proof dish. Add the chicken stock and olive oil and stir in the diced sausage.

3 Slice the pepper into thin rounds and add them to the rice mixture. Mix in the chopped mushrooms, shallot and paprika. Cover and cook in the oven for 20–25 minutes.

4 Meanwhile, if you are using fresh mussels, clean them and heat them gently in a covered saucepan until they open. Remove some of the shells. Simmer frozen mussels in lemon juice until warmed through. Fry the prawns in a little oil on a very low heat.

5 When the rice has absorbed all the liquid, drain the mussels. Top the rice with mussels and prawns, and garnish.

Brown rice supper dish

 1 hour

Serves 4
250 g /9 oz brown rice
5 ml /1 tsp salt
1 large onion, chopped
2 celery sticks, finely chopped
30 ml /2 tbls vegetable oil
1 bunch spring onions, trimmed and
  chopped
1 red-skinned eating apple, cored and chopped
50 g /2 oz raisins
50 g /2 oz flaked almonds
50 g /2 oz roasted peanuts
For the sauce
40 g /1½ oz butter
25 g /1 oz flour
300 ml /11 fl oz milk
15 ml /1 tbls mild wholegrain mustard
100 g /4 oz cheese, grated

1 Put the rice, 600 ml /1 pt water and the salt in a heavy-based pan and bring it to the boil. Stir once, cover, and cook over a gentle heat for 40–50 minutes, or until the rice is tender and the water has been absorbed.
2 While the rice is cooking, make the sauce. Melt two-thirds of the butter in a medium-sized saucepan and stir in the flour. Cook for a minute or two, then add the milk. Stir over a moderate heat, until the mixture thickens, then let the sauce simmer gently for 5–10 minutes to cook the flour. Stir in the mustard and cheese and season to taste. Dot the remaining butter over the top of the sauce and leave on one side while preparing the rice mixture.
3 Fry the onion and celery in the oil for 10 minutes, taking care not to let them brown. Next, add the spring onions and cook for a further 2 minutes.
4 Using a fork, mix the vegetables with the cooked rice and stir in the apple, raisins, almonds and peanuts. Heap the mixture on a warm serving dish; keep it warm while you reheat the sauce, stirring in the butter on its surface. Serve the rice with the sauce.

Jambalaya

 cooking and cooling the rice, then 30 minutes

Serves 4
75 g /3 oz bacon, diced
100 g /4 oz spring onions, chopped
15 ml /1 tbls flour
400 g /14 oz canned, peeled tomatoes
400 g /14 oz cold, boiling long-grain rice
400 g /14 oz boiled prawns, peeled
salt and freshly ground black pepper
a pinch of cayenne pepper
25 g /1 oz finely chopped fresh parsley

1 Cook the bacon in a large frying-pan over a medium heat until the fat begins to run; add the spring onions and cook until golden.
2 Stir the flour into the pan, add the

tomatoes and 125 ml /4 fl oz water and stir until the sauce has thickened. When the mixture boils, stir in the cooked rice and the prawns.
3 Reduce the heat to low and heat the mixture through for 10 minutes, stirring occasionally. Season with salt, cayenne pepper and freshly ground pepper, and sprinkle with the chopped parsley.

Moulded rice salad with egg mayonnaise

This savoury rice mould makes an easy and eye-catching centrepiece for a cold meal or for a buffet table.

 1 hour,
plus cooling

Serves 6–8
250 g /9 oz aubergine
salt
250 g /9 oz long-grain rice
45 ml /3 tbls oil
1 onion, chopped
1 garlic clove, crushed
1 red pepper, seeded and chopped
2 tomatoes, peeled and chopped
2 drops Tabasco
freshly ground black pepper
6 small flat mushrooms
For the filling
4 hard-boiled eggs
30 ml /2 tbls mayonnaise
30 ml /2 tbls soured cream or natural yoghurt
5 ml /1 tsp fresh tarragon, chopped, or
  2.5 ml /½ tsp dried tarragon
several pinches of paprika

Peach condé — A variation on the traditional rice pudding

1 Wash the aubergine and remove the stalk end. Cut the aubergine into 5 mm /¼ in dice, place it in a colander, sprinkle it with salt, and cover it with a plate with a weight on top. Leave for 30 minutes to draw out the bitter juices.
2 Put the rice in a heavy-based saucepan with 600 ml /21 fl oz water and 5 ml /1 tsp salt. Bring to the boil, stir once, then cover and cook over a gentle heat for 15–20 minutes, or until the rice is tender and all the water is absorbed.
3 Drain the aubergine, rinse and pat it dry. Heat 30 ml /2 tbls oil in a medium-sized saucepan; add the onion and fry for 5 minutes, then add the aubergine, garlic, pepper and tomatoes and fry for a further 7–10 minutes, until all the vegetables are tender.
4 Using a fork, gently mix the vegetables into the cooked rice. Add the Tabasco and season with salt and pepper.
5 Fry the mushrooms in the remaining oil. Arrange the mushrooms, black side down, in the base of a 1.5 L /2½ pt ring mould. Spoon the rice mixture on top of the mushrooms, smooth the surface and press down. Leave in a cool place for several hours, until completely cold and firm.
6 To make the filling, chop the eggs and mix them with the mayonnaise, soured cream or yoghurt, and tarragon. Season with salt and pepper.
7 To serve, slip a palette knife around the inside of the mould, then invert a dish on top. Turn out onto the dish. Spoon the egg mayonnaise into the centre of the mould and sprinkle it with paprika.

Traditional rice pudding

Rice pudding is one of those traditional recipes in which the rice protein is enhanced by the dairy protein in the milk to make a very tasty but nourishing dish. It is one of the easiest puddings to make and the actual preparation time rivals that of any 'instant' pudding and forms the basis for delicious variations.

2–3 hours

Serves 4
50 g /2 oz short-grain rice
600 ml /1 pt hot milk
15 ml /1 tbls granulated sugar
butter, for greasing
a pinch of freshly grated nutmeg

1 Heat the oven to 150C /300F /gas 2. Put the rice, the milk and the sugar into a lightly-greased, shallow ovenproof dish. Grate a little nutmeg over the top of the pudding.
2 Place the uncovered dish in the oven. Stir the pudding two or three times during the first hour of cooking — this stirs in the skin and helps to make the pudding creamy. Bake for 2–3 hours, until it is thick.

● To make an extra-rich pudding, soak the rice in milk overnight.
● Rice pudding can be cooked on top of the stove. Put all the ingredients into a heavy-based saucepan, cover and simmer over a very gentle heat for 1½–2 hours until creamy. Remove the lid for the last 40 minutes and stir the mixture from time to time.
● For pressure-cooker rice pudding, melt a little butter in the pressure cooker, add the milk and bring to the boil, then stir in the rice and sugar. Lower the heat, so that the mixture is only just simmering, and put on the lid. Bring up to pressure at room temperature. The top of the pudding can be browned under a moderate grill just before serving, if wished.
● For an extra creamy pudding, fold 150 g / 5 fl oz thick cream, lightly whipped, into the pudding — this can be added to either hot or cold rice pudding.
● A cold rice pudding is delicious served with redcurrant or raspberry purée and toasted flaked almonds.
● To make a peach condé (see the illustration on the opposite page), make a creamy rice pudding and chill it. Divide the rice among 4–6 individual glasses. Top each serving with a peach half and pour a sauce of melted redcurrant jelly mixed with lemon juice over each portion.

Riz à l'impératrice

Riz à l'impératrice

Cold milky rice puddings, flavoured with lemon, are traditional in Spain, where they are served on feast days. Consequently, when the Spanish Eugenia married Napoleon III and became Empress of France, this dessert was created in her honour.

45 minutes preparation, plus chilling and garnishing

Serves 6–8
100 g /4 oz short-grain rice
oil, for greasing
15 ml /1 tbls gelatine
60 ml /4 tbls cream sherry or kirsch
100 g /4 oz mixed glacé fruit, chopped
900 ml /1 pt 12 fl oz milk
25 g /1 oz butter
100 g /4 oz sugar
4 medium-sized egg yolks
5 ml /1 tsp vanilla essence
extra glacé fruit, for decoration
250 ml /9 fl oz thick cream
crystallized fruit, to decorate

1 Bring a large pan of water to the boil and sprinkle in the rice. Boil for 3 minutes, stirring occasionally, then drain it thoroughly. Grease a 1.5 L /2½ pt deep charlotte mould.
2 Meanwhile put the gelatine into a small bowl and stir in the sherry or kirsch. Leave it to soften for 5 minutes, then stand it in a pan of simmering water until the gelatine has dissolved. Add the glacé fruit and mix well.
3 Put 450 ml /16 fl oz of the milk, the rice and the butter into a heavy-based saucepan and simmer, uncovered, over a gentle heat until the rice is tender and all the milk has been absorbed — 25–30 minutes. Then stir in half the sugar.
4 While the rice is cooking, make the custard. Heat the remaining milk to boiling point. Whisk the egg yolks in the top of a double boiler with the remaining sugar. Pour the hot milk onto the egg yolks. Cook the mixture in the double boiler over gentle heat, stirring all the time until the custard thickens. Remove it from the heat and stir in the vanilla essence.
5 Turn the custard into a bowl and stir in the cooked rice and glacé fruit mixture.
6 Before the rice sets, decorate the bottom of the mould with the extra glacé fruit. Whisk the cream until it stands in soft peaks. Fold the cream gently into the custard and rice mixture, then spoon it into the prepared mould. When cold, chill for 2–3 hours.
7 Just before the meal, loosen the dessert by inserting a spatula all the way around the inside of the mould. Invert a serving dish on top, then turn out the mould onto it. Decorate the pudding with crystallized fruit.

● Set the rice in a 1.5 L /2½ pt ring mould and fill the centre with 500 g /1 lb fresh raspberries or strawberries.
● Use an orange-flavoured liqueur in the mixture instead of sherry and garnish the dessert with mandarin orange segments.
● Garnish this dessert with pears poached in a sweet red wine.

PERFECT PULSES

Dried beans, peas and lentils can add an extra dimension to your cooking. Experiment and use your imagination to create tasty and wholesome soups, salads and main courses with a difference.

Pulses have been sadly neglected in the past, relegated to the back of the store cupboard for years or bought only in cans. Now, with a revival of interest in vegetable cooking, peas, beans and lentils are coming into their own: a marvellous standby in the kitchen, they are inexpensive, easily obtainable and they make nutritious, easily-prepared and exciting meals.

Soaking

At one time no one would have contemplated cooking dried pulses without leaving them to soak overnight in cold water first. The pulses were, as likely as not, several years old and practically fossil-hard. Nowadays, although soaking overnight still remains the best method of dealing with dried pulses, it is rarely absolutely necessary except for chick-peas and, occasionally, brown lentils. So, if you have forgotten to put them in to soak the previous evening, it will be enough to place them in a saucepan, cover with plenty of cold water and bring the water to the boil. Once they have boiled, remove the pan from the heat, cover and leave undisturbed for about an hour to soften. It is important to use plenty of water, especially if you are leaving the pulses to soak overnight or in the morning you may find that they have absorbed all the water and could have absorbed more.

Cooking pulses

Each season, dried pulses seem to cook more quickly. I suspect, though I have no evidence to support my theory, that this is largely due to improved drying methods as well as a faster turnover in the shops. Not so long ago, chick-peas always required prolonged soaking, followed by several hours simmering to soften them. Nowadays you may be able to find ones which only take about an hour to cook.

More flavour can easily be added to the pulses by cooking other ingredients with them. Try an unsalted home-made stock, or add wine or cider to the cooking water. Salt is best not added until the end of the cooking time because it tends to slow down the softening process.

Most other pulses are thoroughly cooked in anything from 30 minutes to 4 hours. One thing to remember in the case of red kidney beans is that they are poisonous unless they are boiled vigorously for at least 10 minutes before you start timing their cooking.

Pulses can be cooked in the oven or on top of the stove or, to save time, they can be cooked in a pressure cooker. If you are cooking them in water alone, make sure that they are in at least twice their volume of water.

More flavour can easily be added to the pulses by cooking other ingredients with them. Try an unsalted home-made stock, or add wine or cider to the cooking water. Salt is best not added until the end of the cooking time because it tends to slow down the softening process.

Flavouring vegetables such as onions, garlic or celery, or herbs and spices added during cooking will make any pulse dish extra special. The key word is imagination. Try being creative and adding different ingredients when you are cooking pulses, the results will make your efforts worthwhile.

Using pulses

An ideal way to utilize pulses in the winter is to make soup: puréed beans, peas or lentils, on their own or with additions, make hearty, warming soups. Red or Egyptian lentils need little or no soaking and disintegrate with only a few minutes cooking, so they are ideal for making soups. (German or brown lentils keep their shape after prolonged cooking and are much better suited to casseroles and salads.) Lentils on their own, soaked and then simmered with onion and carrot, stock or milk and then puréed, make a delicious creamy soup. If you vary the quantity of lentils, then the thickness of the soup will vary accordingly, making it either an ideal first course for a dinner party or something more substantial for a lunch or supper. Variations to try are lentil and tomato or lentil and spinach.

Haricot and butter beans make smooth, pale soups and are especially good enriched with cream just before serving. Whole peas or split peas also make excellent soups and add a splash of colour to the menu. For a completely different type of soup, Bessera (see recipe) uses chick-peas with finely chopped garlic and olive oil added just before serving. The black bean — a dark-complexioned cousin of the kidney bean — is frequently used in Spanish and Portuguese cookery.

Salads: use pulses to ring the changes. German lentils, haricot beans, butter beans, kidney beans and chick-peas are all ideal. Simply soak one type of pulse, or a mixture, cook them and then toss in a good vinaigrette with some freshly chopped herbs. Serve the salad well chilled.

Main courses from many parts of the world feature dried pulses. Those which come from Mediterranean countries are often flavoured with thyme, marjoram and garlic. Middle Eastern cookery has several tasty dishes that use pulses puréed and shaped into rissoles. In India, particularly in the vegetarian regions, all kinds of pulses are curried.

One of the most famous dishes is Cassoulet (see recipe), a traditional family meal from France. Good quality white haricot beans form the basis of the dish, with spiced or garlic-flavoured sausage, pork and chicken — this substantial meal is generally eaten at midday. Haricot beans are, of course, also used in another renowned dish, Boston baked beans, which makes a heavy, filling meal. This uses salt pork or bacon (see recipe).

Side dishes to accompany meat can also be made from pulses. They may be quite simply cooked and puréed; dried peas and lentils are well suited to this. Dal is the Indian version of a red lentil purée, flavoured with garlic and spices. Hummus is another spicy purée, this time using chick-peas.

Haricot beans, butter beans or lentils can be served in a cream sauce, and haricot beans provençales (with tomato and garlic) is a classic French accompaniment to a leg of lamb. These pulses are also delicious when served with either garlic or parsley butter (see page 42) for added flavour.

Soaking and cooking times

Soaking

in cold water	4–6 hours
in boiling water	40–60 minutes

Pulse	Average cooking time
Adzuki	30–45 minutes
Black beans	1–1¼ hours
Black-eyed beans	1–1¼ hours
Borlotti beans	1–1¼ hours
Broad beans	1½–2 hours
Butter beans	1¼–1½ hours
Cannellini	1–1¼ hours
Chick-peas	3–4 hours or more
Flageolet	1–1¼ hours
Ful mesdames	1–1¼ hours
Gungo beans	2–3 hours
Haricot beans	1¼–1½ hours
Mung beans	30–45 minutes
Pinto beans	1¼–1½ hours
Red kidney beans**	1–1¼ hours
Soya beans	3–4 hours or more
Split lentils	20–35 minutes
Split peas	30–45 minutes
Whole green peas	1¼–2 hours
Whole lentils	30–45 minutes

** Boil hard for 10 minutes first

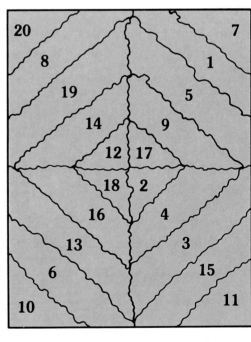

1 Adzuki; 2 Black beans; 3 Black-eyed beans;
4 Borlotti beans; 5 Broad beans; 6 Butter beans; 7 Cannellini; 8 Chick-peas;
9 Flageolets; 10 Ful mesdames; 11 Gungo beans; 12 Haricot beans; 13 Mung beans;
14 Pinto beans; 15 Red kidney beans; 16 Soya beans; 17 Split lentils; 18 Split peas;
19 Whole green peas; 20 Whole lentils

Cassoulet

This filling dish from the Périgord region of France is best served with a green salad and crusty French bread.

soaking the beans,
then 5 hours

Serves 6
350 g /12 oz haricot beans, soaked and
*   drained*
1 large onion, sliced
2 garlic cloves, crushed
1 bay leaf
1 L /1¾ pt unsalted white stock, home-made or
*   from stock cubes, plus extra*
freshly ground black pepper
3 medium-sized tomatoes, skinned, seeded and
*   finely chopped*
500 g /1 lb belly of pork, skinned and cut into
*   thin strips*
2 quarters of chicken, skinned, boned and
*   sliced*
150 g /5 oz chorizo (spiced Spanish garlic)
*   sausage, or similar, skinned and diced*
15 ml /1 tbls chopped fresh parsley
15 ml /1 tbls tomato purée
15 ml /1 tbls whole-grain mustard
75 g /3 oz fresh white breadcrumbs

1   Put the beans, onion, garlic, bay leaf and stock in a large saucepan and bring to the boil. Add freshly ground pepper and cover and simmer for 1 hour.
2   Heat the oven to 150C /300F /gas 2. Drain the beans and reserve the stock. Discard the bay leaf and stir the chopped tomatoes into the beans.
3   Put a layer of the bean and tomato mixture in a 2 L/3½ pt ovenproof casserole. Cover this with a layer of pork, then layers of more beans, chicken, beans, sausage and more beans again, seasoning each bean layer with ground black pepper.
4   Stir the parsley, tomato purée and the mustard into the reserved stock and pour this over the casserole. Make some more stock if necessary, so that the top layer is covered.
5   Sprinkle on half the breadcrumbs, cover and cook the casserole for 3 hours. Next, stir the cooked breadcrumbs carefully into the top layer. Sprinkle on the remaining breadcrumbs and continue cooking, uncovered, for 45 minutes.

Chick-pea and leek salad

cooking the chick-peas,
then 10 minutes

Serves 4
4 small young leeks
225 g /8 oz cooked chick-peas
15 ml /1 tbls lemon juice
45 ml /3 tbls sunflower oil
a large pinch of dried mustard
salt and freshly ground black pepper
8–12 black olives, stoned
15 ml /1 tbls freshly chopped parsley
2 tomatoes, quartered

1   Trim the leeks, discarding most of the green part which you can reserve for making a soup. Wash the leeks thoroughly and slice them thinly into rings.
2   Toss together the leeks and the chick-peas.
3   Shake or beat together the lemon juice, the oil, the mustard and the salt and pepper, and pour this dressing over the vegetables. Stir in the black olives.
4   Turn the salad into a serving dish and sprinkle with the chopped parsley. Decorate it with the tomato wedges and serve as an accompaniment to a main dish.

● When you are cooking chick-peas for another dish, cook enough for this salad, too — it saves time and fuel.

Moors and Christians

This Cuban dish combines pulses and grain. It gets its name from the contrasting black beans and white rice. Serve without eggs (see picture) as a main dish accompaniment.

soaking the beans,
then 2 hours

Serves 4–6
225 g /8 oz black beans, soaked and drained
30 ml /2 tbls vegetable oil
1 medium-sized onion, chopped
1 garlic clove, crushed
1 green pepper, seeded and thinly sliced
1 red pepper, seeded and thinly sliced
2 large tomatoes, skinned, seeded and chopped
salt and freshly ground black pepper
a large pinch of cayenne pepper
225 g /8 oz long-grain rice
4–6 eggs
25 g /1 oz butter
15 ml /1 tbls freshly chopped parsley

1   Cook the black beans in plenty of boiling unsalted water for about 1 hour, until they are barely tender.
2   Heat the oil in a saucepan and fry the onion and garlic over a medium heat for 2 minutes. Add the sliced peppers, stir well and fry for a further 3 minutes, stirring occasionally. Do not brown.
3   Add the tomatoes, salt, pepper, cayenne pepper, rice, drained beans and 600 ml /1 pt water. Stir well, cover the pan and simmer very gently for about 45 minutes, until the rice is tender and the liquid has all been absorbed. Adjust the seasoning.
4   Turn onto a heated serving dish and keep warm. Fry the eggs in the butter and arrange them on top of the beans and rice. Sprinkle with the chopped parsley and serve.

Brown lentils and mint

This simple Italian dish of whole lentils is delicious with lamb or veal. To reduce the cooking time to 30–45 minutes, pre-soak the lentils for 4–6 hours.

1¾ hours

Serves 4–6
45 ml /3 tbls sunflower oil
1 large onion, thinly sliced
2 garlic cloves, crushed
350 g /12 oz whole brown lentils, washed and
*   drained*
2 sprigs of mint
salt and freshly ground black pepper
15 ml /1 tbls freshly chopped mint, to garnish

1   Heat the oil in a large saucepan and fry the onion over a medium heat, stirring occasionally, for 3 minutes. Add the crushed garlic cloves and fry for a further minute.
2   Add the lentils and stir for about 3 minutes, until they have absorbed all the oil.
3   Pour in 1 L /1¾ pt hot water, add the mint sprigs and bring the water to the boil. Cover the pan and simmer for 1¼–1½ hours. Remove the mint and season. Turn into a heated serving dish, sprinkle with the chopped mint and serve.

Bessara

Bessara is a Moroccan pulse soup served with olive oil trickled over the top.

soaking the peas,
then 50 minutes

Serves 8
450 g /1 lb dried split green peas, soaked
3 garlic cloves, finely chopped
5 ml /1 tsp salt
2.5 ml /½ tsp paprika
5 ml /1 tsp cumin powder
1.5 ml /¼ tsp cayenne pepper
125 ml /4 fl oz olive oil
lemon juice, to serve

1 Drain the split peas and place them in a pan. Cover with 1.7 L /3 pt cold water, add the garlic and salt. Bring to the boil and simmer for 30 minutes, stirring occasionally.

2 Purée the peas and the cooking liquid in a blender and pass the purée through a sieve. The soup should be thick but if necessary add a little more water to make it thinner.

3 Add the paprika, the cumin powder and the cayenne pepper to the soup. Reheat and serve hot in individual bowls with 15 ml /1 tbls olive oil poured over the top of each. Serve the bessara accompanied by lemon juice.

Chilli con carne

⏸ 1 hour soaking the chillies,
then 1¼ hours

Serves 4
4 dried red chillies, soaked in hot water for
* 1 hour*
2 medium-sized onions, peeled and chopped
2 large garlic cloves, peeled and chopped
30–45 ml /2–3 tbls vegetable oil
450 g /1 lb chuck steak, trimmed and cubed
7.5 ml /½ tbls dried oregano
salt
freshly ground black pepper
175–225 g /6–8 oz cooked or canned red kidney
* beans*

1 Drain the chillies, reserving the liquid, then seed and coarsely chop the chillies. Combine the chopped chillies, onion and garlic and reduce it all to a coarse purée in an electric blender or with a pestle and mortar.

2 Heat the oil in a large, heavy-based pan. Add the meat and fry it until it is brown on all sides. Carefully remove the meat from the saucepan with a slotted spoon and reserve.

3 Add the chilli purée to the pan and cook it for 5 minutes, stirring constantly. Stir in the oregano and salt and freshly ground black pepper to taste. Return the meat to the pan and moisten it with a little of the reserved chilli liquid. Cover and cook gently for 10 minutes.

4 Drain the beans, reserving the cooking or canning liquid. Add the beans to the pan, together with some of their liquid if the mixture is at all dry. Adjust the seasoning, adding some more of the chilli liquid to taste, if necessary. Simmer for 45 minutes and serve hot.

Lentil salad with tiny sausages

🕐⏸ soaking the lentils,
then 1 hour, plus cooling

Serves 4
225 g /8 oz brown lentils, soaked
4 thick slices streaky bacon, weighing about
* 100 g /4 oz*
16 cocktail sausages, or 8 small chipolata
* sausages*
15 g /½ oz butter
150 ml /5 fl oz olive oil
30–45 ml /2–3 tbls wine vinegar
30–45 ml /2–3 tbls onion, finely chopped
2–3 anchovy fillets, chopped
salt and freshly ground black pepper
30 ml /2 tbls finely chopped fresh parsley
tomato wedges, to garnish

Moors and Christians

1 Soak the lentils for about 4–6 hours or overnight. Drain them and place them in a medium-sized saucepan. Remove the rind from the bacon and cut each slice into 3 pieces. Add the bacon to the lentils with twice their volume of cold water. Bring the water to the boil, then lower the heat and simmer for about 30–40 minutes. The lentils should be tender but not mushy. Drain the lentils and cool. Discard the bacon.

2 Fry the sausages in the butter until they are thoroughly cooked and golden brown all over. Remove them from the pan to cool.

3 In a bowl, mix the lentils with the olive oil, wine vinegar, finely chopped onion and chopped anchovies and season with salt and freshly ground black pepper to taste.

4 Serve the lentil salad in a long shallow serving dish. Sprinkle the finely chopped parsley over the cocktail sausages which should be placed on top of the lentils. Decorate the dish with tomatoes wedges.

Boston baked beans

🕐⏸ soaking the beans,
then 4½ hours

Serves 8
700 g /1½ lb dried haricot beans, soaked
450 g /1 lb salt pork or bacon, cut into 2
* pieces*
2 Spanish onions, finely chopped
50 g /2 oz butter
10 ml /2 tsp dry mustard
60 ml /4 tbls molasses (or black treacle)
60 ml /4 tbls soft dark brown sugar
salt and freshly ground black pepper
60–90 ml /4–6 tbls tomato ketchup

1 Drain the haricot beans and place them in a large saucepan. Cover the beans with twice their volume of water and bring to the boil, reduce the heat and simmer for 30–40 minutes, or until the beans are tender. Next, drain them thoroughly, reserving about 600 ml /1 pt of the cooking liquid.

2 Put the pork or bacon in another saucepan of cold water and bring to the boil; drain the bacon and slash the rind in several places with a sharp knife. Place 1 of the pieces of pork or bacon in the bottom of a deep, ovenproof casserole.

3 Heat the oven to 140C /275F /gas 1. In a medium-sized saucepan, sauté the finely chopped onions in the butter until they are soft and golden. Stir in the dry mustard, molasses or treacle, sugar, 5 ml /1 tsp each of salt and freshly ground black pepper and the reserved cooking liquid. Bring to the boil, stirring. Pour this in with the beans and mix thoroughly and then spoon it over the pork in the casserole.

4 Push the remaining piece of pork into the casserole so that the rind remains sticking up above the surface. Cover the casserole, place it in the centre of the oven and bake for about 3 hours, stirring every hour, and adding a little boiling water if the beans dry out too quickly.

5 Uncover the casserole and gently stir in the tomato ketchup, taking care not to break the beans. Adjust the seasoning, if necessary, and serve immediately.

WHEAT, OATS & CEREALS

Everyone knows that a steaming bowl of oatmeal porridge makes a healthy start to the day, but wheat, rye, barley, millet and buckwheat are rarely used in our meals. Learn to make them into delicious and nutritious dishes.

Named after Ceres, the Roman goddess of the harvest, cereals are the edible seeds of different grasses. They include rice, wheat, oats, rye, barley, millet and buckwheat, which, though not really a cereal, is usually included among them.

Cereals were one of the earliest food crops cultivated by man, and they still play an important part in the diet of most of the world's population. In the richer countries of the world, however, they are more popular with health food enthusiasts, who make them into deliciously chewy and tasty vegetable casseroles, meat accompaniments, salads and breakfast cereals.

Cereals are basically carbohydrates, but they also contain valuable amounts of protein as well as iron and B vitamins. In their natural state they are also one of the richest sources of dietary fibre, although this may be completely or partially removed in milling.

Store cereals in airtight containers for up to 6 months, unless otherwise specified.

Wheat
The staple cereal of most of the world, wheat has been cultivated in Europe and Asia for at least 6000 years. There are three main types of wheat grown these days, see page 32. Flour is the most important wheat product, but whole wheat grains, bran, kibbled wheat, burghul, and wheatgerm are generally available in health food shops and most large supermarkets.

Whole wheat grains are grains of wheat with just the inedible outer husk removed. They look like plump brown grains of rice, with a split down the middle. In medieval England, the grains were boiled in milk with sugar and spices to make frumenty, which is a kind of porridge.

Whole wheat grains are prepared by soaking them in water overnight, then cooking them in a saucepan of boiling water over a low heat until they are tender. This usually takes 1¼–1½ hours (25 minutes in a pressure cooker), although it may take longer if the grains are old.

Combine whole wheat with cooked or raw vegetables to make main course casseroles and salads, or add some sautéed onion and a few chopped herbs to make a side dish. With fruit and milk or cream, whole wheat makes a delicious breakfast cereal. The grains can also be sprouted and used in salads.

Kibbled wheat is whole wheat grains which have been crushed to make them easier to cook and eat. Sprinkle on breads before baking to give an attractive finish, or add to home-made muesli mixes.

Burghul, sometimes called bulgur or bulgar wheat, is wheat which has been cracked by boiling. The grains are quick to prepare: Turn 225 g /8 oz burghul in 25 g /1 oz oil or melted butter in a saucepan, then stir in 300 ml /10 fl oz boiling water or stock, cover and

leave over a very gentle heat for 10 minutes, or until all the water is absorbed and the grains are fluffy and tender.

Cooking is not necessary, however; it can also be prepared by soaking in cold water for 30–60 minutes, until it is tender, then draining, squeezing dry, and combining with a salad dressing. Burghul can also be made into a main course dish by adding vegetables, pulses, meat or cheese.

Bran is the outer layer of the wheat grain which is removed during the milling of white flour. Its main use is as a source of extra fibre in the diet. Add the brown flakes to breads or meat loaves, mix some into breakfast cereals, or use it instead of breadcrumbs for coating rissoles.

Wheatgerm is the inner part of the wheat grain removed in the milling of white flour. Wheatgerm looks like little brown grains, and can be bought in its natural state or toasted. It has a slightly nutty flavour and is good if sprinkled over breakfast cereals, fruit compotes and yoghurt. It can also be added to breads, cakes and crumble toppings to increase the nutritional content. Store it in an airtight jar in the refrigerator for up to 2 months.

Oats
Oats grow further north than any other cereal and this accounts for their importance in the cookery of Scotland, Alaska and Norway. Oatmeal used to be given to Scottish farm workers as part of their wages. Oats have more protein, fat and vitamins than other cereals — and a sweet flavour.

Whole grain oats or oat groats, obtainable from health food shops, are more slender and pointed than whole wheat grains. They are very chewy and can be cooked and used as you would whole wheat grains.

Rolled oats: widely available, these are oats which have had their outer layers removed before being steam-softened and rolled flat. Jumbo oats from health food shops are similar except that less of the outer skin is removed before rolling. Rolled oats keep

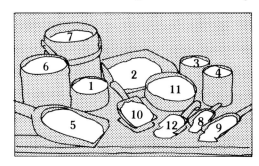

1 Rye; 2 Rolled oats; 3 Kibbled wheat;
4 Jumbo oats; 5 Whole grain oats; 6 Bran;
7 Whole wheat grains; 8 Burghul; 9 Roasted
buckwheat; 10 Pot barley; 11 Millet;
12 Medium oatmeal

better than other kinds of oats because the heat treatment they undergo helps to preserve them. They are useful for making into biscuits, such as Flapjacks (see recipe), and muesli, as well as for adding to stuffings and for coating fish and rissoles.

Oatmeal is oats which have been milled. Oatmeal is available in three degrees of coarseness: fine, medium and coarse, sometimes called pinhead. It is traditionally used for making porridge and it is available from health food shops and most supermarkets. Store it in a glass jar for up to 2 months.

Rye
Rye is another cereal which can survive in conditions which are too cold for wheat. It was used by the early settlers in North America and was the staple bread grain in many parts of northern Europe until the mid-19th century when its popularity declined. Rye bread has, however, increased in popularity in recent years and is especially good as a basis for open sandwiches and for serving with thick soups and stews.

The whole rye grain is a slender, pointed grain like oats in shape but a darker brown in colour which can be bought from health food

shops. It can be cooked like whole wheat grains and used to make an unusual accompaniment to meat and vegetable stews, but it is mainly used for making rye whisky, gin, beer and some kinds of vodka.

Barley

One of the first cereals discovered by man, barley was used before wheat to make bread. Being very hardy, barley will grow in places too cold for wheat and for this reason it was the staple cereal in many northern countries before hardier varieties of wheat had been developed. It does not contain sufficient gluten to rise, however, and is now grown mainly as animal feed.

Pot barley is the grain in its most natural state, with just the inedible outer husk removed. Pot barley grains look very similar to wheat grains, but are paler in colour. It has a chewy texture and a fairly strong flavour. Available from health food shops, it is cooked and used in the same way as whole wheat grains.

Pearl barley is more refined than pot barley, having had the outer layers of the grain removed as well as the husk. This is the most common form of barley available, and can be bought from any supermarket. It can be added to soups and stews before cooking to give extra body and nourishment, as in my Chicken, barley and vegetable broth (see recipe). Alternatively, cook it in boiling water for 25–30 minutes, drain and then add it to vegetable casseroles or serve it as an accompaniment to meat.

Barley water is made from an infusion of pearl barley in boiling water which is then strained, sweetened and flavoured with lemon. Barley sugar is a sweet traditionally made from barley water.

Malt extract, a sweet, dark brown paste, is a barley product useful in bread making.

Millet

Cultivated by the Romans to make flour, millet can tolerate both drought and excess water. Many different varieties of millet are grown, but although it is relatively high in protein, in the prosperous countries of the world millet is grown mainly for animal feed. Millet grains are small, round and pale gold in colour and can be found in most health food shops.

● To cook millet, stir 250 g /9 oz millet in 25 g/1 oz melted butter or oil in a saucepan, then add 600 ml /1 pt boiling water or stock. Cover and cook over a low heat for 20–30 minutes or until tender.

Serve millet as an accompaniment to soak up tasty juices, make it into croquettes or add it to vegetable casseroles.

Buckwheat

Not a true grain, being the seed of a plant belonging to the rhubarb family, buckwheat or kasha is nevertheless treated as one and is a staple food in Russia. The name comes from the Dutch *boek-weit,* meaning beech wheat and refers to the shape of the grain which is triangular, rather like a beech nut. Buckwheat is used in Russia for a porridge, known as *kasha.* Japanese noodles, called Soba, are made from buckwheat flour.

Buckwheat is often treated by being lightly roasted and can be bought from health food shops and delicatessens and used without further preparation as a nutty addition to muesli mixes or as a nibble with drinks.

● To cook, add 175 g /6 oz buckwheat to 700 ml /1¼ pt boiling water and simmer gently until tender, about 8–10 minutes. Add butter or olive oil, or sautéed vegetables: onions, peppers and mushrooms.

Scots porridge

 overnight soaking,
then 25 minutes

Serves 4
75 g /3 oz medium oatmeal
2.5 ml /½ tsp salt

1 Put the oatmeal and 850 ml /1½ pt cold water into a saucepan, cover and leave the oatmeal to soak overnight.
2 Next day, add the salt, then bring the mixture to the boil and allow it to simmer until it is thick, 15–20 minutes, stirring occasionally. Serve immediately with cream or milk and maple or golden syrup, honey or sugar — or salt for the traditionally minded.

Chicken, barley and vegetable broth

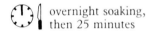 55 minutes

Serves 6
1.5 L /2½ pt chicken stock, home-made or
* from a cube*
1 large onion, chopped
2 celery sticks, chopped
1 medium-sized turnip, chopped
3 medium-sized carrots, chopped
50 g /2 oz pearl barley
salt and freshly ground black pepper
60 ml /4 tbls finely chopped fresh parsley

1 Put the stock into a large saucepan and bring it to the boil, skimming off any fat. Add the onion, celery, turnip, carrots and barley to the stock, together with a little salt and a grinding of black pepper.
2 Simmer, uncovered, for 30 minutes, until the vegetables and barley are cooked.
3 Add the parsley, check the seasoning and adjust it if necessary, then serve at once.

Millet and vegetable pilaff

 55 minutes

Serves 4
250 g /9 oz millet
salt
30 ml /2 tbls oil
2 leeks, trimmed and thinly sliced
1 large carrot, coarsely grated
250 g /8 oz courgettes, diced
5 ml /1 tsp grated fresh ginger root
50–125 g /2–4 oz raisins
freshly ground black pepper

1 Put the millet into a medium-sized saucepan with 600 ml /1 pt water and 2.5 ml /½ tsp salt, bring to the boil, then simmer, with the lid on, for 20 minutes or until the millet is tender and the water absorbed.
2 Remove the saucepan from the heat and leave it on one side, keeping it covered for a further 5–10 minutes.
3 Meanwhile, heat the oil in a frying-pan

Wheaty pea and vegetable salad

and fry the leeks, carrot and courgettes for 5 minutes, until they are just beginning to soften, then stir in the ginger root and cook for a further 2 minutes.
4 Using a fork, gently mix the vegetables with the millet and add the raisins. Season to taste. Cook for a further 2–3 minutes to heat it through, then serve.

Cauliflower, oat and mushroom casserole

This casserole can be served either as a side dish, or as a vegetarian supper dish with a fresh green salad and plenty of crusty French bread.

 1 hour 10 minutes

Serves 6–8 as a side dish, 4 as a supper dish
1 medium-sized cauliflower, in even-sized
* florets*
30 ml /2 tbls flour
300 ml /10 fl oz soured cream
5 ml /1 tsp mild mustard
175 g /6 oz matured Cheddar cheese, grated
salt
freshly ground black pepper
250 g /8 oz button mushrooms, trimmed
25 g /1 oz butter
125 g /4 oz rolled oats
50 g /2 oz walnuts, coarsely chopped

1 Heat the oven to 200C /400F /gas 6. Drop the cauliflower florets in a saucepan of boiling salted water and cook them for about 7 minutes, or until they are just tender. Next, drain them well.

2 Meanwhile, put the flour into a small bowl and blend to a smooth paste with a little of the soured cream. Gradually stir in the remaining soured cream, the mustard, half the grated cheese and salt and freshly ground black pepper to taste.

3 Pour the sauce over the cauliflower, add the mushrooms and turn gently so that the vegetables are thoroughly coated. Then put the mixture into a shallow ovenproof dish.

4 Using a fork, mix the butter with the oats, then add the rest of the cheese and the walnuts to make a lumpy, crumbly mixture. Sprinkle evenly over the cauliflower and mushrooms and bake for 40 minutes, until the topping is golden brown and crisp. Serve the casserole at once.

Wheaty pea and vegetable salad

overnight soaking,
then 2½ hours

Serves 4
125 g /4 oz whole wheat grains
125 g /4 oz green or yellow split peas
30 ml /2 tbls olive oil
15 ml /1 tbls red wine vinegar
salt
freshly ground black pepper
2 carrots, grated
2 celery sticks, chopped
5 cm /2 in cucumber, chopped
4 spring onions, chopped
2 tomatoes, blanched, skinned and chopped
4 lettuce leaves, shredded
30 ml /2 tbls raisins
cress, to garnish
For the dressing
175 g /6 oz curd cheese
60 ml /4 tbls milk
15 ml /1 tbls mayonnaise

1 Cover the whole wheat grains with cold water and leave them to soak overnight.

2 Next day, cook the wheat in a pressure cooker for 25 minutes, or simmer it in plenty of water for 1¼–1½ hours, or until the grains are tender and beginning to burst. Drain and cool slightly.

3 Meanwhile, put the split peas into a saucepan filled with cold water and simmer them for about 25 minutes, until they are tender but still whole.

4 Mix together the oil, vinegar and salt and pepper. Add the wheat and peas and allow the salad mixture to cool completely.

5 Stir in the carrots, celery, cucumber, spring onions, tomatoes, lettuce and raisins, tossing gently until the ingredients are well coated with the oil and vinegar mixture. Divide among 4 bowls.

6 To make the dressing: beat together the curd cheese, the milk and the mayonnaise until the dressing is smooth. Put a spoonful of dressing on top of each bowl, sprinkle with cress and serve.

Crunchy honey grains

30 minutes,
plus cooling

Serves 6
125 g /4 oz rolled oats
125 g /4 oz buckwheat (roasted or plain)
50 g /2 oz unsweetened desiccated coconut
25 g /1 oz sesame seeds
25 g /1 oz kibbled wheat
30 ml /2 tbls sunflower oil
30 ml /2 tbls clear honey
50 g /2 oz chopped nuts or sunflower seeds
50–125 g /2–4 oz raisins

1 Heat the oven to 190C /375F /gas 5. Put the oats, buckwheat, coconut, sesame seeds and kibbled wheat into a large bowl and add the oil and honey. Work the ingredients until they are well blended.

2 Spread the crumbly mixture over a large baking sheet. Bake for 15–20 minutes, stirring the mixture with a fork every 5 minutes, until it is golden brown and crisp. Leave to cool, then add the nuts or sunflower seeds and the raisins.

● Store in an airtight jar for up to 3 weeks.
● Serve with milk as a breakfast cereal or as a crumble topping for cooked fruits.

Sesame and almond flapjacks

35 minutes,
plus cooling

Makes 20
175 g /6 oz butter, plus extra for greasing
125 g /4 oz soft light brown sugar
15 ml /1 tbls golden syrup
225 g /8 oz rolled oats
25 g /1 oz flaked almonds
45 ml /3 tbls sesame seeds

1 Heat the oven to 180C /350F /gas 4. Butter a 28×18 cm /11×7 in Swiss roll tin.

2 Put the butter, sugar and golden syrup into a medium-sized saucepan and then heat gently until melted. Remove from the heat. Add the oats, almonds and 30 ml /2 tbls sesame seeds to the butter mixture and stir until all the ingredients are combined.

3 Spread the mixture evenly in the prepared tin and bake for 20 minutes.

4 Sprinkle the remaining sesame seeds over the top of the flapjacks, pressing them in lightly with a back of a spoon. Next, mark the cooked mixture into 20 pieces and leave until completely cold before removing the flapjacks from the tin.

Cauliflower, oat and mushroom casserole

TEA & COFFEE

There is nothing difficult or mysterious about making good tea or coffee — and once you have produced your brew use it in a variety of recipes from tasty broths and stews to rich cakes and desserts.

Tea and coffee are the most popular drinks in many countries throughout the world. Drunk hot or cold, with or without milk, with or without sugar, they are consumed in vast quantities every day — but have you thought of using them in your cooking? Not only for sweet recipes — cakes, mousses — but also, in the case of tea, in soups and stews. Read on and find out how you can use these commodities to their best advantage.

Tea

Tea originally came from China, and it has been drunk there for thousands of years. The Dutch first brought the leaf to Europe at the end of the 16th century; it was an exotic rarity, commanding as much as £15 a pound — then many a man's yearly income. For generations tea remained costly — those beautiful 18th-century caddies were not provided with strong locks for purely decorative purposes!

By the 19th century tea had become less expensive and it was on its way to becoming the favourite non-alcoholic drink of the British, especially as the emergence of India and Ceylon as producers brought tea within the means of most people.

Tea from India and Ceylon, which has a more robust flavour, largely replaced the delicate, and much costlier, China tea. Just as differing teas from China had been mixed to make a desirable brew, so Indian and Ceylon teas became part of blends established by pioneering companies; these became household names.

Types of tea

Broadly speaking, there are two main types of tea — green and black. The latter is far more popular nowadays. For green tea, the leaf is dried immediately after picking. Black tea is allowed to ferment in its natural moisture before being lightly roasted and slowly dried, then graded for size. There is also another type called Oolong, which is semi-fermented. It is essentially for blending but occasionally sold on its own.

A blend may contain up to 30 teas and, unless it is specifically labelled as being from India, Ceylon or China, it may contain leaf from various countries — other important growers and exporters include Kenya, Indonesia, Bangladesh, Malawi and Taiwan.

From the long list of teas, here is a selection of those most likely to be available to people who prefer special teas as opposed to the mass-market blends:

Assam is an extremely strongly flavoured tea, not usually sold unblended.

Ceylon tea has not been re-named for its country of origin, Sri Lanka. Ceylon teas are of high quality, the best being Dimbula, Kandy, Nuwara and Uva.

Darjeeling is a fine, large-leaved tea, widely considered India's best.

Earl Grey is a blended black tea flavoured with bergamot oil.

English Breakfast tea was once a black China tea; it is now usually a strong India/Ceylon blend.

Formosa Oolong has a peach aftertaste; top grades of it are very highly regarded.

Gunpowder tea is named for its colour and consistency; it is a top-quality green China tea.

Jasmine tea is admirable for drinking with or after Chinese food. It has a flowery taste and should not be drunk with milk.

Keemun is richly aromatic and thought by some to be superior to all other China teas.

Nilgiris is the leading tea from south India; it is quite pungent.

Orange Pekoe is a very fragrant China tea; it is also the name of a size of leaf.

Souchong tea, such as Lapsang Souchong, has a smoky bouquet.

Buying and storing tea

Tea-bags have much improved technically and even the British, who take their tea very seriously, now buy them for preference. Superior teas, such as Earl Grey, which were formerly sold only as loose leaves, can now be bought in tea-bags.

Loose tea, from the original chest in which it was shipped, is confined to specialist retailers, who also have their own blends; however, pre-packed loose tea is available.

Storing: freshness is all-important with good tea. Once you have opened a package of tea-bags, put them in an airtight jar and keep firmly closed. Treat loose tea similarly: if you have a large amount, divide it among several airtight jars and keep it dry and tightly covered.

Making and drinking tea

In the traditional method of making tea, the pot is first warmed. Use one teaspoonful of tea for each person, plus one extra 'for the pot'. Boil fresh water; as soon as it boils, pour it onto the leaves and allow to infuse for not less than five minutes. Whether you put milk in the cup before or after pouring the tea, if at all, is a matter of personal choice, as are the use of a strainer and the addition of sugar or honey.

Milk is not a universal additive; probably the most common flavouring added to tea is mint. Dried or fresh mint (the latter is best) is mixed with the tea before infusion; it is then usually highly sweetened. Mint tea is drunk in North Africa and the Middle East. Russians drink very strong tea, usually with a slice of lemon or a spoonful of jam. Milk tea, made with boiling milk instead of water, is favoured in parts of India, and local herbs are often added. The rancid yak butter tea of Tibet is not generally to Western taste, though the Sri Lanka way, stirring the hot fluid with an aromatic cinnamon stick, might

Some teas and tisanes; back row, left to right: maté, chamomile, Darjeeling; next row, left to right: stinging nettle, Assam, linden, rosehip, jasmine; bottom left corner, gunpowder

very well seem a good deal more attractive.

Iced tea, much favoured in the United States of America, is by no means a modern notion. It was praised in the last century as being stimulating, and it certainly is a splendidly cooling summer drink.

● One way to make iced tea is to soak the leaves in cold water for about 12 hours, then strain and refrigerate it. Or make tea in the normal way, allow it to cool, strain and chill it. For quick iced tea, make it very strong (at least double the quantity of leaf) and strain onto ice cubes. Iced tea may be sweetened to taste and drunk with milk or lemon.

Cooking with tea

Tea is unduly neglected in the kitchen — people who may drink several cups of it while cooking rarely think of using it in their dishes. Apart from its flavour, tea adds extra colour. So keep surplus tea from the pot, strain it and store it in a bottle in the refrigerator. It will not be strong enough for all recipes but will be useful for soaking dried fruits for a compote or a sweet bread.

When making fruit cakes, try substituting cold tea for at least half of the liquid. Try tea in savoury dishes as well, such as a pâté, a stew or a broth (see Country tea stew or Tomato, beef and tea broth).

Make a warming drink for a cold night by infusing lemon zest and whole spices in tea and adding sugar and rum to taste, or make a hot Royal tea punch (see recipe). Tea is also delicious in cold punches.

Herbal teas

Many herbal teas, or tisanes, are of great antiquity, some have medicinal value while others are regarded merely as attractive

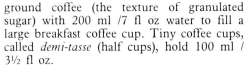

being steeped in water or dried in the sun.

Discovered by merchants and travellers to the Middle East, coffee took Europe by storm in the 17th century. Coffee houses, where coffee was drunk while business was transacted, became immensely popular in the City of London. England, France, Spain and Holland in turn introduced the coffee plant to the Americas, Africa and the Far East.

There are more than 100 kinds of coffee from 40 countries. Quality coffees come from the *Coffea arabica* plant; beans of the *robusta* variety are used for making instant coffees.

Quality coffees

Santos, especially Bourbon Santos, is the finest of the Brazilian coffees. Some of the world's best coffee comes from Colombia which is the largest producer in the world after Brazil. Costa Rican coffee is mild and popular as a breakfast drink. Jamaican coffee is noted for its quality and flavour; the most famous name is Blue Mountain. Mocha is valued as an after dinner coffee; it comes from the Yemen.

Mysore coffee is from Southern India and has a distinctively smooth flavour. Among African coffees, Kenyan is popular for its richness; Tanzanian coffee is similar to Kenyan, but produces a thinner liquid. The heavier coffees come from Java and Sumatra.

Buying and storing fresh coffee

Buy coffee from shops which roast their own beans; that way you can be sure of their freshness. Once roasted, coffee loses its aroma within 3 weeks. It is best to grind your own coffee just before brewing it. Otherwise buy branded vacuum packs.

Store coffee beans and ground coffee in airtight jars. Ground coffee absorbs other smells quickly and goes rancid.

Making perfect coffee

There is really no mystique about making good coffee — just follow these tips.

Amounts to use: make strong coffee rather than weak, as you can always dilute it to taste. The amount of coffee you will need varies according to the method. As a general rule, if you are using a filter or vacuum coffee pot, you will need 15 ml /1 tbls fine ground coffee (the texture of granulated sugar) with 200 ml /7 fl oz water to fill a large breakfast coffee cup. Tiny coffee cups, called *demi-tasse* (half cups), hold 100 ml / 3½ fl oz.

If you are using a jug or percolator coffee pot, you will need medium ground coffee and therefore a larger quantity: about 60 ml /4 tbls to 600 ml /1 pt of water.

Making coffee in a jug: you can make very good coffee using only a jug and a strainer. Measure 60 ml /4 tbls of fine or medium ground coffee into a warmed jug or pot. Pour on 600 ml /1 pt of freshly boiling water and stir well. Leave to stand for 4 minutes, then draw a spoon across the surface to remove any floating grounds. Pour the coffee gently through a strainer into cups.

Ways of drinking coffee

Always drink coffee hot, as soon as it is brewed. Although purists claim coffee is best savoured black and unsweetened, certain flavours go very well with it. Try a squeeze of lemon or a strip of orange or lemon zest, or stir the coffee in the cup with a stick of cinnamon or a vanilla pod. Or sprinkle it very lightly with spices such as ground nutmeg, cloves, cinnamon or cardamom. A tiny pinch of salt brings out the flavour, a black peppercorn gives an extra kick, and honey may be used to sweeten the drink instead of sugar. Or you can buy special coffee crystals (see page 58).

Café au lait: pour 3 parts strong coffee to 1 part hot milk (or half and half) into a large cup or bowl — about 200 ml /8 fl oz.

Capuccino: use equal parts strong coffee and hot milk and top each cup with lightly whipped cream.

Viennese coffee: allow 25 g /1 oz plain chocolate and 15 ml /1 tbls thick cream to each cupful of coffee. Melt the chocolate in a saucepan and add sugar to taste. Stir in the cream, pour in the hot coffee and beat until frothy. Serve topped with whipped cream, sprinkled with cinnamon or chocolate.

Turkish coffee: this strong, sweet coffee is traditionally made in a special small copper pot called an *ibrik*, wider at the base than top and with a long handle. For 2, pour 2 small coffee cupfuls of cold water into the *ibrik* with 10 ml /2 tsp of caster sugar (heaped if you like it sweet). Add 15 ml /2 heaped tsp of pulverized coffee (even finer than very fine ground): a mixture of Mocha and Mysore does well. Stir the coffee, bring it to the boil, then immediately remove it from the heat. Repeat this process twice. Allow the grounds to settle, pour it into small cups and serve.

Iced coffee: chill unsweetened or sweetened coffee, with or without milk, in a covered bowl for at least 2 hours. Serve with a scoop of vanilla, coffee or chocolate ice cream, topped with whipped cream. Alternatively freeze already made coffee in ice cube trays and liquidize the ice cubes when needed.

Laced coffee: for a sophisticated after-dinner drink, fill a coffee cup three-quarters full of strong black coffee. Sweeten it if you

beverages whose ingredients may, excitingly, be found in hedgerows and gardens. Among the more common are those made from camomile flowers, young dandelion or stinging nettle leaves, fennel seeds, elderflowers, lettuce, rosehips, rosemary and sage.

Herbal leaves are best picked immediately before flowering time and used at once. To preserve them for later use though, dry them by spreading them out in an airy place, avoiding direct sunlight. When they are dry, remove any stalks, pack them into tightly closed containers and store in a cool, dark place. Make the tisanes as you would ordinary tea but substitute tablespoon quantities for teaspoon measures.

Coffee

The coffee plant is a small, evergreen tree which bears a fruit that looks rather like a wild cherry: each berry contains 2 green beans, which are released from the fruit by

There are very many different types and blends for, and methods of making, a really good cup of coffee

like and add a generous dash of cognac, armagnac, rum or whisky. Or put a cube of sugar into a tablespoon, pour brandy over it to fill the spoon, heat and set it alight and quickly pour it into the cup. You can then dribble in cream over the back of a spoon. The most famous laced coffee is Irish coffee.

Other coffee products
Try some of these other forms of coffee and coffee products.

Instant coffee: the soluble powder or granules are extracted from a concentrated coffee brew by spray or freeze-drying. In processing the coffee loses flavour and aroma, but instant coffee makes a quick drink, and is useful for flavouring. Dried and powdered chicory is sometimes added to make instant coffee go further.

Decaffeinated coffee is coffee available both in the bean and instant form, from which the caffeine has been removed.

Coffee essence is a syrup made from coffee mixed with chicory, caramel and other flavourings. It is mainly used for flavouring.

Coffee liqueurs are made from coffee extracts which are added to spirits.

Tia Maria is made with Jamaican rum and Blue Mountain coffee extracts. Irish Coffee Liqueur is made with whisky, coffee, honey and herbs, and Old Vienna Coffee Brandy from matured cognac and coffee extracts.

Flavouring with coffee
As a general rule, when a recipe specifies 'strong black coffee', make this with 15 ml /1 tbls fresh fine ground coffee or 10 ml /2 tsp instant to 150 ml /5 fl oz boiling water.

For a cake filling: stir instant or very fine ground coffee into a small quantity of hot water, then beat this into whipped cream or butter cream: allow about 30 ml /2 tbls ground or 15 ml /1 tbls instant coffee to 15–30 ml /1–2 tbls hot water for 225 g /8 oz filling.

For a syrup: bring to the boil 225 g /8 oz sugar with 150 ml /5 fl oz strong black coffee and simmer for 3 minutes. Pour hot onto sweet soufflés, or use cold on ice cream.

Tomato, beef and tea broth

making the tea,
then 30 minutes

Serves 6
100 g /4 oz streaky bacon, diced
1 large onion, finely chopped
225 g /8 oz lean minced beef
1 L /1¾ pt strong tea
2 beef stock cubes, crumbled
2.5 ml /½ tsp dried marjoram
2.5 ml /½ tsp dried mixed herbs
500 g /18 oz canned tomatoes
salt and freshly ground black pepper
croûtons, to serve

1 In a saucepan, fry the bacon until the fat begins to run. Add the onion and minced beef and cook gently for 5 minutes, stirring.

Frozen coffee mousse

2 Add the tea, stock cubes, herbs, the tomatoes with their juice and salt and pepper to taste. Simmer for 15 minutes, stirring occasionally, then transfer to heated soup bowls and serve with croûtons.

Country tea stew

Serve this with boiled or mashed potatoes and lightly cooked, buttered cabbage.

making the tea,
then 2 hours 20 minutes

Serves 4
15 ml /1 tbls oil
2 large onions, chopped
4 carrots, sliced
750 g /1½ lb braising steak, in small cubes
25 g /1 oz seasoned flour
25 g /1 oz butter, more if necessary
600 ml /1 pt strong tea
15 ml /1 tbls tomato purée
5 ml /1 tsp dried mixed herbs
2 beef stock cubes, crumbled
salt
freshly ground black pepper
100 g /4 oz mushrooms, sliced

1 Heat the oven to 150C /300F /gas 2. In a frying-pan, heat the oil and sauté the onions and carrots for 3 minutes. Using a slotted spoon, transfer them to a casserole.
2 Coat the steak in the seasoned flour. Add 25 g /1 oz butter to the frying-pan and, when it is hot, add the steak and brown it lightly. Transfer the steak to the casserole with a

slotted spoon. Add any remaining flour to the pan, adding more butter if necessary, and cook briefly.
3 Stir in the tea and bring to the boil, add the tomato purée, herbs, stock cubes and salt and pepper to taste and pour it into the casserole. Add the mushrooms, stir, cover and cook in the oven for 2 hours, or until the steak is tender, then transfer the stew to a heated serving dish, if wished, and serve.

Royal tea punch

making the tea,
then 15 minutes

Serves 6
4 medium-sized eggs, separated
50 g /2 oz caster sugar
juice of 2 lemons
75 ml /3 fl oz Cointreau
250 ml /9 fl oz brandy
850 ml /1½ pt strong tea

1 Beat the egg yolks. In a large saucepan, combine the sugar, lemon juice, Cointreau, brandy, tea and egg yolks. Heat gently until it is hot, but do not allow it to boil.
2 Whisk the egg whites until stiff, then add to the hot punch and whisk until blended. Serve at once.

Tea cream

45 minutes,
plus cooling and setting

Serves 6
300 ml /10 fl oz milk
25 g /1 oz tea-leaves
600 ml /1 pt thick cream
15 g /½ oz gelatine
45 ml /3 tbls caster sugar
whipped cream, to garnish
glacé fruits, to garnish

1 Bring the milk to the boil in a small saucepan, pour it over the tea-leaves and infuse them for 20 minutes.
2 Pour half the cream into a bowl and strain the milky tea into it. Stir to blend.
3 Pour 60 ml /4 tbls warm water into a small bowl, sprinkle in the gelatine and then place the small bowl in a larger bowl of hot water until the gelatine dissolves. Add it to the tea cream mixture along with the sugar, stir and allow to cool.
4 As soon as the tea cream is cool, whisk the remaining cream stiffly and fold it in. Pour it into a dampened 850 ml /1½ pt mould and allow it to set in the refrigerator.
5 Just before serving, decorate it with the whipped cream and glacé fruits.

Mocha diplomate dessert with praline

Frozen coffee mousse

 30 minutes,
plus 1½ hours freezing

Serves 6
4 eggs, separated
90 ml /6 tbls caster sugar
30 ml /2 tbls instant coffee
275 ml /10 fl oz thick cream
thick cream, whipped, to garnish
coffee beans, to garnish

1 Beat the egg yolks with 60 ml /4 tbls sugar until pale and light. Place the bowl over a pan of hot water and continue to beat until the mixture has thickened. Stir in the coffee and allow to cool.
2 Whip the cream in a large bowl until peaks form; stir in the coffee mixture.
3 Whisk the egg whites until stiff peaks form, then beat in the remaining sugar. Gently fold the egg whites into the cream mixture.
4 Pour this into a glass serving bowl. Cover and freeze in the freezer compartment for at least 1½ hours.
5 Remove from the freezer 20 minutes before serving and garnish.

Coffee and walnut cake

 1¼ hours

Makes an 18 cm /7 in cake
4 medium-sized eggs, separated
100 g /4 oz icing sugar
15 ml /1 tbls fine breadcrumbs
15 ml /1 tbls instant coffee
15 ml /1 tbls powdered drinking chocolate
175 g /6 oz walnuts, coarsely chopped
walnut halves, to decorate
butter, for greasing
flour, for dusting

For the butter cream topping
100 g /4 oz unsalted butter
100 g /4 oz icing sugar
1 medium-sized egg yolk
30 ml /2 tbls very strong coffee

1 Heat the oven to 180C /350F /gas 4. Cream the yolks and sugar in a large bowl until light and fluffy. Add the breadcrumbs, coffee and chocolate powder and mix thoroughly. Stir in the chopped walnuts.
2 Whisk the egg whites until stiff peaks form. Then gently fold them into the yolk mixture, using a metal spoon.
3 Butter and dust with flour an 18 cm /7 in cake tin. Pour in the mixture and bake it for 45 minutes. The cake is cooked when it is springy to the touch and a skewer inserted in the centre comes out clean. Cool it on a wire cake rack.
4 For the topping, cream the butter and sugar. Add the egg yolk and coffee and beat to a smooth, soft cream. Spread this over the cake. Decorate with walnut halves.

Mocha diplomate dessert with praline

This delicious gateau would make an unusual birthday cake. It can also be frozen like an ice cream.

 1 hour,
plus 2 hours chilling or freezing

Makes 12 slices
100 g /4 oz hazelnuts
90 ml /6 tbls caster sugar
275 ml /10 fl oz thick cream
150 ml /5 fl oz thin cream
45 ml /3 tbls instant coffee
200 ml /7 fl oz milk
48 boudoir biscuits (3 packets)

1 First make a praline with the hazelnuts. Brown the nuts lightly in a heavy frying-pan without fat, stirring them with a spatula over a medium heat. When the skins begin to flake, remove the hazelnuts from the heat. Then, when they are cool enough, rub them between your hands to remove the skins completely.
2 Add 60 ml /4 tbls of the sugar to the pan and return it to the heat. When the sugar is melted and lightly browned, add the hazelnuts and stir until they are coated. Pour the mixture onto a lightly greased piece of foil on a baking sheet.
3 When the praline is cool, break it into pieces. Reserve a few whole caramelized hazelnuts for the decoration. Grind the rest to a coarse powder using a blender or a well-cleaned coffee mill.
4 Beat the thick and thin creams together until fairly stiff. Dissolve 30 ml /2 tbls of the coffee in 30 ml /2 tbls of warm milk. Stir this, with the remaining sugar, into the cream.
5 Dissolve the remaining coffee in the rest of the milk. Dip the back of each biscuit into the mixture to moisten it slightly. Do not let the biscuits soak up too much liquid or they will become soggy.
6 Reserve half the coffee cream for coating and 15 ml /1 tbls of the praline for decorating. Grease a loose-bottomed 23 cm /9 in cake tin. Put a layer of boudoir biscuits in the bottom, arranging them in rows, side by side, and trimming them, if necessary, to fit. Spread a thin layer of coffee cream over them and sprinkle with a little praline. Repeat the layers until all the biscuits are used up, ending with a layer of cream.
7 Chill for 2 hours in the refrigerator — or in the freezer compartment if serving as an ice cream.
8 To serve, unmould the dessert from the tin. Spread the reserved coffee cream on the top and the sides. Sprinkle the top with the reserved praline and decorate it with a few whole caramelized hazelnuts.

OILS FOR COOKING

Olive oil, sunflower oil, groundnut oil, 'cooking oil' — the shopper is faced with a wide and confusing variety of oils. Learn what they look and taste like and how to use them successfully.

Oils for cooking are produced from various seeds, nuts and beans; each has its own flavour and range of culinary uses.

Refined and unrefined oils

Except for olive oil, there are basically two types of oil: refined and unrefined. Unrefined oils are best from a nutritional point of view, they have a deep, rich colour and retain the flavour of the nut or seed from which they were produced; however, they are more expensive.

Some unrefined oils are said to be 'cold pressed' because no artificial heat is applied in the extraction process. These oils are the richest in colour and flavour and may contain some sediment.

Cold pressing extracts a relatively small amount of oil. A more economical method of extraction involves the use of a screw or expeller press and it is from this that most unrefined oils are obtained.

The expeller press leaves behind some of the oil. To extract it completely, a chemical solvent is used, and then the oil goes through a further refining process and becomes a refined oil. Refined oils have lost most of their colour, flavour and nutrients, but they have a much longer shelf life.

Types of oil

Almond oil is made from sweet almonds. It is almost colourless and has an extremely delicate flavour. It is used most often for oiling moulds when making confectionery and sweet dishes. It also makes a very delicate mayonnaise which is ideal for serving with seafood (see Prawns mimosa).

Coconut oil, at room temperature, takes the form of a solid white fat with a light texture. To use it, stand the bottle in warm water until it becomes a pale coloured liquid. Unusually for a vegetable oil, coconut oil is very high in saturated fats. It has a strong coconut flavour.

Corn oil is made from sweetcorn. It is deep yellow in colour, with a bland flavour. It has a high smoke point and so is often used for deep frying, but as it has a rather strong smell when heated, it is not ideal for this purpose. Corn oil is the oil most suitable for making cakes and pastries.

Cotton-seed oil is used most often commercially, in margarines, cooking fats and salad dressings, and as one of the ingredients in blended cooking oils.

Groundnut oil, also called arachide or peanut oil, can be used for deep frying, sautéing, stir-frying and salad dressings.

Hazelnut oil, with its delicate flavour, can be used in baking or for salad dressings.

Mustard oil is used in India as a cheap substitute for ghee or clarified butter and for making pickles. It has a strong flavour when cold, but this diminishes when heated.

Olive oil is the favourite oil of most cooks as it has such a delicate flavour. Most of it comes from Spain, Italy, France and Greece.

There are several grades of olive oil. The best, called virgin oil, is made from the finest olives, simply crushed. It has a green colour and has a rich flavour and smell. Oil from a second crushing of the olives is weaker. Then there is second-grade olive oil, which is extracted by pressure under heat. It is whitish in colour, has far less flavour and becomes rancid quickly.

Olive oil can be used for shallow frying and sautéing and is often mixed with butter for this purpose. It gives a very good flavour when used for deep-frying, but has a low smoke point.

Olive oil is delicious in a vinaigrette, for dressing pasta and for pickling and making vegetables à la grecque.

Rapeseed oil is rarely used on its own, but is often added to blends of oils.

Safflower oil has a high polyunsaturated fat content. It has a nutty flavour and is used mainly for shallow and stir-frying and for salad dressings.

Sesame oil has a rich amber colour and a delicious nutty flavour. It is superb in salad dressings, particularly if a few sesame seeds are scattered in as well. In Oriental cookery it is often used for stir-frying and also in curries. It can be used for deep frying, but as it is expensive, this is extravagant.

Soya oil is made from the soya bean. It is pale amber in colour, with a very heavy texture. It can be used for salad dressings and shallow frying, but it does have a fishy flavour. It is used in blended oils, margarines and commercial salad dressings.

Sunflower oil is a good, universal oil to have in the kitchen. It has a pleasant, mild, nutty flavour and can be used for both shallow and deep frying, baking and for making mayonnaise and salad dressings.

Walnut oil is produced in France. It is one of the most expensive oils and is usually available in small cans which, once opened, must be kept in the refrigerator. Walnut oil has a fine nutty flavour and is superb with a green salad to which walnuts have been added (see page 98). It may also be used for shallow frying.

Blended oils are sold as 'cooking oils' or 'frying oils' and consist of a mixture of refined oils. They are pale in colour and have little flavour. They are useful when you want to do large quantities of deep frying as they are cheaper than most other oils.

Buying and storing oils

Oils are available in cans and bottles of varying sizes. Oils will keep longer in cans than in bottles as they deteriorate more quickly when exposed to the light. Larger containers are often more economical to buy than smaller ones, so pour a small amount of oil into a handy-sized container for regular use and store the remainder in a cool larder.

Kept in a firmly closed container in a cool, dark place, unrefined oils should keep for up to six months and refined oils for up to a year.

Using oils

Deep frying: when deep frying, use an oil with a high smoke point — that is the temperature at which the oil will start to smoke, turn a darker colour and break down. Never leave the oil to heat unattended as it may go past its smoke point and burst into flames.

Always heat oil slowly: rapid heating causes deterioration, as does overheating oil. Use a deep-frying thermometer or, failing this, drop a 15 mm /½ in cube of day-old white bread into the oil. It should be crisp and golden in 40 seconds if the oil has reached 200C /400F; in 50 seconds at 190C /375F; in 60 seconds at 180C /350F; in 75 seconds at 170C /325F.

Frying at too high a temperature will not make the food cook more quickly, it will simply burn the outside before the inside is cooked. Cooking food at too low a temperature will allow moisture to mix with the oil, causing early deterioration.

If you look after your oil, you can usually use it for deep frying about 10 times. After use, cool the oil and pour it through a sieve lined with a double layer of absorbent paper into a bowl, then bottle it.

There are several indications that an oil has come to the end of its useful frying life: foamy bubbles appear on the surface; the oil smokes when heated; the colour darkens; the food may absorb too much oil, and there may be an 'off' smell.

Shallow frying: all oils can be used for shallow frying at high or low temperatures. When sautéing, many cooks mix equal quantities of oil and butter for maximum flavour; also the oil will prevent the butter from burning. All stir-frying is done in oil.

Roasting and grilling: meats can be lightly brushed with oil before roasting or grilling; and vegetables can be roasted in oil.

Marinating: oil added to a marinade will make lean or slightly dry meats moister.

Baking: oil can be used to make a quick cake or light and crumbly pastry. When added to bread dough, it will produce a loaf that is soft-textured.

Salad dressings: to make a successful mayonnaise-type salad dressing, oil is mixed with a watery substance such as vinegar to produce an emulsion. To make this stable, an emulsifying agent must be used, such as the lecithin contained in egg yolks. Rapid beating is necessary to break up the oil particles and disperse them evenly.

Vinaigrette-type salad dressings are not stable emulsions — the oil and vinegar separate easily, but fine particles such as mustard powder or spices make the emulsion hold for a short time.

Sauces: many sauces may be made with oil instead of butter.

Preserving: oil is a short-term preservative (see Aubergine and pepper pickle).

Flavoured oils are particularly good for salads. Steep herbs or spices in a bottle of oil in a warm place for two weeks, strain the oil and it will be ready for use.

Prawns mimosa

A mayonnaise made with almond oil has a light, delicate flavour.

15 minutes

Serves 4
4 large lettuce leaves
250 g /8 oz boiled shelled prawns
2 medium-sized eggs, hard-boiled
4 prawns in their shells, to garnish
For the mayonnaise
1 medium-sized egg yolk
1.5 ml /¼ tsp mustard powder
100 ml /3½ fl oz almond oil
about 30 ml /2 tbls lemon juice

1 To make the mayonnaise, beat the egg yolk in a bowl with the mustard powder. Gradually beat in 45 ml /3 tbls of the almond oil, then 10 ml /2 tsp lemon juice, and finally the remaining oil. Add extra lemon juice to taste — it should taste quite lemony.
2 Place a lettuce leaf on each of 4 small plates. Divide the shelled prawns among the plates.
3 Quarter one of the eggs lengthways and garnish each plate with an egg quarter. Cut the other egg in half and remove the yolk. Finely chop the white and mix it into the mayonnaise.
4 Spoon the mayonnaise over the prawns. Rub the yolk through a sieve onto the mayonnaise-covered prawns, garnish each plate with a prawn in its shell, and serve.

Aubergine and pepper pickle

Stir-fried curried vegetables

Stir-frying vegetables in coconut oil gives them a light flavour of coconut.

preparing the vegetables, then 15 minutes

Serves 4
15 ml /1 tbls cornflour
300 ml /11 fl oz chicken stock, home-made or from a cube
90 ml /6 tbls coconut oil
1 small cauliflower, in 20 mm /¾ in florets
250 g /8 oz carrots, thinly sliced
1 medium-sized green pepper, in 25 mm × 5 mm /1 × ¼ in pieces
2 medium-sized onions, thinly sliced
1 garlic clove, finely chopped
5 ml /1 tsp ground turmeric
5 ml /1 tsp ground cumin
2.5 ml /½ tsp ground ginger
1.5 ml /¼ tsp cayenne pepper
salt

1 Put the cornflour in a bowl and gradually mix in the chicken stock.
2 Pour the coconut oil into a large frying-pan or wok and set it over a high heat. When it is hot, put in the vegetables and garlic and stir for 3 minutes. Lower the heat and add the spices, then stir for 3 minutes.
3 Stir the cornflour mixture and pour into

the pan. Bring to the boil, stirring, then cover and simmer for 5 minutes. Add salt to taste, pour the vegetables into a warm serving bowl and serve at once.

Sesame chicken

Sesame oil is the basis for a tasty marinade. Plainly boiled rice is the best accompaniment for this chicken dish.

1 hour, plus 4 hours marinating

Serves 4
125 ml /4 fl oz sesame oil
2 dried red chillies, crumbled
30 ml /2 tbls tomato purée
30 ml /2 tbls soy sauce
1 garlic clove, crushed with a pinch of salt or sesame salt
juice of ½ lemon
1.6 kg /3½ lb roasting chicken, cut in 4 pieces
30 ml /2 tbls sesame seeds

1 In a large, flat ovenproof dish, mix together the oil, chillies, tomato purée, soy sauce, garlic and lemon juice.
2 Turn the chicken in the mixture and leave to marinate, skin side up, for 4 hours at room temperature.
3 Heat the oven to 200C /400F /gas 6 and cook the chicken for 45 minutes, scattering the sesame seeds over the chicken after 30 minutes. Serve from the dish.

Aubergine and pepper pickle

2 hours draining, 1 hour, then 1 week maturing

Fills a 1 kg /2 lb jar
500 g /1 lb aubergines
30 ml /2 tbls salt
300 ml /10 fl oz white wine vinegar
2 large green peppers
2 large red peppers
6 anchovy fillets
1 lemon, thinly sliced
5 ml /1 tsp black peppercorns
olive oil, to cover

1 Cut the aubergines in half lengthways and then in 5 mm /¼ in slices. Layer the slices with the salt in a colander and leave them to drain for 2 hours.
2 Put the vinegar into a saucepan with 150 ml /5 fl oz water and bring to the boil. Rinse the aubergine slices in cold water, drain, then add to the pan and simmer for 5 minutes. Drain again.
3 Cook the peppers under a hot grill until their skins blacken, then peel them and cut them into 5 mm /¼ in strips.
4 Pack the aubergines and peppers in layers in a 1 kg /2 lb jar, adding an anchovy fillet, a lemon slice and 1 or 2 peppercorns here and there.
5 Immerse in olive oil, cover and keep in a cool, dry place for at least 1 week before opening. It should keep for up to 6 months.

Honeyed wheatmeal doughnuts

These doughnuts are delicious served as a dessert with whipped cream. They will keep fresh for up to 2 days if kept in an airtight plastic container.

1 hour 25 minutes, plus 1 hour 10 minutes rising and 2 hours soaking

Makes 12

15 g /¹/₂ oz fresh yeast or 10 ml /2 tsp dried
50 g /2 oz honey, plus 5 ml /1 tsp
100 ml /3¹/₂ fl oz warm milk
250 g /9 oz wheatmeal flour, plus extra for
  kneading and flouring a baking sheet
2.5 ml /¹/₂ tsp salt
1 medium-sized egg, lightly beaten
45 ml /3 tbls sunflower oil, plus extra oil
  for deep frying
60 ml /4 tbls apricot jam
For the syrup
125 g /4 oz honey
30 ml /2 tbls medium dry sherry

1 Cream the yeast in a bowl with 5 ml /1 tsp honey and 30 ml /2 tbls warm milk. Leave the mixture until it is frothy — about 5 minutes for fresh yeast, 15 minutes for dried yeast.
2 Sift the flour and salt into a bowl and make a well in the centre. Put in the remaining honey, the egg, 45 ml /3 tbls oil, the remaining milk and the yeast mixture. Beat to a dough, gradually incorporating the flour from the sides of the well.
3 Turn the dough onto a floured work surface and knead until smooth. Return the dough to the bowl, place the bowl in a polythene bag and leave in a warm place to double in size, about 1 hour.
4 Heat the oven to its lowest setting. Knead the dough again for a few minutes and divide it into 12 small pieces. Flatten out each one and put 5 ml /1 tsp jam in the centre. Bring the sides together, seal them and form the dough into a ball.
5 Place the doughnuts on a floured baking sheet and put them in the oven for 10 minutes to double in size.
6 Heat a deep pan of oil to 190C /375F, or until a cube of day-old bread turns golden brown in 50 seconds. Fry 4 doughnuts at a time for 5 minutes, turning once, until they are a rich brown all over. Lift them out with a slotted spoon and drain them on absorbent paper. Cook the remaining doughnuts in the same way.
7 Make the syrup: put the honey and 150 ml /5 fl oz water into a saucepan and set over a low heat. Cook without boiling until the honey has dissolved. Remove the pan from the heat and stir in the sherry.
8 Put the doughnuts on a large, flat dish and spoon the hot syrup over them. Leave them for 2 hours, turning once, so they soak up all the syrup, then serve.

● If you have no sunflower oil, groundnut or a blended oil can be used instead.

Corn oil lemon cake

Corn oil is considered to be the best oil for making cakes, but you could also use sunflower, groundnut or a blended vegetable oil.

50 minutes, plus cooling and 1 hour setting

Makes one 18 cm /7 in cake
175 g /6 oz flour
a pinch of salt
5 ml /1 tsp baking powder
grated zest of 1 lemon
150 g /5 oz caster sugar
125 ml /4 fl oz corn oil, plus extra for
  greasing
2 medium-sized eggs, separated
60 ml /4 tbls lemon curd
For the frosting
1 egg white
175 g /6 oz caster sugar
a pinch of salt
a pinch of cream of tartar
15 ml /1 tbls lemon juice
2 drops yellow food colouring (optional)

1 Heat the oven to 180C /350F /gas 4. Sift the flour, salt and baking powder into a bowl. Add the lemon zest and sugar and mix with your fingers. Make a well in the centre.
2 Beat together the oil, 90 ml /6 tbls water and the egg yolks and pour them into the well. Beat the mixture together with a wooden spoon. It will be fairly stiff.
3 Stiffly whisk the egg whites and fold them in. Divide the mixture between 2 oiled 18 cm /7 in sponge tins and bake for 20 minutes or until they are firm and have shrunk slightly from the sides of the tins. Turn out onto wire racks to cool.
4 When the cakes are cold, sandwich them together with the lemon curd.
5 To make the frosting, combine the egg white, sugar, salt and cream of tartar in the top of a double boiler and, using a balloon whisk, whisk until they are light and frothy.
6 Place over simmering water. Stir in the lemon juice and optional food colouring and continue whisking until the mixture stands in stiff peaks, about 6–8 minutes.
7 Take the pan from the heat and spread the frosting over the top of the cake. Leave it to set for 1 hour before serving.

Sweet
Ingredients

USING SUGAR

Sugar can be used simply as a sweetener, as the basis of mouth-watering confectionery, or as a special feature when icing a cake to make it look and taste spectacular.

Our bodies manufacture sugar from carbohydrates in starchy food to give us energy. Consuming sugar itself, therefore, is a quick way of gaining and replacing lost energy.

The bad reputation sugar has, perhaps unfairly, acquired as a cause of fat, heart disease and so on can be blamed, in part, on the modern way of life. If we do not take enough exercise, we cannot burn up the calories generated by the sugar-rich foods in our diets.

Yet while excess sugar is bad for all of us, it is important to maintain a naturally balanced diet, so do not be afraid to indulge your sweet tooth from time to time.

The origins of sugar

Sugar is derived from sugar cane and sugar beet. Sugar cane thrives in a tropical climate; it may first have been used as a food by the Polynesians, before spreading to the Far East, Asia, and the Mediterranean.

By the 15th century, cane sugar was the basis of a thriving trade in Europe: sugar was almost as valuable as gold. Columbus took sugar cane to the Caribbean, where it grew so successfully that the sugar trade moved from Europe to the West Indies.

In the mid-18th century a German chemist discovered that sugar could also be made from beet, which grows well in the temperate climates. Nowadays large quantities of sugar beet are grown and processed in Britain, France, West Germany and Poland.

How sugar is made

The sugar is extracted from both cane and beet as a syrup, which is boiled to evaporate and concentrate the liquid and form crystals.

The syrup is then mechanically spun to separate the crystals from the liquid, which is known as molasses. At this stage the sugar is called 'raw', and cane sugar is exported like this, in crystals still coated with molasses. The raw sugar is then further refined to whiten it if required.

Types of white sugar

White sugar from cane and from beet taste identical.

Granulated sugar is the most commonly used and cheapest type of sugar, with relatively coarse, sparkling crystals.

Caster sugar is similar, but with much finer crystals than granulated. This means caster sugar dissolves quickly and it has advantages for certain types of cooking, especially for making cakes and delicate cold desserts.

Icing sugar is granulated sugar milled to a very fine powder, with a tiny proportion of calcium phosphate added to keep it free-flowing. Always sift it before you use it. In an emergency you can make your own icing sugar by grinding granulated or caster sugar in a blender.

Cube sugar is moulded granulated sugar. Convenient to handle, it is mainly used to sweeten tea or coffee. Ordinary cube sugar dissolves more slowly than granulated sugar but a quick-dissolving type is also generally available. Coarsely crushed cube sugar can be useful for decorative purposes. Cubes can be rubbed over an orange rind to remove the zest.

Preserving sugar is ideal for jams, marmalades and jellies because the large white crystals dissolve very slowly, creating a minimum of froth when the jam is boiled. It does not form a coating on the bottom of the pan, as can happen with granulated sugar, and so does not need to be stirred so often; the result is clear, bright jam.

Types of brown sugar

Most brown sugar comes from cane, retaining some of the colour and flavour of molasses. Beet sugar is always refined until white and then it may be coloured and flavoured with cane molasses.

Light soft brown sugar is fine-grained with moist, clinging crystals and a distinctive and mild flavour. It is used mainly for cakes and confectionery.

Dark soft brown sugar, such as that from Barbados, in the Caribbean, has a rich, full flavour and fine, moist crystals. It is used in confectionery and in baking, especially for toffee, gingerbread and fruit cakes.

Molasses sugar is usually cane sugar with an extra high proportion of molasses left in it, making it rich and sticky. Try it in a Christmas cake for a change.

Demerara sugar: originally exported from Guyana in South America, this kind of sugar has larger, light golden crystals which remain well-separated and are slow to melt. Demerara has a rich taste and gives good colour and flavour to fruit cakes. It is also used to sweeten coffee.

Coffee crystals are large, slow-dissolving crystals, even larger than those of Demerara. Brown crystals are pure sugar; the multi-coloured ones are artificially coloured.

Storing sugar

Stored in a cool, dry place, white sugar has an indefinite life. Fine icing sugar may become lumpy, but it can always be sifted before you need to use it.

As brown sugars are moist, they tend to go lumpy when stored for long periods so it is better to buy them in small quantities. Lumpy sugar can, of course, be used in recipes where it needs to be melted.

Tests for boiling sugar — how to tell what stage the sugar has reached without a thermometer

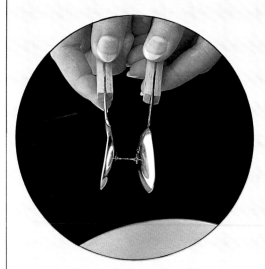

Thread test: dip two spoons into the syrup, then separate them immediately. A thread should form that breaks at a short distance.

Pearl: when the syrup is boiled to 150C / 220F, the surface of the syrup forms bubbles that resemble small pearls.

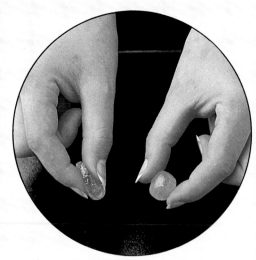

Soft and hard ball: drop a little syrup into cold water. Remove and roll it with your fingers into a ball, either soft or hard.

Cooking with sugar

Sugar syrup is invaluable for poaching fruit and as the base of a fruit salad, as well as for freezing purposes and use in sweet-making. Always use a heavy-based saucepan.

Choose a large pan so that it is only half full when you start, because boiling sugar rises up the sides of the pan.

Boiling sugar: boiling changes the physical characteristics of sugar. If the sugar is to be the main ingredient, as in confectionery, it needs to be boiled to the correct temperature and this demands great care.

The changes in the sugar become more marked as it is boiled to successively higher temperatures. In the tests, shown in the pictures below, you can see how the sugar behaves at each stage, although the simplest way to check the temperature is with a sugar thermometer. Warm this in hot water before using it — otherwise it may shatter with the heat of the sugar.

Heat gently at first, stirring slowly with a wooden spoon. Do not let the syrup boil until the sugar is completely dissolved. It can easily take 20–30 minutes to dissolve 500 g / 1 lb sugar, but rushing this stage will result in a grainy syrup, with crystals that spoil the finished product. When the syrup is absolutely clear, turn up the heat and boil briskly without stirring any more. When the required stage is reached, stop the process by putting the pan in cold water.

Baking: sugar helps to prolong the freshness of baked foods — and also helps to fix the aroma. All sugars are equally sweet and therefore you could use the cheapest — granulated — in most recipes. But granulated will give a slightly grainy result in a sponge cake or a mousse, so choose caster sugar for these dishes, unless otherwise stated.

Use brown sugar for its extra flavour in dark cakes. For gingerbreads, made by the melting method, use any brown sugar. But if you are using the method of creaming the sugar with the butter, only soft brown sugar will give a smooth, velvety texture.

Confectionery and cake decorations: use boiled sugar to make toffee, fudge, caramel and boiled sweets. Caramel and nuts together make praline which is used for flavouring and decorating desserts.

Preserving: sugar will preserve fruit, for example glacé fruit and fruit in jams. It also helps to preserve vegetables in chutney.

Savoury dishes: sweet and sour sauces (see recipe), which balance the natural sweetness of sugar with the acidity of vinegar, are very successful with meat, poultry and vegetables. Sugar boiled to a high temperature loses all sweetness. It can then be used as a colouring, for example as gravy browning.

Sweet and sour sauce

 10 minutes

Serves 4

1 small onion, chopped
2 carrots, cut into thin strips
1 green pepper, seeded and cut into thin strips
salt
50 g /2 oz soft dark brown sugar
15 ml /1 tbls cornflour
60 ml /4 tbls malt vinegar
15 ml /1 tbls soy sauce
15 ml /1 tbls dry sherry
275 ml /10 fl oz chicken stock, home-made or from a cube

1 Blanch the onion, the carrots and the pepper for 2 minutes in boiling salted water. Then drain and refresh them under plenty of cold running water. Leave to drain.
2 Mix the sugar and cornflour with the vinegar, soy sauce and sherry in a small saucepan. Stir with a wooden spoon until smooth, then stir in the stock. Bring to the boil, still stirring, then simmer for 2 minutes. Add the vegetables to the sauce and heat.

Boiling sugar

Temperature, test and uses

101C /215F **Thread** Thin syrups for fruit salads, poached fruit

105C /220F **Pearl.** Fondant, jam

115C /240F **Soft ball.** Soft fudges

130C /260F **Hard ball.** Hard fudges

138C /280F **Crack.** Soft toffees, frostings

155C /310F **Hard crack.** Hard toffees

170C /325F **Caramel.** Caramel coatings

199C /390F **Black jack.** Gravy browning, colour for dark fruit cakes

Italian cake frosting

 30 minutes

Covers a 20 cm /8 in sandwich cake
225 g /8 oz granulated sugar
4 egg whites

1 Put the sugar in a heavy-based saucepan with 75 ml /3 fl oz water. Heat gently, stirring, until the sugar is dissolved.
2 Turn up the heat and boil the syrup to 130C /260F; at this temperature a sample in cold water will make a hard ball. Whisk the egg whites until softly peaked.
3 Pour the syrup onto the beaten egg whites a little at a time, continuing whisking until the meringue is smooth and shiny. Leave it to cool.
4 To use, spread it over the cake with a palette knife, using the tip to make a pattern.

Crack test: drop a little syrup into cold water; it should separate into pieces that are hard but not brittle.

Hard crack test: when the sugar reaches hard crack stage, a drop put into cold water will separate into hard, brittle strands.

Caramel: boil the sugar until the syrup turns golden brown. If boiling is continued, the sugar burns and forms black jack.

about 10 minutes or until the apple is tender. Purée in a blender or rub through a sieve. Allow the purée to cool. Whip the cream and fold all but 45 ml /3 tbls into the purée.

2 Meanwhile, melt the butter in a frying-pan, stir in the crumbs, sugar and cinnamon and stir over a low heat for about 5–7 minutes, until the crumbs are a golden brown. Remove from the heat and allow to cool.

3 In a glass bowl, make a layer of apricot purée, sprinkle this with a layer of crumbs, add another layer of apricot purée and so on, finishing with the fruit. Cover the pudding with the remaining whipped cream and put in the refrigerator to chill thoroughly for about 1½ hours. Arrange the almonds in a pattern on top to serve.

Macaroon sandwiches

For light, crispy macaroon biscuits with added luxury, sandwich them into pairs with a brandy-flavoured chocolate filling.

50 minutes,
plus cooling

Makes 15
melted butter, for brushing
300 g /10 oz blanched almonds, finely ground
175 g /6 oz icing sugar, sifted
30 ml /2 tbls cocoa powder, sifted
4 drops almond essence
4 egg whites

Fondant fancies

1 hour

Makes about 20
450 g /1 lb granulated sugar
a pinch of cream of tartar
15 ml /1 tbls evaporated milk
a good squeeze of lemon juice
icing sugar, for dusting
4–5 glacé cherries, halved
15 ml /1 tbls instant coffee
25 g /1 oz walnut pieces

1 Put the sugar in a large, heavy-based saucepan with 175 ml /6 fl oz water and heat gently until the sugar is completely dissolved. Stir in the cream of tartar and boil to 115C /240F or until a little syrup dropped into a pan of cold water forms a soft ball between your fingers.

2 Remove the pan from the heat, let the bubbles subside and pour the syrup into a large bowl. Cool for about 10 minutes.

3 Using a flat wooden spatula, work the syrup with a paddling motion, turning it over and over until it thickens and becomes opaque. As it thickens, work in the milk.

4 Turn the fondant onto a laminated surface and knead it with your hands until smooth. Then divide it in half.

5 Knead the lemon juice into one-half of the fondant. Next dust your hands with the icing sugar. Divide the lemon fondant into about 10 even-sized pieces. Shape into balls,

Fondant fancies

rolling between your hands. Place each ball in a paper sweet case and press half a glacé cherry on top.

6 Dissolve the coffee in 15 ml /1 tbls boiling water and work it into the remaining fondant. Divide this into about 10 pieces, roll into balls as before, and put in paper sweet cases. Press a piece of walnut on top of each.

Apricot cream pudding

Smooth golden apricot purée and crunchy layers of crumbs make a delicious pudding.

1 hour soaking apricots,
then 30 minutes, plus chilling

Serves 4
225 g /8 oz dried apricots, soaked in warm
  water, to cover, for 1 hour
45 ml /3 tbls orange juice
1 large cooking apple, cored and chopped
150 ml /5 fl oz thick cream
100 g /4 oz butter
100 g /4 oz fresh white breadcrumbs
50 g /2 oz demerara sugar
a pinch of ground cinnamon
25 g /1 oz blanched almonds, toasted

1 Drain the apricots and put them in a pan with the orange juice and the chopped apple. Slowly bring to the boil and simmer for

To finish

225 g /8 oz semi-sweet chocolate, broken
60 ml /4 tbls brandy
15 ml /1 tbls icing sugar
15 ml /1 tbls cocoa powder
wrapping (optional)

1 Heat the oven to 180C /350F /gas 4. Line 2 baking sheets with greaseproof paper, then brush them with melted butter.
2 In a large bowl, combine the ground almonds with the sifted icing sugar, cocoa powder, almond essence and 2 egg whites. Work this to a smooth paste with a wooden spoon.
3 In a clean bowl, whisk the remaining egg whites to soft peaks. With a large metal spoon, fold lightly but thoroughly into the almond mixture.
4 Spoon 30 × 15 ml /1 tbls mixture onto the prepared baking sheets, spacing them 5 cm /2 in apart. Bake for 12–15 minutes, then transfer to a wire rack with a palette knife. Leave until completely cold.
5 Meanwhile, in the top pan of a double boiler, melt the broken chocolate pieces over gently simmering water. Then stir in the brandy.
6 Divide this evenly among half the macaroons and sandwich them together with the remaining halves.
7 Combine the icing sugar and cocoa powder and dust it over the top of the macaroon sandwiches. Leave them to get quite cold. Wrap carefully, if wished.

Macaroon sandwiches

Strawberry and orange sorbet

This delicate and unusual sorbet is displayed to full effect in the attractive orange baskets.

⏱ 🍴 1 hour, plus cooling the syrup, then 6–7 hours freezing

Serves 6

450 g /1 lb caster sugar
575 ml /1 pt orange juice extracted from 6 large oranges, the shells reserved, if wished, as containers (see note below)
550 g /1¼ lb strawberries
juice of 1 lemon
a pinch of salt
crushed ice, to serve (optional)
Grand Marnier (optional)
mint leaves, to serve

1 If using the freezing compartment of your refrigerator, turn it down to its lowest temperature (the highest setting) about 1 hour before you start.
2 Put the sugar and the orange juice in a large, heavy-based saucepan over a low heat. Gently dissolve the sugar, stirring constantly, then boil the syrup rapidly for 1 minute. Plunge the base of the pan into cold water to stop the sugar cooking and leave it to cool completely.
3 Reserve 6 perfect strawberries with their stalks and leaves intact for a decoration. Hull and then purée the rest in a blender. Press

Strawberry and orange sorbet

the pulp through a nylon sieve to remove the seeds. Add the lemon juice and salt. Stir in the cold orange syrup.
4 Pour the mixture into a shallow freezer-proof container, cover and freeze for 2 hours or until it is frozen to a depth of about 25 mm /1 in all around the sides.
5 Stir up the mixture vigorously with a fork, then freeze it again. Repeat every 30 minutes until the sorbet is half-frozen. Cover it and leave it for at least 3 hours or overnight, until it is frozen hard.
7 About 30 minutes before serving, transfer the sorbet to the refrigerator.
8 For a party presentation, about 10 minutes before serving cover a shallow dish with a bed of crushed ice. Set the orange shells on the ice and fill them with the sorbet. Otherwise, simply arrange scoops of the sorbet in individual glass dishes. If wished, dribble Grand Marnier over the top. Decorate each serving with a reserved strawberry and mint leaves.

● To prepare the orange baskets, make two parallel cuts from the top down to just above the centre of the orange, leaving a strip 5 mm /¼ in wide between the cuts (this forms the handle). Cut in at right angles to meet the base of the cuts and remove the two wedge-shaped pieces. Holding the orange in 1 hand, cut round between the flesh and the skin. Scrape out the flesh with a teaspoon, leaving the shell clean. Remove the flesh and pith from inside the handle.

CHOCOLATE

Chocolate is a great favourite with people of all ages. Its main use is in confectionery, but with it you can make drinks, sauces, cakes and biscuits, puddings and desserts — you can even add it to savoury dishes.

The cocoa tree (*Theobroma cacao*) is a native of the equatorial Americas, although today it is also cultivated in West Africa and Malaya. Its fruit grow on the trunk and the main branches and look rather like tapered melons: the pods inside contain up to 40 seeds which, when fermented and dried, become what we know as cocoa beans. It is from these that cocoa and chocolate are made.

In the 1520s cocoa was taken to Spain from the New World and the secret of growing and preparing it was closely guarded for a century.

Chocolate became highly fashionable at the French court, and chocolate houses opened in London and Amsterdam, although the high price meant that only the wealthy could enjoy the beverage. Dessert chocolate in solid bars, however, was not produced for nearly 200 years, when a Dutchman, Van Houten, discovered how to press cocoa butter out of the beans.

Making cocoa and chocolate
The cocoa beans are processed by roasting, crushing and sieving them before they are blended and milled. Because the beans contain 50% fat, called cocoa butter, the milling results in a liquor rather than a powder. This liquor is the basis of all chocolate products.

Cocoa is made by extracting about half of the cocoa butter from the liquor, leaving a solid block which is then ground to a fine powder. Chocolate, on the other hand, has extra cocoa butter added to the basic liquor, with sugar for sweetening, and milk solids for milk chocolate. This mixture is then refined and moulded.

Kinds of block chocolate
Choose the sort of chocolate you require for each recipe.

Cooking chocolate is unsweetened chocolate made from cooled and solidified cocoa liquor, but true cooking chocolate is not easy to find. Chocolate that is sold for cooking broken up into chunks in bags, without any identifying label, is unlikely to be pure chocolate; it will contain some cocoa powder and other edible fillers, and the cocoa butter will probably have been replaced with other fats such as coconut and palm kernel oils which increase the melting properties, but at the expense of flavour. If you choose to use unsweetened cooking chocolate in a recipe which requires plain chocolate, remember that you will need to add sugar to compensate.

Plain chocolate may be labelled as bitter or semi-sweet, according to the amount of sugar it contains. Any type of plain chocolate is suitable for cooking.

Milk chocolate, which contains powdered or condensed milk, is perhaps the most popular eating chocolate; it is not suitable for cooking, as it separates quickly on heating, but it can be used for decoration on cakes and desserts.

Storing cocoa and chocolate
Both cocoa and chocolate should be stored in a cool, dry place. Cocoa will keep for about a year in a tightly sealed can. Chocolate should have a shelf life of 6 months, but it is always better to buy what you need month by month. Keep any chocolate well wrapped up since it absorbs other flavours easily. A bloom sometimes appears on chocolate, but this does not affect the taste.

Chocolate drinks
There are several forms in which you can drink chocolate.
Cocoa powder (allow 5–10 ml /1–2 tsp per

Making chocolate caraque

Use a small, sharp knife in order to shave the chocolate into long curls.

cup) must be blended carefully with a little boiling water or milk to make a paste before the rest of the boiling liquid is added. Stir thoroughly. Sweeten to taste.
Drinking chocolate is a ready-made mixture of cocoa and powdered sugar, treated to blend evenly with hot or cold milk. Allow 15 ml /1 tbls per cup of milk.
Block chocolate can also be used to make a delicious drink. In a saucepan, melt 40 g / 1½ oz plain chocolate for each cup of milk, with just enough milk to moisten, then stir in boiling milk until evenly blended. Beat with an egg whisk to make it frothy.
Flavouring hot chocolate drinks: for Viennese chocolate beat an egg yolk into each cupful of cooled chocolate drink and then warm the mixture through over a gentle heat, stirring so that it does not boil. Remove it from the heat, whisk, pour into a cup and

top it with a spoonful of whipped cream.
For Mocha chocolate, melt 40 g /1½ oz plain chocolate in 90 ml /6 tbls strong black coffee over a low heat. Remove from the heat, pour in boiling milk to make a cupful, whisk and top with whipped cream.
Add any of the following to flavour hot chocolate: ground cinnamon; marshmallows; finely grated orange zest; chocolate mints, broken up and stirred until dissolved; rum, brandy, sherry or a chocolate-based liqueur.
Cold chocolate drinks are refreshing in the summer. Make a basic chocolate syrup for use in these by mixing 50 g /2 oz cocoa powder with 275 ml /10 fl oz boiling water. Add sugar to taste and 2.5 ml /½ tsp vanilla essence. Stir well to dissolve the sugar. Store in a sealed jar in the refrigerator and use to taste to make chocolate milk shakes by blending with ice cream and ice-cold milk; make chocolate ice cream soda with the syrup, ice cream and soda water.

Cocoa and chocolate for cooking
Surprisingly, cocoa and chocolate can be used in many different dishes, including several savoury ones.
Savoury ways: chocolate is used in savoury dishes in the cuisine of various countries — most often with game. The amount of chocolate added is minimal, but it enriches the sauce in an interesting and subtle manner. From Sardinia there is a recipe for leg of wild boar which includes chocolate; the Spaniards stew partridge with chocolate; in France, in the Médoc, they add chocolate to a beef, rabbit and pork stew, and the Mexicans serve a rabbit casserole (see recipe) and a sauce containing chocolate with turkey.
Sweet ways: the flavour of chocolate can be allied to a great number of different ingredients — fruit (especially citrus fruit, cherries, raspberries), nuts, coffee, ginger and mint.
Cocoa is the economical way to provide chocolate flavour in cooking. It is most often used where the mixture is to be thoroughly cooked, as in cakes, steamed or baked puddings and flour-based sauces. Use block chocolate rather than cocoa for dishes requiring little or no cooking; it gives a better flavour and texture in cold desserts.
Cocoa or chocolate can be used for cake icings and fillings and you can also try easy-to-use plain or milk chocolate chips.
Coating with chocolate: melted chocolate gives a hard, glossy finish to biscuits and cakes. Nuts, candied peel and crystallized ginger coated with chocolate make delicious sweets, perfect with after-dinner coffee.
● For chocolate nuts, melt broken-up chocolate in a bowl over simmering water and add some whole hazelnuts. Stir to coat thoroughly, then place clusters of 3 or 4 nuts on a sheet of waxed paper or in small paper sweet cases and leave to set.

Garnishing with chocolate
Chocolate can be used in some delightfully attractive ways to decorate cakes, ice cream, mousses and whipped cream.
Chocolate caraque: melt plain chocolate in a bowl over simmering water. Turn the chocolate onto a cold, flat surface and spread

Chocolate-coated orange sorbet

it out evenly. Leave until set. Use a sharp knife to shave the chocolate into long curls.

Grated chocolate: use the coarse section of a sharp grater. It is only worthwhile using an electric grater if you are making a large amount of grated chocolate.

Chocolate curls: use a sharp potato peeler to scrape the chocolate from the bar.

Chocolate shapes: melt plain chocolate in a bowl over simmering water. Trace small designs on greaseproof paper and fill in the shapes by piping the melted chocolate through a very fine nozzle. When the chocolate is set, peel off the paper carefully.

Chocolate flake: this is available from confectioners and makes a very effective decoration for ice cream and cakes.

Chocolate vermicelli are tiny, fine strands of chocolate or chocolate-flavoured sugar for sprinkling over cakes or desserts.

Drinking chocolate looks pretty sprinkled over whipped cream. It also makes an attractive garnish for a cake: dredge the surface with icing sugar, place strips of foil on top to form a pattern, sieve drinking chocolate over the cake, then carefully remove the foil.

Chocolate liqueurs

Chocolate liqueurs are produced either by macerating or percolating cocoa beans, followed by distillation and sweetening. Crème de cacao is the usual name for chocolate liqueurs. Flavours added to chocolate liqueur include mint, citrus fruit and coconut.

Chocolate liqueurs are excellent in mousses, added to hot sauces and soufflés, poured over ice cream or folded into cream.

Rabbit casserole

 2 hours

Serves 6–8
2 rabbits, jointed
45 ml /3 tbls olive oil
1 large garlic clove, crushed
2 bay leaves
2 cloves
30 ml /2 tbls freshly chopped parsley
400 ml /14 fl oz full-bodied red wine
25 g /1 oz plain chocolate
salt and freshly ground pepper

1 Wipe the rabbit pieces. Heat the oil and fry the rabbit until it is lightly browned.

2 Add the garlic, bay leaves, cloves and parsley and stir well. Add the wine, bring it to the boil and then reduce the heat. Transfer to an oven-proof casserole.

3 Break the chocolate into pieces and add it to the casserole, stirring until it has melted. Season with salt and pepper. Cover and cook over a gentle heat for about 1½ hours. Check the liquid during the cooking time and add a little wine or water if necessary.

Chocolate-coated orange sorbet

3 hours, plus overnight freezing

Serves 4
vegetable oil, for greasing
250 g /8 oz dark (semi-sweet) cooking chocolate, broken into pieces
crushed ice, for chilling
125 g /4 oz sugar
finely grated zest of 1 orange
375 ml /13 fl oz orange juice
60 ml /4 tbls lemon juice
1 egg white
For the garnish
150 ml /5 fl oz thick cream, whipped
zest of 2 oranges cut into julienne strips

1 Using vegetable oil, generously grease a dry 850 ml /1½ pt plain plastic mould. Turn the mould upside down on absorbent paper for 10 minutes to drain. Place the mould in the refrigerator to chill.

2 In the top part of a double boiler, melt the chocolate over a low heat, stirring frequently. As soon as the chocolate has melted remove the pan from the heat.

3 Remove the chilled mould from the refrigerator and pour in the melted chocolate. Tip and rotate the mould to coat the inside completely. Place the mould in a large bowl of crushed ice and continue tipping and rotating until the chocolate has set in an even layer. Return the chocolate-lined mould to the refrigerator to chill.

4 Bring the sugar and 150 ml /5 fl oz water to the boil, boil for 5 minutes. Remove it from the heat, add the grated orange zest and cool.

5 Strain the orange juice and lemon juice into the flavoured syrup, stir once and allow to cool completely.

6 Pour the orange mixture into a freezer-proof container and freeze the liquid to a depth of about 25 mm /1 in around the sides of the container. Whisk the sorbet with a fork to break up the ice particles and return to freezer for 30 minutes.

7 Whisk the sorbet again with a fork or wire whisk until smooth then beat the egg white lightly and whisk it into the sorbet. Remove the chocolate-coated mould from the refrigerator and spoon the sorbet into it, smoothing it down. Cover the mould and freeze overnight.

8 Just before serving remove the mould from the freezer. Place a chilled serving dish over the top of the mould. Turn the plate and the mould upside down, giving the mould a sharp shake — the dessert should come out easily. To decorate the mould, pipe a border of whipped cream around the base and scatter the orange julienne strips all over the top.

9 To serve cut with a serrated knife, heated in a jug of hot water.

Chestnut meringue basket

3 hours, plus cooling

Serves 6–8
250 g /9 oz icing sugar, sifted
4 egg whites
a pinch of cream of tartar or salt
3 drops of vanilla essence
75 ml /5 tbls whipped cream
chocolate caraque, to decorate
  (see introduction)
For the filling
100 g /4 oz plain chocolate
50 g /2 oz unsalted butter, softened
100 g /4 oz caster sugar
grated zest of 1 orange
450 g /1 lb unsweetened chestnut purée
30 ml /2 tbls cognac

Chestnut meringue basket

1 Heat the oven to 140C /275F /gas 1. Line 2 baking sheets with non-stick baking paper. Draw a circle on each one, using a 23 cm /9 in plate as a guide.

2 Sift the icing sugar into a bowl. In a separate bowl whisk the egg whites lightly with the cream of tartar or salt, then add the icing sugar 15 ml /1 tbls at a time, whisking continuously. Add the vanilla essence at the same time, a drop at a time.

3 When all the sugar has been added, place the bowl over a saucepan of simmering water (the bowl must not touch the water) and continue to whisk until the meringue is very thick and stiff — about 5–8 minutes. It must hold its shape firmly when the whisk is lifted. Be careful to whisk continually around the sides and bottom.

4 To make the top of the meringue basket, spoon ⅓ of the meringue into a piping bag fitted with a 25 mm /1 in star nozzle and pipe an ornamental ring around one circle (see picture). Spoon the rest of the meringue into the piping bag and make the base: piping in a circular motion, completely fill in the second circle. Finish off the edge with an ornamental ring.

5 Place the ring on the centre shelf of the oven and bake the base on the shelf above that for 1½ hours. Take from the oven and allow to cool. Stick the ring onto the base with the whipped cream.

6 To make the filling, break the chocolate into small pieces and melt them in a small bowl over hot water. Beat the butter in a mixing bowl until it is pale and creamy. Add the sugar and orange zest and beat well. Add the melted chocolate, chestnut purée and cognac and beat until smooth. Spoon the chestnut mixture into the meringue basket and cool before serving. Decorate with chocolate caraque.

Florentines

 1¼ hours

Makes 14
40 g /1½ oz butter, plus extra for greasing
60 ml /4 tbls caster sugar
4 glacé cherries, quartered
75 ml /5 tbls blanched and finely chopped
  almonds
60 ml /4 tbls blanched and flaked almonds
45 ml /3 tbls candied orange peel, finely
  chopped
15 ml /1 tbls thick cream, whipped
125 g /4 oz chocolate

1 Heat the oven to 180C /350F /gas 4. Lightly butter 2 or 3 baking sheets.

2 Put 40 g /1½ oz butter and the sugar in a small, heavy saucepan. With a wooden spoon, stir over a low heat until the sugar has dissolved. Bring it to the boil, then remove the pan from the heat.

3 With a metal spoon, fold the cherries, chopped and flaked almonds, candied peel and whipped cream into the butter mixture. Mix well and leave to cool thoroughly.

4 Drop 10 ml /2 tsp of biscuit mixture for each florentine onto the baking sheets 10 cm /4 in apart, as they spread considerably. Bake

in the oven for 6–7 minutes, or until the florentines have spread to thin discs. Remove from the oven and with a plain pastry cutter ease the edges of the florentines in, to make circles. Turn the baking sheets, return them to the oven and cook for a further 2–3 minutes, or until they are a beautiful golden colour. Leave the florentines on the baking sheets to become lukewarm before transferring them to a wire rack. Allow them to become completely cold.

5 Melt the chocolate and 5 ml /1 tsp butter in a bowl over a pan of hot water. Using a palette knife, spread the smooth side of each florentine with a thin layer of melted chocolate and mark wavy lines over it with the prongs of a fork. Leave them to harden at room temperature. Store the florentines in an airtight container.

Chocolate cookies

 25 minutes

Makes 35
75 g /3 oz butter, plus extra for greasing
75 g /3 oz caster sugar
75 g /3 oz soft brown sugar
5 ml /1 tsp vanilla essence
1 egg, beaten
125 g /4 oz self-raising flour
2.5 ml /½ tsp bicarbonate of soda
75 g /3 oz walnuts, coarsely chopped
75 g /3 oz plain chocolate, coarsely chopped

1 Heat the oven to 190C /375F /gas 5. Next, lightly grease 2 or 3 baking sheets with butter.

2 In a large bowl, cream the butter until it is soft. Gradually add the sugars and whisk until light and fluffy. Add the vanilla essence, then the beaten egg, a little at a time, whisking continuously until well blended.

3 Sift the flour and bicarbonate of soda into the butter mixture. Next, add the nuts and

Florentines

the chocolate to it and fold them in.

4 Drop 10 ml /2 tsp of chocolate mixture for each cookie onto the prepared baking sheets 5 cm /2 in apart and bake in the oven for 10–12 minutes, or until slightly golden and firm to the touch. Turn the baking sheets occasionally during cooking. Transfer the cookies to a wire rack with a spatula and allow them to cool. When completely cold, store the cookies in a box or jar with a loosely fitting lid or they can be frozen.

Rum truffles

 20 minutes,
plus chilling and setting

Makes about 30
15 ml /1 tbls instant coffee
225 g /8 oz plain chocolate
100 g /4 oz butter
30 ml /2 tbls dark rum
a little icing sugar
chocolate vermicelli, for coating
  (see introduction)
paper sweet cases

1 Dissolve the instant coffee in 30 ml /2 tbls hot water. Break the chocolate into small pieces and place them in a bowl with the coffee. Set the bowl over a pan of hot water and stir until the chocolate has melted.

2 When the chocolate has melted, remove it from the heat and beat for a moment to cool it. Cut the butter into dice and gradually beat this into the chocolate until it is smooth and thick. Beat in the rum gradually.

3 Chill the chocolate mixture for about an hour or until it is firm. Dust your hands with icing sugar and roll the chocolate mixture into walnut-size balls. Next, roll the balls in the chocolate vermicelli to coat them thoroughly. Put the truffles in sweet cases and leave to set.

HONEY, SYRUPS & TREACLE

For a change, try sweetening your cooking with honey, treacle, golden syrup or maple syrup. They add extra flavour, colour and interest to dishes as far-ranging as pancakes, gingerbread and glazed carrots.

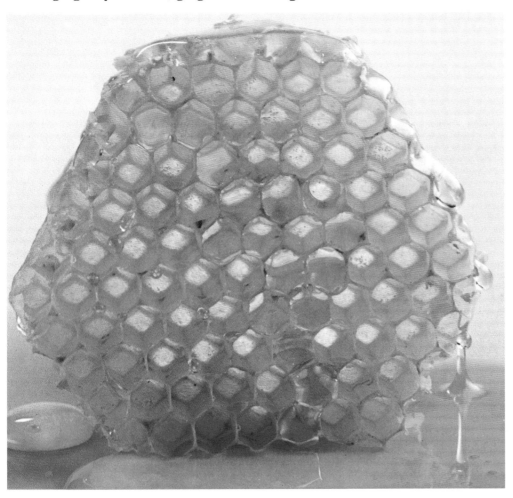

A section of honeycomb

Sugar is not the only way of sweetening your cooking. There are synthetic products for those who watch their weight, but these may leave a bitter after-taste. The best natural sweeteners are honeys and syrups.

Types of sweetener

Honey is a natural syrup manufactured by bees from the nectar of flowers and plants, and used to be the only sweetener for cooking. The Romans baked with honey, while the ancient Greeks combined honey with ground nuts and poppy seeds to make a filling for a simple flour dough. Before this, in Egypt, it was used not only as a sweetener but as a healing aid, to soothe burns and wounds. Today honey is valued as a rich source of vitamins, minerals, enzymes and acids, and for its energy-giving properties.

Honey is usually sold in jars and sometimes, on the comb from the hive. There are many different types of honey, ranging from pure nectar honey to blended varieties. It can taste of all sorts of flavours; wild thyme from Greece (said to be the finest in the world), heather, orange blossom, jasmine, lime flower and clover. The flowers, the weather and the season, the degree of heat and pressure applied to extract the honey from the combs all affect the end product. The colour may vary from a deep brown to a creamy white.

Light-coloured honey is usually more delicately flavoured and scented than darker types. Cloudiness is quite natural and is caused by the pollen contained in the honey (clear honey has been heat-treated). For general cooking purposes, thin clear honey blends easily and dissolves readily.

Maple syrup has a very smooth, rich taste, rather like rum. The best grades are light in colour. Pure 100% maple syrup is expensive and consists entirely of boiled-down sap; 'genuine' maple syrup must contain at least 35% maple sap. Maple-flavoured syrup can be used in the same way as pure maple syrup.

Molasses is a dark, thick and sticky syrup, made from either sugar cane or sugar beet, although the molasses from sugar cane is the one usually used for cooking. It is a nourishing, energy-giving sweetener, rich in iron and other minerals, various B vitamins, calcium and a lot of natural sugar. It varies in colour from mid-brown to black and has a very concentrated sweet flavour. The darkest type of molasses is called blackstrap and has a raw, slightly bitter taste.

Treacle is refined from molasses. It is thick and dark but it is less sweet than molasses. It can be used in the same way as molasses and as a substitute for it in many recipes.

Golden syrup is a by-product of the sugar-refining process, and is thin and runny. Light amber in colour, it has a mild butterscotch flavour which goes well with sweet spices like ground cinnamon and ginger. It combines well with coconut.

Corn syrup made from corn (maize) starch, is more common in the United States of America than in Europe. It can be light or dark in colour. Light corn syrup is more refined and less strongly flavoured than the darker varieties.

Storing liquid sweeteners

If they are correctly stored most liquid sweeteners have a shelf life of up to one year. Honey will keep longer, although it may crystallize if kept too long, and the colour and the flavour will deepen with age. Corn and maple syrup will deteriorate more quickly as they are susceptible to mould. After opening, store them in a refrigerator.

Measuring liquid sweeteners

Place the container in a pan of hot water for a few minutes until the syrup is warmed and runny. Rinse measuring spoons in very hot water and dry thoroughly before use. If you only need a small quantity, pour the warmed sweetener directly into the measuring spoon, because if you dip the spoon into the container, some of the syrup will cling underneath and this may result in too much being added. When a large quantity is called for, pre-weigh the mixing bowl and measure the liquid sweetener into the bowl by weight.

Using liquid sweetners

Because they are liquid rather than solid ingredients, these sweeteners do not behave in exactly the same way as sugar, so adjustments will have to be made.

Honey is wonderful in cakes, sponge puddings and yeast doughs where it helps produce a soft, moist texture and an appetizing golden colour. Baked food containing honey will stay fresh longer than if sugar is used. Honey also makes an excellent glaze. Brush it over scones and tea-bread when they are still warm from the oven. In yeast-raised doughs honey can replace sugar weight for weight. In cakes you can replace up to half the sugar in the recipe with honey. To compensate for honey's extra sweetness and liquidity, the general rule is to use only 225 g /8 oz honey in place of each 275 g /10 oz sugar and to reduce the liquid in the recipe by 45 ml / 3 tbls. Unless the recipe calls for sour cream, add a pinch of bicarbonate of soda to counteract the acidity of honey.

Honey is a delicious substitute for sugar in syrups, especially for poached apples and pears. Because it is sweeter than sugar you need only use 22.5 ml /1½ tbls honey in place of each 75 g /3 oz sugar in the recipe.

Make your own exotic honey — as a gift or just for yourself. By adding the flavour of summer roses to a pot of ordinary honey it becomes something special. Remove the petals of 10 cabbage roses, discard any that are not in good condition and wash the rest carefully. Put them in a pan with 60 ml /4 tbls water and heat for 5 minutes, stirring constantly. Add 450 g /1 lb clear honey to the pan, bring it to the boil and simmer, covered, for 30 minutes. Remove the petals, cool the honey and repot it.

Honey can also be used in some savoury dishes, for example honey-glazed roast gammon, while a little honey included in the basting juices for roast chicken will give it a rich mellow flavour.

Maple syrup has a sweet assertive flavour, so it is often used alone as a sauce for pancakes, ice-cream and waffles. It is also delicious poured over baked or steamed sponge puddings, particularly those flavoured with orange zest, sweet spices or coffee. Use maple syrup to flavour sweet mousses and fillings and icings for cakes, as well as for sweets like toffee. Its affinity with nuts, — pecans and walnuts in particular — is often used to best effect in sweet open pastry tarts. It is seldom included in savoury dishes but sometimes is used in American marinades for pork spare ribs. Maple syrup can replace up to half the amount of sugar in cakes in the proportion of 175 ml /6 fl oz syrup for each 225 g /8 oz caster sugar and a reduction of other liquid in the recipe by 45 ml /3 tbls.

Molasses is used for extra flavouring in milky drinks, to flavour cakes and puddings, or combined with nuts to make fillings for sweet pies. Some traditional American dishes based on pork or dried beans also call for molasses: Boston baked beans (see page 45) is probably the most famous example; barbecued spare ribs — pork spare ribs glazed with molasses syrup and eaten with your fingers — is another.

In baking, molasses can replace up to half the sugar in cakes and will give a denser, moister texture and a deep brown colour. Because it is acidic you should reduce or omit any baking powder called for and add 2.5 ml /½ tsp bicarbonate of soda for each 225 g /8 oz molasses used. You should also reduce the liquid called for in the recipe by 45 ml /3 tbls.

Treacle in English cooking is most strongly associated with baking; a small quantity is included in very rich fruit cakes and puddings to give a good rich colour and flavour. It is also an important ingredient in gingerbreads (see Welsh gingerbread).

Golden syrup can be thickened with breadcrumbs and used as a filling for open pastry tarts or suet rolls. Warmed golden syrup can be sharpened with lemon juice or cooked with butter and brown sugar as a sauce for pancakes, sponge puddings or ice cream.

In baking it can replace treacle and is often used in biscuit-making — it is the ingredient which puts the snap in ginger biscuits and the chewiness in flapjacks.

Corn syrup is an important ingredient in confectionery where it helps to prevent sweets drying out. In baking it can replace up to half the amount of sugar in cakes. But you need twice as much to achieve the equivalent degree of sweetness. The general rule is to use 600 ml /1 pt corn syrup in place of each 250 g /8 oz caster sugar and to reduce the other liquids by 50 ml /2 fl oz.

Breakfast pancakes

These pancakes are best eaten fresh from the pan — so give your family breakfast in the kitchen and cook the pancakes in batches, spreading them with maple syrup and stacking them as you go.

 40 minutes

Serves 4
100 g /4 oz flour
2.5 ml /½ tsp salt
30 ml /2 tbls caster sugar
2 good pinches of ground mixed spice
6 eggs, separated
225 g /8 oz cottage cheese, sieved
45 ml /3 tbls milk
30 ml /2 tbls melted butter
a pinch of cream of tartar
oil or melted butter, for greasing
warmed maple syrup, to serve

1 Sift the flour, salt, sugar and spice into a mixing bowl and make a well in the centre. In a separate bowl, beat the egg yolks into the sieved cottage cheese until smooth. Pour the egg and cheese mixture into the flour, add the milk, blend lightly, then stir in the melted butter.

2 Whisk the egg whites with the cream of tartar until they stand in soft peaks. Stir a spoonful of the whisked whites into the batter, then fold in the rest.

3 Place a griddle or heavy-based frying-pan over medium-high heat and rub the surface with an oiled or buttered cloth to grease it lightly. When a faint haze rises, drop the batter — a scant 45 ml /3 tbls at a time — into the pan. Cook for about 3 minutes until the pancakes puff up and bubbles begin to burst on the surface, then turn them over and brown the other side. Continue in this way until all the batter is used up, lightly regreasing the pan if necessary. You should make 16 pancakes in all.

4 Spread the cooked pancakes generously with warmed maple syrup as you make them and stack them, four at a time, on warmed serving plates. Spoon a little more syrup over the top of each stack and then serve them immediately.

Breakfast pancakes

Honey-glazed carrots with coriander

 30 minutes

Serves 4
500 g /1 lb carrots, trimmed and scrubbed
8 coriander seeds, finely crushed
a pinch of salt
25 g /1 oz butter
30 ml /2 tbls thin honey

1 Slice young carrots into rings; scrape old carrots, cut them into quarters, remove the central woody cores and then chop them into even lengths.
2 Place the carrots in a heavy-based saucepan and add the coriander, salt, 20 g /¾ oz of the butter and the honey. Pour in enough water to come three-quarters of the way up the carrots. Bring to the boil, then cover and simmer the carrots until they are just tender in texture.
3 Remove the lid and bring the liquid back to the boil. Boil vigorously until the liquid has reduced to a syrupy glaze, shaking the pan as often as necessary to prevent the carrots sticking to the bottom. Swirl in the remaining butter and turn the glazed carrots into a warm serving dish.

Veal cutlets with apples and port

 30 minutes

Serves 6
125 ml /4 fl oz clear honey
125 ml /4 fl oz tawny port
a pinch of dried mixed herbs
a pinch of freshly grated nutmeg
50 g /2 oz unsalted butter
6 best-end veal cutlets or small leg steaks
    about 20 mm /¾ in thick
salt
freshly ground white pepper
450 g /1 lb crisp eating apples, peeled, cored
    and sliced
45 ml /3 tbls lemon juice

1 Warm the honey until it is liquid. In a jug, mix it with the port, the mixed herbs and the nutmeg.
2 Heat the butter in a large, deep frying-pan with a lid over a moderately high heat. Add the chops and brown them quickly on each side. Sprinkle them with salt and pepper and reduce the heat to low.
3 Pour in the port mixture, cover and simmer for 4 minutes. Add the apples and sprinkle them with salt and pepper. Spoon some of the sauce over the apples. Cover the pan and simmer for 5 minutes.
4 Stir the lemon juice into the sauce and simmer, uncovered, for 3 minutes. Turn the contents of the pan into a warmed, shallow serving dish and serve at once.

Nutty treacle tart

Honey vinaigrette

Use this Persian salad dressing to put on crisp lettuce leaves. Serve the salad with a hard cheese such as Wensleydale after a main course or for lunch.

⏲ 10 minutes,
plus chilling

Makes 150 ml /5 fl oz
300 ml /10 fl oz malt vinegar
45 ml /3 tbls clear honey
salt and freshly ground black pepper
15 ml /1 tbls lemon juice
2 drops of orange water (optional)

1 Put the vinegar in a small pan and boil it for 10 minutes to reduce the liquid. Add the other ingredients and cool before use.

● Use honey to make a salad dressing with yoghurt. Stir 5 ml /1 tsp each honey and lemon juice into 150 ml /5 fl oz yoghurt. Add 1 garlic clove, crushed with salt, and season. This is an excellent dressing with tomato salads, cucumber and grated root vegetables.

Nutty treacle tart

Despite its name, this good old-fashioned sweet is made with golden syrup. In this version a buttery wheaten pastry is used to complement the hazelnut filling. This pastry is more crumbly than the usual shortcrust — keeping it cool makes it easier to handle.

⏲⏲ 1½ hours

Serves 4–6
100 g /4 oz wholemeal flour
50 g /2 oz self-raising flour
a pinch of salt
75 g /3 oz butter, diced
a little iced water, to mix
beaten egg or milk, to glaze
For the filling
120 ml /8 tbls warmed golden syrup
75 g /3 oz fresh brown breadcrumbs
grated zest of ½ lemon
50 g /2 oz hazelnuts, toasted, skinned and
  coarsely chopped

1 Sift the flours with the salt into a mixing bowl. Tip the residue of bran left in the sieve into the bowl and stir lightly to mix.
2 Cut the butter into the flour with a palette knife, then rub it in with your fingertips until the mixture resembles even-sized breadcrumbs. Gradually stir in just enough iced water to bind the mixture together. Knead briefly until smooth. Wrap it in cling film and leave it to relax in the bottom of the refrigerator for 15 minutes.
3 On a lightly floured surface, roll out the dough to a circle about 22 cm /9 in in diameter. Line an 18 cm /7 in diameter flan tin, reserving the trimmings for 15 minutes.
4 Heat the oven to 200C /400F /gas 6. Measure the warm syrup into a heavy-based saucepan. Stir in the breadcrumbs, lemon zest and chopped nuts.

5 Spread the syrup mixture evenly over the base of the pastry case. Roll out the pastry trimmings thinly and cut into long, narrow strips. Arrange the strips in a lattice over the filling. Neaten the edges, then lightly brush the strips with the beaten egg or milk.
6 Bake the tart for 30–35 minutes, until the pastry is cooked and the filling is a rich, dark brown colour.

Maple, rum and raisin ice cream

Luxuriously rich, this ice cream is worth every calorie! It is important to beat the mixture thoroughly during the freezing process otherwise the texture will not be smooth and creamy. Soften the ice cream in the refrigerator for half an hour before you serve it.

⏲⏲ 1 hour,
plus 4½ hours freezing

Serves 6–8
275 ml /10 fl oz thin cream
75 ml /5 tbls maple syrup
2 medium-sized egg yolks
1 medium-sized egg
275 ml /10 fl oz thick cream, lightly whipped
15 ml /1 tbls rum
50 g /2 oz seedless raisins, chopped

1 Set the refrigerator to its lowest temperature (the highest setting). Chill a metal container.
2 Pour the thin cream into a small, heavy-based saucepan, add 60 ml /4 tbls of the maple syrup and stir well to mix. Bring the mixture to boiling point, then remove it from the heat.
3 In the top part of a double boiler, lightly beat together the egg yolks and whole egg. Put the egg mixture over a double boiler containing simmering water. Pour the hot cream mixture onto the beaten eggs in a thin stream, stirring constantly.
4 Cook the custard for 15 minutes, continuing to stir, then strain it into a jug standing in a bowl of ice cubes. Leave it for about 30 minutes or until it is cold, stirring occasionally.
5 Turn the cold custard into the chilled container, cover it with foil and freeze for 45 minutes or until it is firm around the edges.
6 Turn the mixture into a large chilled mixing bowl and whisk thoroughly. Next, stir in the lightly whipped cream and the rum. Return it to the container, cover it and freeze for a further 1½ hours.
7 Beat the ice cream thoroughly again, then stir in the chopped raisins. Return the ice cream to its container. Drizzle the remaining 15 ml /1 tbls maple syrup to and fro across the surface, then swirl it through the ice cream with a metal skewer.
8 Smooth the surface of the ice cream, cover and freeze for 2 hours or until firm. Soften the ice cream in the main body of the refrigerator for 30 minutes before serving.

● Use honey, brandy and mixed chopped fruit to replace the syrup, rum and raisins.

Applejacks

These keep well for 2–3 days in an airtight tin and become moister and more chewy with storage.

🍴 1 hour 10 minutes,
plus cooling

Makes 18
75 g /3 oz butter, plus extra for
* greasing*
50 g /2 oz Demerara sugar
90 ml /6 tbls golden syrup
225 g /8 oz rolled oats
a large pinch of salt
For the topping
45 ml /3 tbls apricot jam
10 ml /2 tsp orange juice
2 medium-sized dessert apples, peeled,
* quartered, cored and thinly sliced*
15 g /½ oz butter
2.5 ml /½ tsp ground cinnamon or mixed
* spice (optional)*

1   Heat the oven to 180C /350F /gas 4. Grease a 28 × 18 cm /11 × 7 in Swiss roll tin.
2   In a medium-sized, heavy-based saucepan, combine the butter, the sugar and the golden syrup over a low heat. Stir until the sugar has dissolved. Remove the pan from the heat and stir in the rolled oats, one third at a time. Next, stir in the salt. Blend thoroughly. Then the mixture into the prepared tin, spreading it evenly over the base, pressing it down well with the back of a spoon and smoothing the surface.
3   Sieve the jam into a small saucepan and add the orange juice. Stir over a low heat

Applejacks

until it is runny. Spread some of the jam thinly over the top of the flapjack. Arrange the apple slices — slightly overlapping — in three rows across the length of the base, leaving a gap between each row.
4   Add the butter, with the ground spice (if using), to the remaining jam and return to a low heat, stirring until the butter has melted, then pour the jam mixture over the apples. Spread the jam over the top of the fruit.
5   Bake the applejack for 30–35 minutes, until the apples are tender and the edges of the flapjack mixture are golden brown. Cut the cooked applejack into oblongs while still warm, then leave it to cool completely before removing it from the tin.

Pears ambrosia

🍴 35 minutes,
plus chilling

Serves 4
4 small, firm dessert pears, peeled, cored and
* thickly sliced*
For the syrup
60 ml /4 tbls thin honey
1 vanilla pod
For the topping
175 g /6 oz fromage blanc (see note below)
10 ml /2 tsp thin honey
3 drops vanilla essence
2 drops almond essence
For the praline
50 g /2 oz sugar
50 g /2 oz toasted almonds
oil, for greasing

1   To make the syrup, place the honey and 300 ml /10 fl oz water in a heavy-based saucepan and stir together until the honey is dissolved. Then bring to the boil and boil the syrup for 3–4 minutes without stirring.
2   Take it off the heat and add the vanilla pod and the pear slices to the syrup. Poach the fruit for 10–15 minutes until the slices are tender. Turn the pears and syrup into a bowl, cool, then cover and chill for 2 hours.
3   Meanwhile, mix together the fromage blanc, honey and essences. Cover and chill.
4   Make the praline. Cook the sugar and almonds over a low heat until they caramelize. Pour onto an oiled tray and cool until set. Crush it with a rolling pin.
5   When ready to serve, drain the pears (reserving the syrup) and remove the vanilla pod. Divide the fruit among 4 dessert plates, arranging the slices in a cartwheel. Dip a pastry brush into the reserved syrup and brush lightly over the pears. Spoon the fromage blanc into the centre of each plate and scatter the praline on top.

● Substitute cream cheese for the fromage blanc if desired.

Welsh gingerbread

🕐🍴 1¼ hours,
plus 2 days maturing

Makes one 25 cm /10 in square cake
100 g /4 oz butter, plus extra for
* greasing*
450 g /1 lb flour
45 ml /3 tbls ground ginger
15 ml /1 tbls ground mixed spice
a pinch of salt
5 ml /1 tsp bicarbonate of soda
100 g /4 oz chopped mixed peel (optional)
450 g /1 lb treacle
50 g /2 oz soft brown sugar
2 medium-sized eggs, lightly beaten
150–200 ml /5–7 fl oz milk

1   Heat the oven to 180C /350F /gas 4. Grease a fairly shallow 25 cm /10 in square cake tin and line the base with greaseproof paper. Lightly grease the lining paper.
2   Sift the flour with the spices, salt and soda into a large mixing bowl. Stir in the chopped peel if used.
3   In a heavy-based saucepan, warm together the treacle, butter and sugar over a low heat, stirring frequently until the sugar dissolves. Cool slightly.
4   Make a well in the centre of the sifted dry ingredients and pour in the melted mixture, the eggs and most of the milk. Stir thoroughly, adding enough of the remaining milk, if needed, to bring the mixture to the consistency of a heavy batter.
5   Turn the cake mixture into the prepared tin and allow it to find its own level. Bake for 40–45 minutes until the surface of the cake is firm and a thin, warmed skewer inserted into the centre comes out clean.
6   Allow the baked cake to cool in the tin for 10 minutes before turning it out onto a wire rack. Remove the lining paper and leave the cake until it is completely cold. Store for at least 2 days before cutting.

Seasonings

SALT & PEPPER

Salt and pepper are our most common seasonings, giving flavour to food both in cooking and at the table. They are generally used in tandem and are thought of as a pair, but in character and origin they are very different.

Salt is without a doubt the most important flavouring in cookery, while pepper must be the most useful spice. They are both readily available from supermarkets, health food shops and delicatessens in many forms, depending on the purpose for which you need them. Salt and pepper cellars and mills are usually made and sold in matching pairs.

Salt

Salt is one of the many minerals which are absolutely essential to our diet, although it is needed in only the tiniest amounts. Intake of salt is closely related to intake of water: cutting down on salt can be an aid to slimming, but a drastic shortage of salt in the diet or an excessive loss of salt through perspiration can be a serious health hazard.

Salt is either mined from the earth (rock salt) or produced by the evaporation of sea water (sea salt). Sea salt is usually produced by the application of artificial heat; salt produced by natural evaporation through sunlight is known as bay salt. There is no significant chemical or nutritional difference between any of these salts in their basic forms, it is the state in which they are offered to the market which differs.

There is relatively little natural salt in meat, but most vegetables and dairy products contain quite a large amount of salt. If these are eaten raw or cooked without water, little extra salt is needed; however, if vegetables are cooked in water, and the water is thrown away, extra salt has to be added either during cooking or when the food comes to the table.

Kitchen salt is not often seen these days. It comes as a rough block from which small pieces are broken off for use in cooking.

Cooking salt, which is usually rock salt, is more common. It is loose salt but with no added chemicals to keep it free-flowing. It is usually sold in packets.

Table salt, again usually rock salt, has magnesium carbonate added to keep it free-flowing. It has a fine crystal and can be poured straight from the packet or drum into a salt cellar. Iodine, another trace mineral vital in our diet, is sometimes added.

Sea salt is generally sold under that label. It comes in coarse or fine crystals, but the fine crystal is not as fine as table salt. For sea salt you need either a salt mill or a mortar and pestle in which to grind the crystals to a fine powder. The blades of the mill should be hard nylon or plastic, not metal, which the salt will quickly corrode.

Sea salt tastes 'saltier' than rock salt and it offers an advantage to those who do not like additives in their food as, unlike table salt, it does not contain magnesium carbonate, although some brands do contain iodine.

Try my recipe for Chicken baked in salt, where the thick crust of salt seals in the natural juices of the meat.

Rock salt is sometimes sold under that label,

as a coarse crystal salt with no additives. Grind it in a mill, as for sea salt.

Flavoured salts: fine salts seasoned with celery, garlic, onion and spices are available for seasoning meat.

Buying and storing salt

Most supermarkets sell only cooking salt and table salt. Pure sea and rock salts are usually available from delicatessens and health food shops.

When storing salt, the most important factor is to keep it dry. Salt attracts moisture and even the 'free-flowing' varieties will quickly clog into lumps in a damp atmosphere. A few grains of rice in the salt container will help to keep it dry.

Salt as a preservative

The main use of salt is as a seasoning in cooking and as a condiment at table. But it is also a preservative. A great number of foods are traditionally preserved in salt to extend their life in storage. Some foods are dry salted, that is, packed with salt between the layers as in making sauerkraut. My recipe for Orange spiced duck calls for dry salting.

Meat, poultry and fish are more often soaked in brine, which is a solution of salt in water or other liquid. Its advantage over dry salting is that it penetrates further and more quickly into the food, making the preservative more thorough. Spices or other flavourings are often added to the brine, which gives the brined products characteristic flavours.

Other uses of salt in cooking

Apart from seasoning and preserving, salt also has the effect of 'stabilizing' some foods. For instance, a pinch of salt added when whisking egg whites will help them to hold their maximum whisked volume for longer. Freeze eggs without shells (because they will crack at low temperatures) with a pinch of salt beaten in.

As salt has the effect of attracting or drawing out water, vegetables which contain an excess of water or acidic juices benefit from being well salted and drained — a process known by the French term *degorger*. This applies particularly to aubergines and cucumbers, which are inclined to be acidic and thus indigestible. If the cut surfaces are well salted and the vegetables then left in a colander for 30–60 minutes, the excess water and the worst of the acidity will drain out, leaving them sweeter and more digestible. Vegetables salted in this way should, of course, be rinsed and dried before use.

The same principle of drawing out the juices applies when salting meat for cooking. To achieve a crisp crackling on roast pork, rub the skin well with salt before starting to cook, using oil to help the salt stick and give the crackling a gloss as well.

Conversely, never salt the cut surface of

lean meat such as rump steak before cooking, as this will make it dry out and harden: cook the meat first and season it lightly if you wish, just before serving.

Pepper

The berries of the climbing plant *Piper nigrum*, native to India and grown chiefly in southern Asia, are the source of pepper. One of our most important spices, with its hot and fiery taste, it is used simply for flavouring; it has no nutritional value. Although it is used only lightly in Western recipes, most savoury recipes are seasoned with at least a small amount of pepper, and it can even be introduced into a few sweet dishes (see recipes for Hot strawberries with peppercorns and Pepper biscuits). In hot climates pepper is used in large quantities — probably because the fiery character of the spice encourages perspiration, which in turn cools the body. Pepper is a major ingredient in curry powder and is heavily used in Asian dishes.

White pepper comes from the fully ripened berries. The hard outer husks are removed.

Pink peppercorns are the ripe berries with the red husks still on.

Black pepper comes from the unripened berries. They are picked green and dried in the sun until they turn a dark, greenish-black. The resultant spice is more subtle than white pepper and can be used rather more freely in cooking and at the table.

use a mixture of ground black and white pepper, which is called *mignonette*.

Whole peppercorns may be used to give extra spark to marinades or, included in a bouquet garni, to flavour stocks, soups and stews; they are then discarded.

Green peppercorns are not often used in general cooking, but they make a pleasant, lightly peppered sauce to serve with white meat such as chicken or turkey, or boiled bacon (see recipe). Mash the peppercorns lightly to release their flavour, before stirring them into the sauce. Try my Green peppercorn tomato salad (see recipe), an attractive dish including whole green peppercorns.

Green peppercorn tomato salad

 10 minutes,
plus making the vinaigrette

Serves 4
500 g /1 lb tomatoes
salt and freshly ground black pepper
5 ml /1 tsp green peppercorns
2 spring onions, thinly sliced
15 ml /1 tbls finely chopped fresh parsley
For the vinaigrette
15 ml /1 tbls wine vinegar
salt and freshly ground black pepper
45 ml /3 tbls olive oil

1 Cut the tomatoes into thin slices and arrange in overlapping rows on a round or oval serving dish, seasoning each row with salt and freshly ground black pepper to taste.
2 Sprinkle the tomato slices with the green peppercorns, thinly sliced spring onions and the finely chopped parsley. Chill lightly.
3 To make the vinaigrette: whisk together the wine vinegar, salt, pepper and olive oil until they form an emulsion.
4 Pour over the vinaigrette and serve.

Chicken baked in salt

As no fat is added to the chicken during cooking, this is a good recipe for slimmers. The thick crust of salt on the skin seals in the natural juices and also seasons the flesh.

1¼ hours

Serves 6
1.8 kg /4 lb chicken, jointed into 6 pieces
275 g /10 oz coarse sea salt

1 Heat the oven to 200C /400F /gas 6.
2 Spread half the salt in a thick layer in a baking tin just large enough to take the chicken joints. Lay the joints on top and cover them with the remaining salt. Avoid using a tin that is too large or you will find yourself wasting salt.
3 Bake the chicken for 1 hour 10 minutes, or until just tender. Break open the salt covering, remove the joints and brush off the excess salt. Serve hot or cold.

Green peppercorns are also unripe berries. They can be bought canned in brine, or pickled in a vinegar solution or just dried, to be used in a mill. Their taste is mild and light.

Buying and storing pepper
Both black and white pepper are available ready-ground and can sometimes be convenient in this form. However, they lose their flavour and aroma quickly so it is best to buy whole peppercorns and grind them in a pepper mill immediately before use. Even so, they still deteriorate fairly quickly, so it is best to buy them in small quantities. Although it is often tempting to buy spices cheaply in bulk, it is rarely wise; peppercorns packaged in sealed containers are likely to be in a much better condition. Ground pepper can be seasoned with other spices and these are also available from supermarkets.

Keep the peppercorns in their sealed container in a cool, dark cupboard. An open spice rack on the kitchen wall looks attractive, but unless the jars are tinted black, it is not actually very good for the spices. Use separate pepper mills for black and white and green peppercorns. When buying a pepper mill, make sure that it has strong, metal blades: nylon or plastic blades are not strong enough to grind the corns.

Green peppercorns are not as commonly available as black and white; look for them in specialist food shops. Canned green peppercorns keep indefinitely provided the can

Back row (in scales): garlic and spice salts; on beam (left to right): kitchen salt, coarse sea salt (as block and in mortar), cooking salt (in 'pig'); foreground (clockwise): table salt (in cellar), Breton sea salt, celery salt, onion salt, whole pink peppercorns, with white, green and black peppercorns above, rock salt, crushed black peppercorns, fine sea salt, lemon flavoured pepper

remains undamaged. Once the can is opened, transfer the peppercorns to a screw-top jar and keep it in the refrigerator, where the peppercorns should last about 6 weeks.

Cooking with pepper
Make sure you use the right sort of pepper to complement the recipe.

Ground pepper should, generally speaking, be used sparingly. Exceptions to the rule are specific recipes which call for particularly large amounts. Black pepper is used most extensively in cooking because of its more subtle flavour. However, white pepper is often preferred in a white or light-coloured sauce and in dishes such as scrambled eggs (see page 10), where the specks of black pepper spoil the natural colour of the dish. When coarsely ground or crushed pepper is called for, as in James Beard's steak au poivre (see recipe), use either a mortar and pestle or an electric mill such as a coffee grinder. Experiment with different seasoned peppers to give exciting flavours to meat. The French

Bacon with green peppercorn sauce

3–4 hours soaking,
then 1¾ hours

Serves 6
1.4 kg /3 lb boneless bacon joint
bouquet garni
1 large onion, halved
1 carrot, halved
1 celery stick, halved
25 g /1 oz butter
25 g /1 oz flour
15 ml /1 tbls green peppercorns
salt (optional)
thin cream or milk (optional)

1   Soak the bacon for 3–4 hours in cold water to cover. Drain off the soaking water, put the bacon in a large saucepan with fresh water to cover it and add the bouquet garni, onion, carrot and celery.
2   Bring the water to the boil, then reduce the heat, cover the pan and simmer for 1 hour 20 minutes until the bacon is tender.
3   Take the bacon out of the pan. Strain the stock into a measuring jug and discard the flavourings.
4   Melt the butter in a small saucepan and stir in the flour. Cook over a gentle heat, stirring, for 3–4 minutes until the roux is a pale straw colour. Remove from the heat and gradually stir in 300 ml /10 fl oz of the reserved bacon stock.
5   Return the pan to the heat and cook, stirring, for a further 3–4 minutes. Mash the peppercorns lightly, stir them into the sauce and check the seasoning. You are unlikely to

Green peppercorn tomato salad

need any extra salt; if the sauce is too salty, stir in a little thin cream or milk.
6   Remove the skin from the bacon and carve the meat into thick slices. Serve with a little sauce spooned over each portion.

Orange spiced duck

The duck is garnished with orange slices to emphasize its orange flavour.

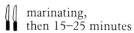 4 days marinating, 2 hours cooking, plus cooling

Serves 4–6
1.8 kg /4 lb duck
a strip of thinly pared orange zest
60 ml /4 tbls orange juice
a few sprigs of fresh parsley
orange slices, to garnish
For the preserving mixture
100 g /4 oz coarse salt
50 g /2 oz fine salt
10 ml /2 tsp saltpetre or potassium nitrate
5 ml /1 tsp dried thyme
5 ml /1 tsp orange zest, grated
2.5 ml /½ tsp ground cinnamon

1   Clean and prepare the duck and wash and dry it thoroughly. Do not truss it. (Use the giblets to make soup or a sauce.)
2   To make the preserving mixture, grind or crush the salts, thyme, orange zest and cinnamon to a fine powder.
3   Choose a casserole or dish, with a lid, that the duck just fits into and scald it in boiling water. Dry the dish well.
4   Rub the duck all over, inside and out,

with the salt mixture, taking care not to forget the crevices: under the wings and in the ridges between the bones. Put the duck in the scalded dish and cover it with a scalded and dried cloth and then the lid. Put it in the refrigerator.
5   Rub the duck inside and outside with the preservatives each day for a further 3 days. The salt will draw the moisture from the meat and the mixture will become a liquid with which to rub the duck.
6   Heat the oven to 150C /300F /gas 2. Wash the duck thoroughly and scrape off any spices and herbs that may be clinging to it. Put the duck into a deep ovenproof dish; cover it with cold water.
7   Add the orange zest, the orange juice and parsley. Stand the dish in a roasting tin and pour cold water into the tin so that it comes halfway up the side of the dish.
8   Cook the duck in the uncovered dish for 2 hours or until it is tender. Lift the duck from the liquid and stand it, breast side up, on absorbent paper to drain. Cover the duck loosely with greaseproof paper and leave it to cool.
9   When the duck is cold, carve into thin slices and garnish with orange slices.

James Beard's steak au poivre

marinating,
then 15–25 minutes

Serves 4
48 black peppercorns
4 × 225 g /8 oz rump steaks
135 ml /9 tbls brandy
beef suet or oil, for greasing
salt
watercress sprigs, to garnish

1 Place the peppercorns between 2 sheets of greaseproof paper and crush them with a rolling pin.
2 Put the crushed peppercorns in a small screwtop jar. Sprinkle them with 15 ml /1 tbls of the brandy. Screw on the lid, shake and leave to marinate for at least 3 hours.
3 Bring the steaks to room temperature. Nick the fat in several places to prevent the steaks curling as they cook.
4 Press the marinated crushed peppercorns onto both sides of the steaks.
5 Select 2 heavy frying-pans large enough to take 2 steaks each. Heat the pans until a sprinkling of water sizzles and evaporates on contact. Spear a piece of beef suet or a trimming of fat from a steak onto a long fork. Alternatively, use a thick wad of absorbent paper dipped in oil. Grease the base and sides of the hot pans. They should start smoking immediately.
6 Slap the steaks into the pans. Sear them quickly on both sides. Then reduce the heat to medium and continue to cook until the steak is done to your taste, 2 minutes each side for blue, 2½ minutes for rare, 3½–4 minutes for medium and 4½–5 for well-done.
7 Transfer the steaks to a hot plate and sprinkle with salt.
8 Divide the remaining brandy between the 2 pans. Stir briefly, then scrape the bottom and sides of the pans with a wooden spoon. Quickly pour the hot brandy over the steaks. Garnish with sprigs of watercress.

● Created by the American cookery writer, James Beard, this recipe for steak au poivre marinates the crushed peppercorns in brandy before using them. It makes an excellent dish for a dinner party, served with simple and quickly cooked vegetables such as Chinese-style mushrooms and stewed fresh tomatoes.

Hot strawberries with peppercorns

Hot strawberries with peppercorns

The green peppercorns bring out the flavour of the strawberries in this attractive dish.

 35 minutes

Serves 4
2 oranges
1 lemon
225 g /8 oz sugar
30 ml /2 tbls brandy
15 ml /1 tbls green peppercorns
500 g /1 lb strawberries, hulled

1 Grate the zest of 1 orange into a heavy-based saucepan. Squeeze the juice from the 2 oranges and the lemon, put it in a bowl and set aside.
2 Add the sugar to the grated orange zest and place over a medium heat. When the sugar has dissolved and formed a light brown caramel, carefully add the brandy. Remove the pan from the heat and ignite the contents. Carefully add the reserved fruit juices to the pan with 225 ml /8 fl oz water and return to the heat. Boil for about 10 minutes, or until you have 225–275 ml /8–10 fl oz syrup.
3 Remove the pan from the heat and pour the syrup through a metal sieve into a clean saucepan. Add the green peppercorns, drained and rinsed, if necessary, to the strained syrup and bring it to the boil.
4 Plunge the whole strawberries into the syrup and heat them for 1 minute only.

Bacon with green peppercorn sauce

5 To serve, remove the strawberries with a slotted spoon and divide among individual heated serving plates. Spoon the syrup over the fruit and serve immediately.

Pepper biscuits

Try serving these unusual biscuits with strawberries and cream.

 30 minutes

Makes about 20 biscuits
50 g /2 oz butter
50 g /2 oz soft dark brown sugar
100 g /4 oz golden syrup
175 g /6 oz self-raising flour
5 ml /1 tsp ground white pepper
butter, for greasing

1 Put the butter, sugar and golden syrup in a saucepan and heat very gently, stirring, until the sugar is dissolved. Remove from the heat. Heat the oven to 180C /350F /gas 4.
2 Sift the flour and pepper together into the saucepan and stir this into the liquid ingredients until thoroughly mixed.
3 Shape heaped teaspoons of the mixture into balls. Place them on a greased baking sheet and flatten them lightly with a fork.
4 Bake for 15 minutes, until they are lightly browned. Remove the biscuits from the oven and leave them on the baking sheet for 2 minutes. Transfer them to a wire rack and leave the biscuits until they are cold.

MUSTARD

Mustard has long been one of the most popular flavourings in cooking and there is certainly much more to it than just a traditional condiment to be eaten with hot roast beef or cold ham sandwiches.

As a seasoning for food mustard has been known to man since prehistoric times and was used by the Greeks, the Romans and the ancient Chinese. The Romans introduced the plant throughout Europe and it has been grown and used since then in many temperate countries.

Originally, ground mustard was sprinkled onto foods as a condiment, rather in the same way that salt and pepper are used today. In medieval times, cooks in France introduced spiced mustards, which consisted of the roughly ground powder mixed with spices, honey, wine or vinegar. It was the favourite accompaniment to a festive boar's head. Later, mustard became the traditional accompaniment to roast beef and goose, and was often flavoured with horseradish and vinegar.

Dijon in Burgundy was a centre of mustard making in the early Middle Ages and in the 17th century was granted exclusive rights in France. The ground mustard was combined with vinegar, the by-product of the local wine trade, to make a paste. Since 1937 this mustard has had an *appellation*, controlled by French law.

English mustard developed along different lines from the French and it was sold chiefly in powder form until after World War II. When the English powder was first produced it was a coarse one as it included the husks. Then millers in Durham began producing a very fine, dry powder. In the 19th century a Norwich miller, Jeremiah Colman, set up a factory, and today his name is synonymous with English mustard. He is quoted as saying that he made his fortune from the mustard people left on the side of their plates!

Types of mustard

Mustard is made from the seeds of three species of plant: white or yellow mustard (*Sinapis* or *Brassica alba*), black mustard (*Brassica nigra*) and brown mustard (*Brassica juncea*). Yellow mustard is native to the Mediterranean but now grows wild in both Britain and the United States of America. This is the mustard of the salad mix 'mustard and cress'. The seeds are a creamy yellow colour and are the least pungent of the three, with a slightly bitter flavour. Mixed with black mustard seeds (in reality they are dark grey in colour), wheat flour and a little turmeric, yellow mustard seeds form the basis of English mustard.

The mild American mustard is also largely based on yellow mustard seeds. Their strong preserving qualities make yellow mustard seeds popular for pickling, as for instance in piccalilli pickle where they are used whole.

Black mustard (sometimes called true mustard) also comes from the Mediterranean. Once very widely cultivated, it is difficult to harvest mechanically, so it is gradually being superseded by brown mustard (also called

Indian mustard), which is of Asian origin. Black mustard seeds have the hottest, most pungent flavour of the three types from which mustard is made, while brown mustard seeds are slightly milder.

Dijon mustard is made from dehusked black mustard seed, mixed with white wine and spices. This mustard is a great favourite for flavouring sauces and mayonnaise, as it does not colour the final product.

Bordeaux mustard, from the other great French wine centre, is also made from black mustard. It includes the finely ground husks (which make the mustard darker), vinegar, sugar, herbs and spices.

German mustard is of the Bordeaux type, but with a milder sweet-sour flavour; it is quite dark in colour.

The granular Moutarde de Meaux is made from whole crushed black and yellow mustard seeds and has a very pungent, spicy flavour. It is of medium strength and light in colour.

Green pepper mustard is subtle, smooth and delicious. It is flavoured with unripe green peppercorns, which generally come from Madagascar.

Buying and storing mustard

Yellow mustard seeds are those most commonly found. Look for ground yellow seeds and black mustard seeds in some specialist delicatessens, wholefood and Asian shops, and for brown mustard seeds, ground or whole, in Oriental food stores. Imported mixed mustards are fairly widely available in most supermarkets.

Store the seeds for a year or more in a cool dry place and the powder for up to 9 months. The essential oils in the seeds are only released when the ground seeds are mixed with water or another liquid. Jars of mustard will keep unopened for up to 1 year and once they have been opened they keep fresh for about 2 months.

Using mustard

To use a powder, add a little cold or tepid water (never boiling) and mix it to a paste. Leave the mixed mustard to stand for 15 minutes for the flavour to develop, then use it as soon as possible. Made mustard loses its taste and pungency after about 4 hours and begins to dry and discolour.

To grind your own mustard, powder 15 g / ½ oz each black and white mustard seeds in a blender or in a mortar. Add a pinch of fine sea salt and ground black pepper and mix to a thick paste with a herb vinegar. Store, covered, for up to one month.

Use it in sautéed or braised dishes, mixed into marinades, soups, sauces, salad dressings and savoury butters. A thin coating on lamb or pork chops before grilling gives a special, spicy flavour, while 5 ml /1 tsp mustard powder mixed with 90 ml /6 tbls dry white

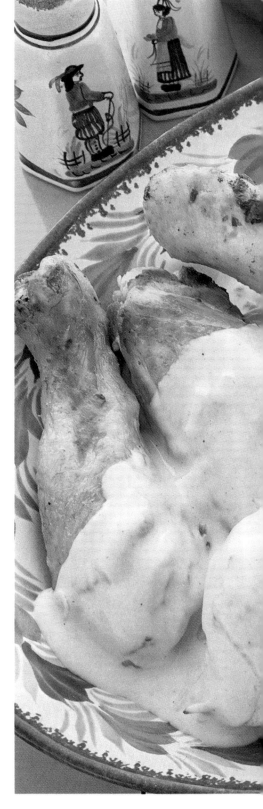

wine and 30 ml /2 tbls olive oil makes a good coating for a white fish which is to be grilled or baked.

Vary the flavours of made mustards. For serving with lamb, mix the mustard powder with a little water, let it stand for 15 minutes (to avoid any bitterness), then add some tarragon vinegar. For pork, mix the mustard powder with honey and dry cider. For beef, add about 2.5 ml /½ tsp grated horseradish to every 20 ml /4 tsp mustard powder before mixing with water.

Ground brown mustard powder, often called Chinese mustard, is much used in

also be finely chopped and then added to salads, where they will impart a flavour similar to that of watercress.

Cabbage salad with white wine dressing

🔪 25 minutes

Serves 4
½ small white cabbage, shredded
125 g /4 oz Florence fennel or celery, thinly sliced
1 medium-sized green pepper, chopped
125 g /4 oz white grapes, halved and seeded
50 g /2 oz raisins
10 ml /2 tsp white wine-flavoured, granular mustard
60 ml /4 tbls olive oil
30 ml /2 tbls dry white wine
15 ml /1 tbls white wine vinegar
1 garlic clove, crushed with a little salt

1 Put the cabbage, fennel or celery, pepper, grapes and raisins into a large salad bowl.
2 Put the mustard into a small bowl and beat in first the oil, then the wine and the vinegar. Mix in the garlic.
3 Pour the dressing over the salad and then toss it well. Leave it to stand for 10 minutes before serving.

Veal in tarragon mustard sauce

🔪🔪 50 minutes

Serves 4
4 veal escalopes
25 g /1 oz seasoned flour
25 g /1 oz butter
1 large onion, finely chopped
1 garlic clove, finely chopped
150 ml /5 fl oz dry white wine
150 ml /5 fl oz white stock, home-made or from a cube
10 ml /2 tsp granular tarragon mustard
60 ml /4 tbls soured cream
sprigs of fresh tarragon, to garnish

1 Beat the escalopes to make them thin and flat. Coat them in the seasoned flour.
2 Melt the butter in a frying-pan or sauté pan over a high heat. Put in the escalopes and brown them on both sides. Remove them and lower the heat.
3 Put in the onion and garlic and cook them until they are soft, about 5 minutes.
4 Pour in the wine and stock and bring them to the boil. Stir in the mustard.
5 Add the escalopes to the pan, cover and cook over a low heat for 20 minutes.
6 Remove the escalopes with a slotted spoon, put them on a warmed serving dish and keep them warm.
7 Stir the soured cream into the juices in the pan, heat the sauce through without letting it boil, pour it over the veal, garnish with tarragon sprigs and serve immediately.

Oriental cooking. Try serving it, mixed with a little water, with crispy Chinese pancake rolls to give them a spicy flavour.

Add dry mustard powder to the flour in the proportion of 5 ml /1 tsp to every 100 g /4 oz flour before making savoury pastries and breads, scones, dumplings and batter puddings. A little mustard powder added to the emulsion will stabilize a vinaigrette. Add 5 ml /1 tsp to the flour when making 300 ml /10 fl oz cheese sauce to bring out the flavour of the cheese and add extra bite.

Add a little of any bought, made mustard to salad dressings and sauces. A little

French mustard chicken

mustard mixed into winter soups such as leek, turnip, carrot, Jerusalem artichoke or celeriac gives added piquancy, as it does to braised vegetables.

Whole mustard seeds can be added to pickles, or they can be coarsely ground and added to marinades, sauces and sautéed dishes. Mix them with mustard powder and water or cider for a different type of topping for grilled meats.

Perhaps less well known is the fact that the young leaves of black or yellow mustard can

French mustard chicken

1¼ hours

Serves 4
1.5 kg /3½ lb oven-ready chicken
salt and freshly ground black pepper
50 g /2 oz butter
45 ml /3 tbls olive oil
1 medium-sized onion, finely chopped
300 ml /10 fl oz thick cream
3 egg yolks
15–30 ml /1–2 tbls Dijon mustard
flat-leaved parsley, to garnish

1 Cut the chicken into 8 portions and blot each with absorbent paper. Season with salt and freshly ground black pepper.
2 Choose a frying-pan large enough to take the chicken portions in one layer. In it heat the butter and oil. When the foaming subsides put in the chicken and sauté over a medium heat on each side until lightly browned. Remove and keep warm.
3 Add the finely chopped onion to the pan and cook for 2–3 minutes, stirring with a

Cabbage salad with white wine dressing and Beef with mustard peppercorn butter

wooden spoon. Return the chicken portions to the pan, and cover tightly with foil or a lid. Cook over a very low heat for 40–45 minutes, or until tender. Turn the chicken portions halfway through the cooking time.
4 Remove the chicken portions, arrange them on a heated dish and keep them warm. Over a high heat, boil the pan juices hard until they have reduced to a quarter of the original quantity.
5 In the top pan of a double boiler, whisk the cream and egg yolks until blended. Add the reduced pan juices to the cream mixture, whisking continuously. Place over simmering water and cook for 7–10 minutes, stirring with a wooden spoon until the sauce has thickened. Do not let the sauce boil or it will curdle. Stir in Dijon mustard to taste and adjust the seasoning.
6 Pour the sauce over the chicken portions and serve, garnished with flat-leaved parsley.

Beef with mustard peppercorn butter

Add green peppercorn mustard to the marinade and to the butter for a luxury meal of grilled fillet steak.

4 hours marinating, plus 35 minutes

Serves 4
750 g /1½ lb fillet steak
For the marinade
200 ml /7 fl oz dry white wine
10 ml /2 tsp green peppercorn mustard
1 small onion, finely chopped
15 ml /1 tbls freshly chopped thyme
30 ml /2 tbls olive oil
1 garlic clove, crushed with a pinch of salt
For the green peppercorn butter
125 g /4 oz butter, softened
15 ml /1 tbls green peppercorn mustard
grated zest and juice of ½ lemon

1 Cut the meat into 2 cm /¾ in steaks.
2 Combine the marinade ingredients in a shallow dish. Add the slices of steak to the marinade and leave for 4 hours, preferably at room temperature, turning or basting them several times.
3 Meanwhile, make the green peppercorn butter: cream the butter in a large bowl, adding the mustard 5 ml /1 tsp at a time. Beat in the lemon zest and then the lemon juice, again 5 ml /1 tsp at a time.
4 Form the butter into a roll about 25 mm / 1 in thick. Wrap it in greaseproof paper and put it into the refrigerator to firm.
5 When you are ready to cook the steak, remove the meat from the marinade, brushing off any pieces of thyme or onion that stick to the slices.
6 Remove the wire rack, lightly grease the grill pan, heat the grill to high and then heat the pan.
7 Replace the rack, place the steaks on the rack and sear them for 2 minutes on each side to seal in the juices. Next, reduce the heat (or lower the pan) and cook to your liking, a further 1 minute for rare, 1½ minutes for medium and 2–2½ minutes for well done. Remove the steaks quickly to a warmed serving plate.
8 Cut the butter into rounds about 3 mm / ⅛ in thick. Place one round on each steak and serve immediately. Any left-over butter rounds can be served separately.

● This green peppercorn butter also makes a good accompaniment to grilled lamb cutlets or a non-oily fish, such as cod.

Kidneys with mustard and port

This dish can be served as a starter or with rice for a main course.

35 minutes

Serves 4
8 lambs' kidneys
75 g /3 oz butter
60 ml /4 tbls finely chopped onion
15 ml /1 tbls Dijon mustard
150 ml /5 fl oz thick cream
2 slices of white bread
45 ml /3 tbls olive oil
salt and freshly ground black pepper
60 ml /4 tbls port
30 ml /2 tbls brandy
15 ml /1 tbls finely chopped fresh parsley

1 Skin and halve the kidneys, snipping the cores out with scissors. Slice each kidney into 3 and pat them dry with absorbent paper. Set them aside.

2 In a medium-sized frying-pan, melt 25 g / 1 oz of the butter and gently simmer the finely chopped onion for 10 minutes over a moderate heat, or until soft, stirring occasionally with a wooden spoon.

3 Stir in the Dijon mustard and then the cream. Simmer gently for 2 minutes or until thickened. Remove it from the heat and keep warm.

4 Remove the crusts from each slice of bread and cut into 2 triangles.

5 In a frying-pan large enough to take the triangles of bread in one layer, heat the olive oil and 25 g /1 oz butter. When the foaming subsides, lay the triangles side by side in the pan and sauté for 2 minutes each side, or until they are all golden brown, turning them with a spatula. Remove the triangles with a slotted spoon and drain them on absorbent paper. Keep them warm.

6 Add the remaining butter to the pan and sauté the prepared kidneys in the hot butter, turning them with a spatula, for 3 minutes, or until they are lightly browned all over but still slightly pink on the inside. Season to taste with salt and freshly ground black pepper.

7 Pour the port into the pan and simmer for 1 minute. Heat the brandy in a ladle. Standing well back, carefully ignite it with a lighted taper and pour it, still flaming, over the kidneys.

8 When the flames have died down, add the reserved mustard sauce.

9 Put the kidneys and sauce into a heated serving dish. Dip one end of the croûtons into finely chopped parsley, arrange on the dish and serve immediately.

Kidneys with mustard and port

Glazed gammon with mustard sauce

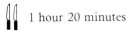 12 hours soaking, then 2¼ hours

Serves 8
2.2 kg /4¾ lb joint lightly smoked gammon
about 20 whole cloves
30 ml /2 tbls olive oil
For the mustard glaze
50 g /2 oz soft dark brown sugar
2.5 ml /½ tsp dry mustard
15 ml /1 tbls cider vinegar
For the mustard sauce
425 ml /15 fl oz milk
½ chicken stock cube, crumbled
25 g /1 oz butter
30 ml /2 tbls flour
60 ml /4 tbls thick cream
2 medium-sized egg yolks, beaten
10–15 ml /2–3 tsp dry mustard
salt and freshly ground black pepper

1 Place the gammon in a large bowl, cover with cold water and leave to soak for about 12 hours. Change the water several times.

2 Drain the soaked gammon and place it in a large saucepan. Cover it with fresh cold water. Slowly bring it to the boil and simmer for 30 minutes, or until the skin can be taken off easily. Leave the pan containing the gammon under running cold water until the gammon is cool enough to handle. Heat the oven to 200C /400F /gas 6.

3 Remove the string from the gammon and strip off the skin. Score the fat of the gammon and spike each diamond with a

whole clove. Lay the gammon in a roasting tin, brush with the olive oil and roast for 1 hour, basting occasionally.

4 Meanwhile, prepare the glaze: mix the sugar with the mustard, vinegar and 15 ml /1 tbls water. Set aside.

5 Prepare the sauce: heat the milk with the crumbled chicken stock cube. Melt the butter in a heavy pan, add the flour and stir over a gentle heat for 3 minutes, to make a roux. Gradually add the milk, and bring to the boil, stirring continuously. Simmer for 20 minutes, stirring regularly. Set aside.

6 When the gammon is cooked, remove it from the oven. Pour the glaze over the top, then return the gammon to the oven and cook, basting frequently, for 30 minutes.

7 When the gammon is cooked, transfer it to a hot serving platter. Leave it in a warm place to 'settle' while finishing the mustard sauce. Gently heat the sauce mixture. Strain in the juices from the roasting tin and stir in the thick cream. Remove the pan from the heat and beat in the egg yolks. Place the dry mustard in a small cup, add 15 ml /1 tbls of the hot sauce and stir until smooth. Beat this mixture back into the sauce, then season to taste with salt and freshly ground black pepper, bearing in mind that the gammon is likely to be a little salty. Gently reheat the sauce if necessary, but do not allow it to boil or it will curdle. Transfer the sauce to a heated sauceboat.

8 Carve the gammon, discarding the cloves, and serve hot, with the hot sauce.

Cheese and mustard sticks

1 hour 20 minutes

Makes about 100
250 g /9 oz flour
salt
10 ml /2 tsp ground yellow mustard seeds
125 g /4 oz butter, plus extra for greasing
30 ml /2 tbls English mustard
175 g /6 oz Cheddar cheese, finely grated
1 egg, beaten

1 Sift the flour, salt and ground yellow mustard seeds into a bowl. Rub in the butter and mix to a dough with 45–60 ml /3–4 tbls cold water. Leave the pastry in the refrigerator for 10 minutes to rest.

2 Heat the oven to 200C /400F /gas 6.

3 Roll the pastry out into an oblong about 3 mm /⅛ in thick. Spread it with one-third of the English mustard. Scatter 50 g /2 oz of the cheese over two-thirds of the area of pastry and fold the pastry into three. Return this to the refrigerator for 5 minutes.

4 Roll out the pastry again; repeat twice.

5 Next, roll out the pastry to 3 mm /⅛ in thick and cut it into sticks 10 mm × 7.5 cm / ⅜ × 3 in.

6 Lightly grease a baking sheet, lay the sticks on it and brush with the beaten egg.

7 Bake the sticks in the oven for 15 minutes until they are golden brown, then cool on wire racks. Store them in an airtight tin for up to 3 days.

VARIOUS VINEGARS

Vinegar is often limited to salad dressings and pickles, yet it lends its unique flavour to a whole range of recipes. Here I show you how to use vinegar successfully in main courses and desserts.

Vinegar has been used in cookery since ancient times. Its name is derived from the French *vin aigre* or sour wine, but it has come to mean any liquid that has been twice fermented to make an acid product that can be used for flavouring and preserving. In the 18th and 19th centuries, sugar vinegar was often made at home from brown sugar and molasses, and then used for pickling and preserving.

Wine and beer are the most common basic ingredients, but vinegar can also be made from cider, perry (made from the juice of fermented pears), mead, rice wine, fruit wines and even fermented milk. In tropical countries it is made from such exotic fruits as tamarind and mangosteen (which has a thick, reddish-brown rind and white, juicy pulp). Palm sugar or maple syrup can also be used to provide a base.

Buying and storing vinegar

The wise cook will always keep a selection of vinegars in the store cupboard. Many types of vinegars can be found in supermarkets, but you will have to look in specialist food stores for the more unusual varieties.

Unflavoured vinegars will keep for up to two years in a cool, dark place. After a while, especially if there is only a little left in the bottle, you may find that 'mother of vinegar' (a thick, folded skin) has started to develop. If the vinegar is strained off, it will still be fit for use.

Vinegars which contain herbs, spices or other ingredients, such as lemon, are best used within a year.

Types of vinegar

Wine vinegar may be made from red, white or rosé wine. The vinegar should be clear and paler in colour than the original wine, and with a wine-like aroma. Wine vinegar is much more acidic than most other vinegars.

The finest wine vinegar is that made by the Orléans method. Wines for this are specially produced and graded, then matured over a long period. The final product has a fine, delicate flavour which is perfect for salads and sauces, although it is more expensive than other wine vinegars.

The Italians also produce a fine wine vinegar known as balsamic vinegar, which improves as it gets older — in fact it's said to be at its best after 100 years!

Other wine vinegars are made by a much quicker process. Use them for classic sauces, salad dressings and marinades, in court bouillons and for pickling.

Sherry vinegar is made from the Andalusian wines of Cádiz. It has a dark, rich brown colour and a mellow, raisin-like flavour. It is best used in salads and sautéed dishes.

Cider vinegar is made by adding 'mother of vinegar' to cider. It is less acid than wine vinegar and has a slight taste of apples. It is generally a pale yellow colour, but some health food shops also sell richer, dark brown vinegars made from sweet, matured cider.

Use cider vinegar in salad dressings, in sweet and sour dishes instead of rice wine vinegar, in marinades for pork and in the liquid for boiling pork.

Malt vinegar is produced from a specially made unhopped beer and it has a slightly bitter, beer-like flavour. When it is first produced, it is a clear amber colour, but for general use it is coloured with caramel.

Malt vinegar can be used for salads containing robustly flavoured ingredients, and it is very good for strongly flavoured pickles and some chutneys and sauces, including tomato ketchup.

High-strength malt vinegar is specially made for pickling. It has a clear amber colour and a high acid content.

Distilled malt vinegar is clear and colourless and also has a high acid content. It is produced by distilling malt vinegar and is used chiefly for pickling. Use it for vegetables such as cucumbers, which are very watery and which may dilute the percentage of acetic acid in the pickle.

White vinegar is a colourless and flavourless vinegar sometimes used for pickling. It is made either by removing the colour from malt vinegar or by diluting acetic acid.

Spiced vinegar is a ready-flavoured pickling vinegar. It is generally made from distilled malt vinegar with added spices such as mustard seeds, cloves, peppercorns, etc.

Herb vinegars are white wine vinegars which contain sprigs of herbs for flavour. Many different herbs are used but the most popular is tarragon (see page 86).

Rice wine vinegar is used in Chinese and Japanese dishes and is usually only available from Oriental food shops. Red, black and white varieties are made, but the white is the most common of the three.

Milk vinegar is made in Switzerland where it is recommended for stomach ailments. It goes particularly well with salads which contain Gruyère cheese.

Fruit vinegars are fruit-flavoured vinegar syrups which can be diluted to serve as drinks or added to sweet or savoury sauces (see recipe).

Other vinegars can be flavoured with chillies, green peppercorns, garlic, lemon, and rose or violet petals.

Flavouring vinegars

Light-coloured cider and white wine vinegars are the best for flavouring. Pour off a little from a full bottle and insert a sprig of herbs — you can use any herb of your choice. Replace the cap and leave in a sunny window for three weeks. Exchange the herb sprig for

Herb vinegars, red wine vinegar and white wine vinegar

a fresh one and the vinegar is ready for use. Alternatively, you can add a string of green peppercorns to make a green peppercorn vinegar. It will be ready for use after three weeks, and there is no need to change the peppercorns. Or make lemon vinegar: add half a finely chopped lemon — peel, pith and pips — and let it stand for at least three weeks. For garlic vinegar, add two peeled and crushed garlic cloves, infuse for 24 hours and then strain.

A lovely idea is to make Rose-petal vinegar, preferably using old-fashioned pink or crimson moss or shrub roses. Pour 600 ml /1 pt white distilled vinegar and 15 ml /1 tbls cider or white wine vinegar into a wide-necked jar. Add 1 cup of washed and dried chopped rose petals. Cover and leave at room temperature for 1 week, shaking the jar occasionally. Strain the liquid and add a few whole petals or scented leaves for effect. Use the rose-petal vinegar within 6 months to flavour biscuits, cakes, puddings, pancakes, candies, sauces, salad dressings and preserves.

Uses of vinegar

Vinegar is one of the essential ingredients in vinaigrette dressing and other salad dressings, and in classic sauces such as bearnaise, poivrade and ravigote. In pickles, chutneys and bottled sauces it acts as both a flavouring and a preservative.

Try this tasty Korean recipe for Vinegar soy sauce. Fried foods are dipped into this savoury sauce just before eating. Mix together 90 ml / 6 tbls soy sauce, 90 ml /6 tbls wine vinegar, 30 ml /2 tbls sugar and 15 ml /1 tbls walnuts, pine or other nuts, finely chopped. Pour the sauce into 6 individual dishes and sprinkle with the finely chopped nuts when you serve it.

Vinegar can be added to stews, casseroles, such as Neck of lamb with tarragon vinegar (see recipe), sautéed dishes, such as Sautéed chicken with sherry vinegar (see recipe), to the liquid for boiling meats and also to marinades, as the acid helps to tenderize the meat. It is an essential ingredient in Chinese and Italian sweet and sour dishes.

Add a dash of vinegar to a court bouillon for poaching fish and to soused fish dishes;

add a little to braised red or white cabbage, too. A small amount added to water for poaching eggs stops them spreading out.

Vinegar can add piquancy to fruit sauces and will lift the flavour of custards and soufflés. It acts as a raising agent when added with soda to cakes and scones; and a little vinegar mixed into pastry will help to make it flaky. Sometimes meringues have a little malt vinegar added to them, to make them crisp outside and soft in the centre.

Neck of lamb with tarragon vinegar

2 hours 10 minutes

Serves 4
15 g /½ oz butter
1 kg /2¼ lb neck of lamb, chopped into
  small pieces
2 medium-sized onions, finely chopped
1 garlic clove, finely chopped
150 ml /5 fl oz chicken or beef stock,
  home-made or from a cube
30 ml /2 tbls tarragon vinegar
bouquet garni
a pinch of salt
a pinch of cayenne pepper
30 ml /2 tbls chopped fresh parsley

1 Heat the oven to 180C /350F /gas 4. Melt the butter in a flameproof casserole on a high heat. Add the pieces of lamb, a few at a time if necessary, brown them all over and remove them from the pan.
2 Lower the heat and pour off all but 30 ml /2 tbls fat. Add the onions and garlic and cook them until they are soft. Pour in the stock and bring it to the boil. Add the vinegar, bouquet garni, salt and cayenne pepper. Replace the lamb, cover the casserole and cook it in the oven for 1 hour 20 minutes, or until the lamb is tender and the liquid is reduced to a glaze.
3 Place the pieces of lamb on a warmed serving dish, pour the sauce over, garnish with the parsley and serve at once.

Perfect vinaigrette

Makes 125 ml /4 fl oz
2.5 ml /½ tsp Dijon mustard (optional)
30 ml /2 tbls wine vinegar
salt and freshly ground black pepper
90 ml /6 tbls olive oil

1 Put the mustard into the bottom of a small jug or cup and add the wine vinegar.
2 Add the salt and pepper and the olive oil and beat vigorously to make an emulsion.

● To vary the taste of your vinaigrette add any of the following: 15–45 ml /1–3 tbls finely chopped fresh herbs (choosing from tarragon, chives, fennel and parsley), a little crumbled Roquefort cheese, a finely chopped garlic clove, onion juice or a pinch of curry powder.
● Substitute lemon juice for the vinegar or half the quantity of mustard powder for the Dijon mustard.

Sautéed chicken with sherry vinegar

 1 hour 40 minutes

Serves 4
15 g /½ oz butter
1.5 kg /3½ lb roasting chicken, jointed
400 g /14 oz carrots, cut into julienne sticks
1 large onion, thinly sliced
1 garlic clove, finely chopped
125 g /4 oz mushrooms, thinly sliced
200 ml /7 fl oz chicken stock, home-made or
  from a cube
45 ml /3 tbls sherry vinegar
15 ml /1 tbls tomato purée
salt and freshly ground black pepper
bouquet garni
watercress sprigs, to garnish

1 Melt the butter in a large frying-pan over a medium heat. Put in the chicken pieces, skin side down, and cook them until they are brown, then turn and brown the other side. Remove them from the pan.
2 Lower the heat. Add the carrots, onion and garlic and cook, stirring frequently, until they begin to brown.
3 Stir in the mushrooms, pour in the stock and bring it to the boil. Stir in the vinegar and tomato purée. Season with salt and pepper and add the bouquet garni.
4 Replace the chicken pieces, cover and cook them on a low heat for 45 minutes, turning them once, halfway through. Place the chicken and vegetables on a warmed serving dish, spoon any sauce on top, garnish with the watercress and serve.

Wheatmeal vinegar pie

Wheatmeal vinegar pie, with its light, moist, souffle-like filling, is an American favourite.

 1½ hours, including chilling

Serves 6–8
25 g /1 oz wheatmeal flour
5 ml /1 tsp ground mixed spice
a pinch of salt
4 medium-sized egg yolks
175 g /6 oz light Barbados sugar, or soft
  light brown sugar
200 ml /7 fl oz soured cream
45 ml /3 tbls cider vinegar
40 g /1½ oz butter, melted
200 g /7 oz sultanas
2 medium-sized egg whites
whipped cream, to serve
For the pastry
250 g /9 oz wheatmeal flour
5 ml /1 tsp salt
150 g /5 oz shortening, or a mixture of
  butter and lard

1 To make the pastry, sift together the flour and the salt. Rub in the shortening or the butter and lard. Bind them together with about 60 ml /4 tbls iced water. Wrap the pastry in cling film or a polythene bag and chill it for 15 minutes.
2 Heat the oven to 230C /450F /gas 8. Roll out the pastry and use it to line a 25 cm /10 in diameter tart tin.
3 To make the filling, sift the flour with the mixed spice and salt. Place the egg yolks

and sugar in a bowl and beat with an electric beater for about 10 minutes, or until the mixture is light and thick, and a little of it dropped from the beaters leaves a trail.
4 Stir in the flour mixture, the soured cream, cider vinegar and melted butter. When it is smooth, add the sultanas.
5 Stiffly whisk the egg whites and fold them in. Pour the mixture into the pastry shell, making sure that that sultanas are evenly distributed. Put the pie into the oven. After 10 minutes, turn the heat down to 180C /350F /gas 4 and cook the pie for a further 20 minutes, until the filling is firm and browned. Serve the pie warm, accompanied by a bowl of lightly whipped cream.

Old-fashioned vinegar cake

 1½ hours, plus cooling

Makes 8–10 slices
butter, for greasing
225 g /8 oz flour
a pinch of salt
100 g /4 oz butter or margarine, diced
75 g /3 oz soft light brown sugar
100 g /4 oz seedless raisins
5 ml /1 tsp bicarbonate of soda
45–60 ml /3–4 tbls milk
15 ml /1 tbls distilled malt vinegar
15 ml /1 tbls Demerara sugar

1 Heat the oven to 190C /375F /gas 5. Next, grease and then line a deep, 15 cm /

Sautéed chicken with sherry vinegar

6 in square cake tin with greaseproof paper.
2 Sift the flour and salt into a large mixing bowl. Rub the fat into the flour with your fingertips until the mixture resembles fine breadcrumbs. Stir in the sugar and raisins and make a well in the centre.
3 Dissolve the bicarbonate of soda in 15 ml /1 tbls milk and pour it into the flour mixture. Add 30 ml /2 tbls milk and the vinegar. (The liquids will foam slightly.) With a large metal spoon, quickly mix all the ingredients together, adding the remaining milk if necessary to give a stiff dropping consistency.
4 Turn the mixture into the prepared tin and spread it evenly. Level the surface with the back of a wet metal spoon and make a deep hollow in the centre so that the cake rises evenly. Sprinkle the Demerara sugar over the top of the cake.
5 Bake for 10 minutes, then reduce the oven heat to 180C /350F /gas 4 and bake for 1 hour. The cake is cooked when a fine metal skewer inserted into the centre comes out clean.
6 Cool the cake in the tin for 15 minutes, then turn it out onto a wire rack and remove the lining paper. Leave the cake until it is completely cold before cutting.

Pickled pears

2¼ hours,
then 3 weeks maturing

Fills 4 × 500 g /1 lb jars
2 kg /4½ lb small hard Conference or other cooking pears
600 ml /1 pt white wine vinegar
10 cm /4 in piece cinnamon stick
2 dried red chillies
5 ml /1 tsp whole cloves
6 allspice berries
750 g /1 lb 11 oz sugar

1 Peel the pears, dropping them into a bowl of cold water as you do so. If they are very small, keep them whole; otherwise quarter and core them.
2 Put the vinegar into a stainless steel or enamel saucepan with the spices and the sugar. Set the pan on a low heat and stir until the sugar has dissolved. Bring it to the boil, then remove the pan from the heat.
3 Bring a large saucepan of water to the boil, add the pears and simmer them for 50 minutes. Lift them out with a slotted spoon and place them in the vinegar.
4 Bring the vinegar to the boil and simmer until the pears are soft and transparent — about 30 minutes.
5 Lift out the pears with a slotted spoon and place them in warmed preserving jars. Bring the vinegar to the boil again and boil it for 10 minutes, or until it thickens slightly and becomes syrupy.
6 Remove the vinegar syrup from the heat and strain it carefully. While it is still hot, pour it over the pears to cover them completely. Seal the jars immediately and let them stand for 3 weeks in a cool, dry place before opening them.

Raspberry vinegar

Dilute raspberry vinegar with hot or cold water or with soda water to make a refreshing drink; use it in salad dressings or add it sparingly to savoury sauces, sautéed dishes and fruit sauces. Note that you will have to buy the raspberries in 3 lots 4 days apart.

13 days

Makes 400 ml /14 fl oz
400 ml /14 fl oz white wine vinegar
3 × 250 g /9 oz fresh raspberries
350 g /12 oz sugar

1 Put the vinegar into a jar or bowl with 250 g /9 oz raspberries. Cover it and leave it for 4 days in a cool place.
2 Strain the vinegar through a sieve and then return it to the jar with a further 250 g /9 oz raspberries. Cover it and leave it for another 4 days.
3 Repeat once more.
4 After the final 4 days, strain the vinegar through a jelly bag into a saucepan. Add the sugar, set it on a low heat and stir until the sugar has dissolved. Next, boil it for 5 minutes, skimming well.
5 Pour the vinegar into a clean jar and cover it with a clean tea-cloth, folded in half. Tie down the cloth and leave the vinegar for 24 hours.
6 Bottle the vinegar and cover it tightly. It is now ready for use, and it will keep well for up to 1 year.

Spiced malt vinegar

This is a hot, spicy vinegar suitable for using with pickled onions or walnuts.

5 minutes,
then 2 months

Makes 1.1 L /2 pt
1.1 L /2 pt malt vinegar
15 ml /1 tbls black peppercorns
15 ml /1 tbls mustard seeds
15 ml /1 tbls whole cloves
8 dried red chillies

1 Put the vinegar and spices into a large bottle or jar. Cover and leave in a warm place for 2 months, shaking occasionally.
2 After 2 months, strain the vinegar. It is now ready for use, and will keep for 1 year.

Mint sauce

1½ hour

Makes about 150 ml /5 fl oz
50 g /2 oz fresh mint leaves, finely chopped
15 ml /1 tbls sugar
60 ml /4 tbls red wine vinegar

1 Pour 45 ml /3 tbls boiling water over the mint leaves, cover and leave them to cool.
2 Stir in the sugar and vinegar and let it stand for 1 hour.
3 Stir the sauce before serving.

KNOWING YOUR HERBS

It is impossible to imagine our cuisine without the wonderful flavours of herbs; they are invaluable for tasty soups, exquisite sauces, omelettes, flans, herb jellies and drinks. They transform everyday cooking into an art.

The leaves and the seeds of herb plants have been used throughout the ages for flavouring food. Wild plants, herbs among them, were man's first food. Over the centuries herbs also became valued for their soothing and healing properties; they were used as preservatives and for making dyes, cosmetics, perfumes and essences. Herbs were used in fragrant pot-pourris and strewn on floors to sweeten the air.

Types of herb
Here is a comprehensive list of the herbs most commonly used, fresh or dried, in the kitchen today.

Basil: this originally came from India where it was revered as a sacred herb and regarded in particular as symbolizing the protection of the poor. In Italy it symbolized love; and the Jews believed that holding a sprig gave moral support on fast days. Medicinally, the herb was used to treat digestive disorders and headaches, and it was also grown indoors as an insect repellent.

Of the 40 or so types of basil, the most common are sweet basil (*Ocimum basilicum*), whose large, shiny, bright green leaves give off a heady scent at the slightest touch, and bush basil (*Ocimum minimum*), which in fact grows to a height of only 15–30 cm /6–12 in, and has tiny, scented leaves. In cooking, basil is particularly associated with hot and cold tomato dishes: the chopped raw leaves make a tomato salad a delicacy, and fresh or dried basil is delicious used in tomato sauce. With Parmesan cheese and olive oil, basil is a basic ingredient of the superb green sauce the Italians often serve with pasta (see page 109). You will also find that the flavour of basil enhances egg dishes of all kinds, and goes specially well with vegetables such as beans, peas, marrows and courgettes. Cream cheese pounded with a few basil leaves makes a delicately flavoured sandwich spread.

Basil dries and freezes well. To dry the leaves for winter, lift the whole plant before the first frost and hang it upside down in a warm, dry place. Freeze a few basil sprigs in cubes of concentrated stock to flavour soups and sauces, and in cubes of syrup for fruit salads. Basil can be used in a bouquet garni.

Bay: this is native to most Mediterranean countries, and the ancient Greeks honoured poets and other heroes with wreaths of bay leaves — hence the title 'poet laureate', from *Laurus nobilis*, the Latin name for bay.

The tough, oval bay leaves are dark green and have a strong, almost sweet scent; fresh or dried, a bay leaf is an essential part of a bouquet garni. Add a bay leaf to the cooking liquid when poaching fish or casseroling meat, or to the milk when you are making a bechamel sauce; it is also a good addition to the brine when salting or pickling meat or fish. A sprig of bay makes a very attractive decoration for the top of a pâté, meat loaf or savoury flan, or as a leaf for a tomato 'rose' garnish.

There is little point in freezing bay leaves as they dry well. Strip the leaves from their stems after drying and store them in an airtight container away from the light. They will keep their fragrance for a long time. You can also buy powdered bay leaves, which make a tasty garnish for cream soups and quiches.

Chervil (*Anthriscus cerefolium*): this is rather like parsley, with delicate cut leaves. Its very slightly aniseed flavour complements other herbs well. One of the first fresh herbs of springtime, it is traditionally used in Easter cookery. It grows well in a kitchen atmosphere, but remember to harvest it by cutting leaves off with scissors — pulling them off is liable to damage the root system. Chop fresh leaves into green salads, mix them with mayonnaise or a soured cream dressing for potato or cucumber salads, or sprinkle them onto soups as a garnish. They should be used sparingly in egg and cheese dishes, and with beef and fish. *Sauce messine*, combining cream, egg yolks, chopped shallot and equal quantities of chervil and tarragon, is a classic dressing for turbot. Chervil is best added towards the end of the cooking time — long cooking makes it slightly bitter. The leaves can be dried or frozen.

Chives (*Allium schoenoprasum*): they have long been cultivated as herbs; they were used in China as early as 3000 BC, but not introduced to Europe until the 16th century. Chives belong to the same genus as garlic, leeks and onions and they grow from bulbs. They have pretty, clover-like mauve flowers which should be cut off as soon as the buds appear, and long, straight, grass-like leaves with a mild onion flavour. Snip the leaves finely with sharp kitchen scissors to garnish soups and salads, particularly tomato and egg, cucumber and potato. Blend snipped chives with soured cream as a filling for baked potatoes, beat them into cream cheese, or use them to flavour omelettes and fried potato cakes. Chives do not dry well, but snipped small, they can be successfully frozen.

Dill (*Anethum graveolens*): this has fine, feathery leaves, which grow in sprays and have a faintly aniseed flavour. When dried, dill is sold as dillweed. Use the leaves or seeds to flavour vinegar, which you will find excellent for pickling vegetables and fish. Dill seeds give piquancy to soups and stews, especially beef, and are delicious in coleslaw and with cooked cabbage. Cooked dill leaves combine well with bechamel sauce to serve with fish or poultry. Dry or freeze the leaves; dry the seeds.

Lemon thyme (*Thymus citriodorus*): with softer leaves than garden thyme and a delicate lemon scent, lemon thyme is extremely good with fish and chicken and in custard-based dishes. This thyme cannot be grown from seed, only from healthy cuttings.

Thyme freezes and dries well. You can dry the flowers and rub them on grilled meat and use them in marinades, as the Greeks do.

Marjoram (sweet or knotted marjoram, *Origanum marjorana*): this is native to Asia, southern Europe and North Africa. It was traditionally used as a dye, a strewing herb and, medicinally, for cramp and rheumatism, stomach ailments, toothache, headache and many nervous disorders. In Greece, where marjoram grows wild on the hillsides, it is the clusters of white or purple flowers, called *rigani*, rather than the soft grey leaves, that are valued. Sprinkled over lamb or beef kebabs or spit-roasted pork or goat, they impart an aroma slightly reminiscent of lavender. Marjoram is used in cooking to flavour poultry, veal, sausages and pulses in particular. Like basil, marjoram has a special affinity with tomatoes, and with mushrooms as well. It is very good baked in bread and scones, and makes excellent tea and jelly. It can be included in a bouquet garni.

Marjoram freezes and dries well: if drying, cut the stems just before they flower.

Mint (*Mentha spicata*): there are many varieties of mint, which is among the oldest of European herbs. Spearmint with its long, oval, greyish-green leaves, is the best for the

1

2

3

sweet-sour mint sauce that is such a favourite with lamb.

Other varieties are applemint, which has round, variegated leaves, and peppermint, which is good for drinks and some dessert dishes. Experiment with the different mints: cook mint with new potatoes, peas and other spring and early summer vegetables, chop it into green salads or stir it into yoghurt to dress a cucumber salad. Use it in tea and alcoholic drinks, like a wine cup or a julep, or chopped with cream cheese as a sandwich filling. The leaves make pretty garnishes, and dry and freeze well.

● Mint sauce can be bought ready made but since it is so easy to prepare, if you have fresh mint available it is well worth making it yourself (see recipe, page 83).

Oregano (*Origanum vulgare*): this is a form of wild marjoram and shares many of the marjoram's characteristics, but its small, roughish leaves are much more pungent than those of any other marjoram — almost spicy-hot and sweet at the same time. Oregano is perhaps best known for the piquancy it brings to pizza toppings (see recipe) and pasta sauces. It is also good with grilled meat and, in moderation, in fish, egg and cheese dishes. Oregano freezes and dries well.

● For an appetizer with an unusual flavour to serve with drinks, steep some black olives in oregano-flavoured oil. First prick the olives with a sterilized needle, then pack them into a screwtop jar. Add 5 ml /1 tsp lightly crushed black peppercorns and 15 ml /1 tbls fresh chopped oregano if available (or half that quantity of dried oregano). Fill the

1 Flat-leaved parsley; 2 Applemint;
3 Spearmint; 4 Mint; 5 Dill; 6 Chives

Bouquet garni

Fresh or dried, strong flavoured herbs are especially associated with the bouquet garni. This is a bunch of fresh herbs (or a sachet of dried herbs) which is used to flavour food ranging from stocks and soups to stews, casseroles and sauces. It is discarded at the end of cooking.

The basic herbs usually included in the bouquet garni are a bay leaf and a few sprigs of both thyme and parsley: the number and size of the sprigs can be varied according to the nature of the dish. Other herbs such as rosemary, marjoram, basil or tarragon (particularly for fish and chicken dishes) are sometimes included, as well as celery stalks and leaves and a pared lemon or orange zest.

Tie the herbs in a piece of scalded and dried muslin. Use a bouquet garni for any dish in which broken leaves would be undesirable.

Tie together a bay leaf, thyme, a parsley sprig and orange zest with fine string. Leave a long end of string to attach to the pan handle.

---

jar with olive oil, cover, shake well and leave for about 2 weeks, shaking the jar from time to time.

Parsley (*Petroselinum crispum*): there are many different varieties, the most common of which are curly and crisp, but there is a flat-leaved type. Parsley is rich in Vitamin C and is good for the digestion. To be friendly, chew it after eating garlic! Sprigs of the bright green leaves are a most popular garnish, and finely chopped fresh parsley is used in sauces, stuffings and breadcrumb toppings for poultry, fish and vegetable dishes, as well as in meat, egg and cheese dishes of all kinds. Parsley stalks and roots are highly flavoured and lend piquancy to soups and stocks.

Freeze large parsley sprigs still on the stems. Dried parsley is not very successful since it looses its flavour.

Rosemary: this is a native of the Mediterranean that thrives particularly well by the sea. Mentioned in ancient Greek, Roman and medieval legends, it has been valued medicinally as a tonic and, because of its abundance of natural oils, as an ingredient in skin fresheners, hair rinses and perfumes. There are a number of varieties of rosemary, with white or light mauve flowers, and arching or straight growth, but no cottage or kitchen garden is complete without a bush of the ordinary form, *Rosemarinus officinalis*, with its thin, spiky green leaves which are a greyish colour underneath, and with small mauve flowers.

Tuck a sprig of rosemary inside a chicken when roasting or boiling, against the bone in loin of lamb, pork or veal for roasting, or on top of chops and fish for braising or grilling. Remove the herb before eating. When rosemary is an integral part of a dish, snip the leaves very finely, several at a time, with sharp kitchen scissors. Include a sprig of rosemary in a bouquet garni, or push a few sprigs of the fresh herb into a jar of sugar to lend an interesting flavour to sweet dishes.

Rosemary does not freeze well; for drying, cut the stems when the plant is just coming into flower. The dried leaves can be easily crumbled between the fingers.

Sage: this is native to the Mediterranean. It can be used medicinally as a mouthwash, and is also considered to be beneficial in warding off winter ills and curing failing memory! There are a large number of garden varieties, differing in the shape and colour of the leaves. The type most frequently used in cooking, *Salvia officinalis*, has furry, greyish-green leaves and purple flowers. Sage helps to make rich meat and oily fish more digestible: sage and onion is a traditional stuffing for duck, goose and pork. Sage is also cooked with eel and mackerel and used in spicy sausages and pâtés. The Italians cook fresh sage leaves with liver — a simple and delicious combination (see recipe). Sage freezes and dries well.

Savory: there are 2 main types of *Satureia* — summer and winter. Summer savory has a slightly more subtle spiciness than the winter variety, which is stronger and more pungent. Savory is sometimes known as the 'bean herb' as it is traditionally cooked with fresh beans of all kinds, in the same way that mint is with peas. Use small quantities of the long, pointed leaves to flavour, or chop and add to stuffings, soups, casseroles, salads, fish dishes or herb butter — whenever a slightly peppery flavour is required.

Tarragon (*Artemisia dranunculus*): this is a classic accompaniment to chicken; and is equally good with veal, pork, lamb, white fish, shellfish and eggs. Be sure to use the true French tarragon and not the Russian variety, which is coarser and more bitter. Chop the long, thin leaves into salads, stuffings and sauces, especially bearnaise, tartare and mustard sauces. Tarragon leaves dry and freeze well.

Thyme: of Mediterranean origin, there are numerous types. The ordinary garden thyme (*Thymus vulgaris*), with tiny, round, greyish green leaves and pale pink flowers, is most often used in cooking. A sprig of thyme is one of the basic herbs in a bouquet garni and is used in that role to flavour soups, stews and casseroles. Combined with parsley and grated lemon zest, it also makes tasty flavourings for stuffings for meat and poultry, and is good in fish and cheese dishes and with many root vegetables. The tiny leaves are very highly scented and a little goes a long way, whether in herb butter, bread or a salad.

Herb combinations
A term used in classical French cookery is *fines herbes*. It refers to a mixture of fresh chervil, chives, parsley and tarragon, which is used in savoury flans and omelettes and with poultry and fish dishes to give a delicate herb flavour.

Traditionally Mixed herbs consist of marjoram, thyme and sage, usually 1 part of each of marjoram and thyme and 2 parts of sage. Try making your own blend from dried home-grown herbs, varying the proportions to your personal taste; store in small screw-top jars in a dry, dark place.

Keeping herbs
As well as enlivening all kinds of dishes and sauces, fresh herbs offer you the added delight of their fragrance and sometimes their flowers: enjoy their beauty and keep them fresh by arranging them in a jar of water. Cut herbs can be bought in season and will keep fresh for several days in a covered container in the refrigerator.

You can freeze herbs on the stem, tied tightly in plastic bags or packed into small containers, then strip off the leaves as you need them. You can save space and freeze just the leaves, which crumble at a touch when frozen, or chop the herbs, pack them into ice-cube trays, fill these with water or stock and freeze them, so that you can add a whole cube of flavour to a soup or stew in moments. For a luxury touch, freeze tiny sprigs of mint in ice cubes and then float them in long summer drinks.

Dried herbs: there is nothing to beat the flavour of fresh herbs, but for longer-term storage, try drying your own. Cut the herbs on a dry day, when there is no excess moisture on their leaves. Hang them in bunches in a warm, dark, airy place — not the kitchen — until the leaves feel papery. By then the water content will have evaporated, leaving the aroma and flavour intact. Strip off the leaves, gently crumble or snip them

and store them in labelled screw-top jars in a cupboard. Leave herb seeds such as dill to ripen on the plants. Cut the heads when they turn brown and hang them upside-down in a paper bag until the seeds drop out, then store them in the same way as you store the leaves.

You can buy a wide range of dried herbs. Whenever you use dried herbs, use half, or a little less than half, the quantity of fresh herbs listed in the recipe ingredients.

Other uses for herbs
Try some of these unusual ideas for using herbs.

Herb teas: use herb leaves or seeds to make hot or iced teas: mint and dill seeds make especially good teas. Mint tea is very popular in the Middle East, and in France herb tea or *tisane* is often drunk after a meal (see also page 50).

● To make tea allow 15 ml /1 tbls fresh or frozen leaves or 5 ml /1 tsp dried herbs to each teacupful of boiling water, infuse for 5–10 minutes, sweeten if you like with a little honey, reheat or chill, and garnish with a thin slice of lemon.

Herb jellies: a traditional delicacy to serve with roast, grilled or cold meats, herb jellies are simple to make (see recipe). Parsley and mint jellies are favourites.

Herb butters: these, when stored in the refrigerator or freezer, are useful in many ways, melted onto freshly cooked young vegetables or baked potatoes, as a topping for lamb, pork or beef in grills, or spread in sandwiches.

● To make herb butter, beat about 10 ml /2 tsp chopped individual or mixed herbs into 125 g /4 oz unsalted butter, season with a dash of lemon juice and salt and pepper to taste. Shape into a roll, wrap closely in foil, and chill or freeze.

Herb bread: make evenly spaced diagonal slits along the length of a loaf of French bread. Spread the herb butter of your choice in each slit, wrap the bread in foil and heat in

Parsley and apple jelly

a moderate oven for 15 minutes until the butter has melted and the bread is crisp.

Herb oils and vinegars: another way to capture the aroma of herbs is to flavour vegetable oil or wine vinegar with them (see pages 54 and 80). Try using tarragon, mint or dill.

Chopping herbs
A herb mill makes short work of chopping herbs but tends to produce rather wet results. If you want to use herbs as an attractive garnish on top of a salad as opposed to lending flavour to a dressing, there is nothing really to beat snipping them up inside a cup with a good sharp pair of scissors.

Cultivating herbs
The first formal herb gardens were established by the monks and by the nobility. These beautifully laid out gardens brought together herbs imported through trade with foreign lands, as well as those planted centuries before by the Romans.

If you are an enthusiastic do-it-yourselfer, you can easily grow herbs from packets of seeds. For more instant results you can buy most herbs ready grown in small pots from a market, garden centre, health food shop or flower shop. An annual plant lasts one year, a biennial two, and a perennial, several years.

The obvious place to grow herbs is in the garden, although you can use a window box or individual flower pots. Indoors, let the herbs bask on the sunniest windowsills, but in extremely hot, sunny weather you may have to provide a little shade.

Most herbs need watering once every 2–3 days in summer, when they are making vigorous growth, and every 5–7 days in winter. The soil should dry out between waterings, but not too much (dry soil can encourage herbs to run to seed). Once a week during the growing season, mix a few drops of liquid fertilizer into the water.

Parsley and apple jelly

Serve this parsley-flavoured apple jelly with ham, pork and veal dishes.

50 minutes, plus overnight draining and cooling

Makes about 1 kg /2 lb jelly
500 g /1 lb cooking apples
about 600 g /1 lb 6 oz sugar
45 ml /3 tbls lemon juice
75 g /3 oz chopped fresh parsley
a few drops of green food colouring (optional)

1   Wash and roughly chop the apples without peeling or coring them. Put them in a saucepan with 600 ml /1 pt water and simmer until soft and pulpy.
2   Scald a large piece of muslin or cheesecloth by immersing it in boiling water, or use a jelly bag if you have one. Hang the material or jelly bag over a bowl, tip in the contents of the pan, and leave undisturbed overnight to drain. Do not squeeze the bag or the jelly will be cloudy.
3   Measure the apple juice, and to each 600 ml /1 pt allow 500 g /1 lb sugar. Put the juice and sugar in a large saucepan, stir over a low heat until the sugar has dissolved, then bring to the boil. Boil for 15–20 minutes until 5 ml /1 tsp of the syrup will set on a saucer when left to cool.
4   When the setting point has been reached, remove the pan from the heat and stir in the lemon juice, parsley, and food colouring if using. Set aside for 10–15 minutes to cool.
5   Stir it well to distribute the parsley evenly through the jelly, pour into small, sterilized jars and cover with discs of waxed paper and then cap tightly. Label and store in a cool, dark, dry place. The jelly will keep for 1 year. If a slight mould develops on the top of the jelly after it has been opened, scrape it off with a spoon.

● You can substitute other herbs for the parsley: try mint, savory or tarragon.

Herb soda bread

55 minutes

Makes 2 × 18 cm /7 in loaves
500 g /18 oz wholemeal flour
5 ml /1 tsp bicarbonate of soda
10 ml /2 tsp salt
30 ml /2 tbls chopped fresh herbs, or 15 ml / 1 tbls dried herbs
275 ml /10 fl oz buttermilk or milk soured with 5 ml /1 tsp lemon juice

Herb pâté

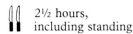

1   Heat the oven to 230C /450F /gas 8. Sift the flour, bicarbonate of soda and salt into a mixing bowl and add the bran that remains in the sieve. Stir in your chosen herb or herbs.
2   Add the buttermilk or soured milk and mix well, adding a little tepid water (up to 45 ml /3 tbls) if necessary, to make a firm but not sticky dough.
3   Divide the dough into two, shape each piece into a 6.5 cm /2½ in thick round, about 15 cm /6 in in diameter. Score the top of each round into 4 sections. Place the dough rounds on floured baking sheets and cover with 20–23 cm /8–9 in inverted deep cake tins. (Using the tins means the bread is steamed for the first part of cooking, with a really moist result.)
4   Bake the dough rounds slightly above the centre of the oven for 30 minutes. Remove the covering tins and bake for a further 10–15 minutes, until the loaves sound hollow when rapped on the base with the knuckles. Cool on a wire rack.

Herb pâté

2½ hours, including standing

Serves 6 as a starter, 4 as a main course
1 kg /2 lb courgettes
15 ml /1 tbls salt
50 g /2 oz butter
4 medium-sized eggs
300 ml /10 fl oz thick cream
30 ml /2 tbls chopped mixed fresh herbs, such as chervil, parsley, mint and tarragon
a pinch of cayenne pepper
freshly ground black pepper
For the garnish
45 ml /3 tbls thick cream
chopped mixed fresh herbs
sprigs of fresh herbs
lettuce leaves
tomato slices

1   Coarsely grate the courgettes into a colander. Sprinkle in the salt, stir well and set aside for 1 hour. Then strain, discarding the liquid which will have formed. Rinse the courgettes under cold running water and leave to dry.
2   Melt the butter in a saucepan, add the courgettes and cook over a low heat for about 10 minutes, stirring occasionally, until they are soft. Leave to cool.
3   Meanwhile heat the oven to 180C /350F / gas 4. Line a 1.5 L /3 pt loaf tin with greased greaseproof paper.
4   Mix together the eggs and cream in a bowl. Add the courgette and butter mixture and the herbs. Stir well and season with a pinch of cayenne pepper and black pepper.
5   Pour the mixture into the prepared tin, cover with foil and stand in a roasting tin. Pour enough cold water to come halfway up the sides of the loaf tin.
6   Bake in the centre of the oven for 1¼ hours, until the pâté is firm. Leave it to cool in the tin, then turn it out carefully onto a serving dish.
7   Whip the cream and spread it over the top of the pâté. Scatter with chopped mixed

fresh herbs and decorate with herb sprigs. Arrange the lettuce leaves and the tomato slices round the edge of the serving dish.

Spinach and chervil soup

 50 minutes

Serves 4
500 g /1 lb fresh spinach leaves or 375 g /12 oz frozen spinach, thawed
50 g /2 oz butter
1 medium-sized onion, thinly sliced
850 ml /1½ pt chicken stock, home-made or from a cube
salt
freshly ground black pepper
30 ml /2 tbls lemon juice
1 bay leaf
15 g /½ oz flour
30 ml /2 tbls chopped fresh chervil or 10 ml / 2 tsp dried chervil
30 ml /2 tbls soured cream

1 Thoroughly wash the fresh spinach, if using, and discard the stalks.
2 Melt half the butter in a large saucepan. Add the onion and cook over a moderate heat for 3–4 minutes, stirring occasionally, until it is soft but not coloured.
3 Add the fresh or thawed frozen spinach to the pan and cook for 5 minutes, stirring frequently. Add the chicken stock, salt,

pepper, lemon juice and bay leaf, reduce the heat, cover the soup and simmer gently for 20 minutes.
4 Discard the bay leaf. Blend the soup to a purée in a liquidizer, or sieve it.
5 Melt the remaining butter in a saucepan, add the flour and stir over a low heat to form a roux. Gradually add the soup to the roux, stirring continuously. Add the fresh or dried chervil, and simmer over a low heat for 5 minutes.
6 Pour the soup into a heated tureen or individual bowls, top with soured cream and serve very hot.

Oregano pizza

 1 hour 20 minutes

Serves 4
1 medium-sized onion, sliced
1 glove garlic, crushed
800 g /1¾ lb canned tomatoes
10 ml /2 tsp dried oregano
5 ml /1 tsp caster sugar
salt
freshly ground black pepper
For the pizza base
225 g /8 oz self-raising flour
5 ml /1 tsp baking powder
5 ml /1 tsp salt
25 g /1 oz butter, softened
freshly ground black pepper
2.5 ml /½ tsp dried mixed herbs
150 ml /5 fl oz milk

Oregano pizza

For the topping
175 g /6 oz Cheddar cheese, grated
100 g /4 oz salami, sliced
1 red pepper, seeded and cut in rings
1 green pepper, seeded and cut in rings
50 g /2 oz stuffed olives, sliced
50 g /2 oz mushrooms, sliced
salt and freshly ground black pepper
10 ml /2 tsp chopped oregano or 5 ml /1 tsp dried oregano

1 To make the tomato sauce for the topping, put the onion and garlic in a small saucepan with the tomatoes, and their juice, and the oregano and sugar. Season with salt and pepper. Cook over a moderate heat, stirring occasionally, for 30 minutes, or until the mixture is thick. Leave to cool while you prepare the dough.
2 Heat the oven to 200C /400F /gas 6. To make the pizza base, sift the flour, baking powder and salt together into a mixing bowl. Rub in the butter until the mixture resembles fine breadcrumbs, season with black pepper and stir in the dried herbs. Mix to a soft dough with the milk.
3 Turn the dough onto a lightly floured board and roll out to a 25 cm /10 in circle. Transfer to a greased baking sheet.
4 Spread the tomato sauce over the base to within 25 mm /1 in of the edge and sprinkle it with three-quarters of the grated cheese.
5 Arrange the slices of salami over the tomato and cheese topping, in overlapping circles. Reserve three mushroom slices to garnish. Arrange rings of pepper on top of the salami, then arrange olive and mushroom slices inside the rings. Season with salt, pepper and the oregano. Sprinkle the remaining grated cheese on top, and garnish with the reserved mushroom slices.
6 Bake in the oven for 30–40 minutes, until the base is well risen and the topping is brown and bubbling. Serve very hot.

Pork chops in cider

 1 hour

Serves 4
4 pork chump chops
salt and freshly ground black pepper
15 ml /1 tbls vegetable oil
25 g /1 oz butter
1 medium-sized onion, finely chopped
1 clove garlic, crushed
300 ml /10 fl oz sweet cider
2 sprigs of rosemary
2 dessert apples, cored but not peeled
15 ml /1 tbls flour

1 Heat the oven to 180C /350F /gas 4. Trim most of the fat from the chops and season them with salt and pepper.
2 Heat the oil and half the butter in a flameproof casserole and fry the chops over a moderate heat for 3–4 minutes, turning them so that they brown on both sides.
3 Stir the onion and garlic into the casserole and cook until the onion is lightly coloured. Pour the cider in, add one sprig of

rosemary and bring the sauce to the boil. Cover and cook in the oven for 30 minutes.
4 Slice the apples into rings, add to the casserole and stir to coat them with sauce. Cook for 10 minutes. Discard the rosemary.
5 In a small bowl, beat together the remaining butter and the flour to make a *beurre manié*. Using a slotted spoon, transfer the chops and apples to a heated serving dish and keep warm. Stir the beurre manié into the sauce in the casserole and whisk it until the sauce thickens and becomes glossy.
6 Pour the sauce over the chops and garnish with the other sprig of rosemary.

Liver with sage and Madeira sauce

20 minutes

Serves 4
450 g /1 lb calf's liver, sliced
22.5 ml /1½ tbls flour
2.5 ml /½ tsp dried sage
salt and freshly ground black pepper
40 g /1½ oz butter
about 20 fresh sage leaves
60 ml /4 tbls chicken stock, home-made or from a cube
60 ml /4 tbls Madeira or medium-dry sherry
a few sprigs of sage to garnish

1 Cut the slices of liver into very thin strips (about 10 mm /½ in). Shake the flour and dried sage together in a polythene bag, empty out onto a plate and season with salt and pepper. Coat the liver strips in the seasoned flour and shake off the excess.
2 Heat the butter in a frying-pan. Fry the liver pieces for 2 minutes, turning them so they brown on all sides. Add the sage leaves to the pan and continue to fry the liver pieces, turning them once or twice, for 1–2 minutes more, or until the liver is just cooked: it should be slightly pink inside.
3 Pour in the stock and Madeira or sherry, stir to take in all the pan juices, and bring it to the boil. Adjust the seasoning if necessary. Turn the liver onto a heated serving dish and garnish with sprigs of sage.

Quiche aux fines herbes

45 minutes, plus chilling

Serves 4
300 g /10 oz flour
1 medium-sized egg
90 ml /6 tbls vegetable oil
2.5 ml /½ tsp salt
about 30 ml /2 tbls iced water
butter, for greasing
For the filling
600 ml /1 pt thick cream
4 medium-sized eggs
salt and freshly ground black pepper
60 ml /4 tbls chopped fresh fines herbes (mixed chervil, chives, parsley and tarragon)

1 Tip the flour onto a pastry board, make a well in the centre; add the egg, the oil and the salt.
2 Using your fingertips, work all the ingredients together to form a dough. Add enough iced water to bind, but do not let the dough become sticky. Form the dough into a ball, wrap tightly in cling film or foil, and leave to rest in the refrigerator for 2–3 hours.
3 Heat the oven to 220C /425F /gas 7. Lightly grease a 20 cm /8 in flan tin.
4 Lightly flour a board and roll out the pastry on it with a floured rolling pin. Lift the pastry onto the flan case, ease it into the case and trim the edges. Prick the base with a fork.
5 Line the pastry case with foil and baking beans and bake blind in the centre of the oven for 10 minutes.
6 Meanwhile, mix together the cream and eggs in a bowl, season with salt and pepper and stir in the herbs.
7 Remove the baking beans and foil from the partly baked pastry case, pour in the filling and return to the oven for 15–20 minutes, or until the custard is just set. Serve the quiche warm.

Mint sorbet

20 minutes, infusing, then 6–7 hours freezing

Serves 8
450 g /1 lb sugar
20 mint leaves
juice of 1 lemon
90 ml /6 tbls crème de menthe
2 egg whites
8 small sprigs of mint

1 If using the refrigerator, turn it down to its lowest temperature (highest setting) about 1 hour before you start.
2 In a large saucepan, heat the sugar and 1.1 L /2 pt water over a gentle heat, stirring until the sugar is dissolved. Bring it to the boil, increase the heat and boil it rapidly for 8 minutes.
3 Add the mint leaves and boil for a further 2 minutes.
4 Remove it from the heat. Stir in the lemon juice and leave it to infuse for at least 30 minutes.
5 Strain the infused mint liquid into a shallow freezer-proof container. Cover and freeze for 1 hour, or until it is frozen to a depth of 25 mm /1 in all around the sides of the container.
6 Stir up the sorbet mixture with a fork or wire whisk to break up the ice particles, then freeze again for 30 minutes.
7 Add the crème de menthe and whisk the sorbet again with a fork or wire whisk until smooth and well blended. (This can be done in a food processor).
8 In a clean dry bowl, whisk the egg whites until stiff and glossy, then whisk them into the mint sorbet, or add them to the food processor. Return it to the freezer container and freeze it again until the sorbet is firm.
9 Transfer to the main part of the refrigerator about 30 minutes before serving, to soften it slightly.
10 To serve, scoop balls of sorbet into 8 individual glasses, and decorate each with a sprig of mint. Alternatively, pile the sorbet attractively in a glass serving dish and arrange the sprigs of mint in a cluster on top. Serve immediately.

Mint sorbet

SUGGESTIONS FOR SPICES

Hot green chilli and scarlet paprika pepper, dried flower-bud cloves and sandy sweet cinnamon sticks — spices are some of the most pungent and aromatic ingredients available to the cook.

Spices are usually associated with hot, strongly flavoured dishes. Used sparingly, though, they can be quite subtle and can give a delicious lift to food without being too obvious — try adding celery seeds to soups and stews, for example. Spices are used in many foreign and homely dishes — sesame seeds in Greek and Middle Eastern cookery, and poppy seeds sprinkled over cakes and breads. Juniper berries, too, have a popular use — as a main ingredient in gin-making.

In past centuries, spices added interest to dull diets, and helped to disguise the flavour of stale or salted food. They were highly valued commodities and the object of much international trade. Today, when spices are easy to buy, it's hard to imagine that men once risked their lives for them; that they were the cause of war or that the wealth of nations depended on them.

Besides their value as flavourings, spices were also used in preserving. Both cinnamon and cloves have some preservative properties; cinnamon contains phenols which help to discourage decay in meat. Present-day recipes for British mincemeat developed from a way of preserving meat with spices, although suet is the only meat-associated ingredient in the modern recipe.

Spices were also highly prized for their use in medicines and perfumes. Cloves have a powerful antiseptic action; chilli stimulates the flow of gastric juices, while paprika contains more vitamin C than citrus fruit. Fenugreek acts as an emollient and used to be administered for inflammations of the digestive tract. Cumin seeds contain up to five per cent essential oil which is used in some medicines as well as in perfumery. And in Elizabethan times sensitive ladies and gentlemen carried pomanders — oranges stuck with cloves and then dried — to sniff when visiting less salubrious areas of the city.

Hot spices
Experiment with some, or all, of these spices to enliven your cooking.

Cardamon, the most expensive of this group of spices, has a warm, slightly pungent flavour. It is the pod of *Eletaria cardamomum*, a leafy member of the ginger family. The plant is a native of East India, Sri Lanka and Guatemala. The pods are bleached to a creamy or pale green colour and contain numerous dark seeds. Black cardamom is a different variety, with large, dark, hairy pods. It is slightly cheaper but less aromatic.

Buy cardamom in the pod and add the whole pod to a recipe, or extract the seeds and crush them lightly before use. It is a very important ingredient in many Near and Far Eastern recipes, and it enhances any curry or rice dish in which it is used. It is also used in meat dishes in northern Europe.

Cayenne pepper is made from pulverized red capsicums which are mixed with wheat flour, made into hard biscuits and then ground to a powder. Although hot, cayenne pepper is not as fiery as chilli powder. It is added to some curry powders and used in many traditional Mexican dishes. Try adding a pinch of cayenne pepper to a cheese or leek soufflé or to a quiche.

Chilli is the fruit of a variety of capsicum or pepper, *Capsicum frutescens*, which is a native of tropical America. The small pointed fruit may be either red or green and can be bought in various forms: fresh or dried, flaked or powdered.

One of the hottest spices known to man, chilli is used extensively in South American cookery. The powder is also an important ingredient of curry powder. It should be used sparingly — although it does come in a milder form called 'chilli seasoning' which may be more suitable for European palates.

Chilli sauce and Tabasco sauce are flavouring liquids made from chillies. They are very hot and only a few drops are needed. The sauces are convenient to use because they blend in easily. Try adding a dash of chilli sauce or Tabasco to tomato juice, cream cheese, or to the dressing served with avocado.

Coriander seeds have a burnt orange flavour when crushed or ground into powder. They are used in pickling spice and are an ingredient of curry powder. They go especially well with chicken, pork, lamb and mushrooms.

Cumin is the seed of an annual herb, *cuminum cyminum*, a member of the parsley family. Although native to the Mediterranean, cumin is more commonly found in the cooking of North Africa, the Far East and South America.

The thin, yellowish-brown seeds are about 6 mm /¼ in long and have a strong, aromatic flavour. They can also be bought ground, as a light brown powder. It is useful to have both seeds and powder available, for while the powder is more convenient for most purposes, the whole seeds are very pleasant in curries, rice dishes, pickles and chutneys. They can also be sprinkled on top of loaves of bread. Always warm the seeds or powder before use, as this helps to release the aromatic oils and bring out the flavour.

Curry powder is another spice blend. Though not used in traditional Indian cookery, it is useful for making Western-style curry. A pinch added to gravy or mayonnaise will give the flavour a subtle lift. If you're adding curry powder to an uncooked mixture, warm the powder in a small saucepan first to release the maximum flavour.

Fenugreek is the seed of *Trigonella foenum-graecum*, an annual belonging to the pea family. The plant is indigenous to the Mediterranean but is most often used in Asian cooking. You can buy it in seed or powder form but the seeds — small, flat and yellowish-brown — are difficult to crush, so buy fenugreek in powdered form.

Bittersweet in flavour, this spice is used mainly in curries, chutneys and spicy vegetable mixtures. It is the dominant taste in commercial curry powder. Combined with cumin and mango chutney, fenugreek will give a spicy but not too hot flavour to stuffed eggs.

Garam masala is the Indian name for a special blend of spices. A typical mixture would be three parts each of cardamom and cinnamon, one part cloves and one part cumin. Some mixtures have black pepper added but the overall flavour is meant to be mild rather than hot. In India there are numerous combinations as each cook makes up an individual favourite blend. If you are very enthusiastic about making curries, you may find it worthwhile making your own, but the canned ones are satisfactory for most purposes. Unlike other curry spices, garam masala is added towards the end of the cooking time, to deepen the flavour.

Paprika pepper is a scarlet powder made from the dried sweet peppers of the capsicum family. It is chiefly made in Hungary and is widely used there and in central Europe. Several grades of paprika are produced: the best quality is called 'rose' paprika and this has a full, sweet, slightly smoky flavour and a glowing colour.

Paprika is the essential flavouring for goulash and in Hungary it is included in many other stews and casseroles. Unlike peppers and chilli powder, it can be used in generous quantities and many dishes can be enhanced both in flavour and colour by the use of paprika. Try adding a teaspoonful to tomato soup or sauce; sprinkle it onto mashed potatoes, potato or onion soup, creamed fish or chicken dishes, vegetables in cream sauce and hard-boiled eggs.

Tamarind, which looks like a lump of dark brown sticky fibres, is actually the pulp from the pods of an evergreen tree, *Tamarindus indica*, a member of the pea family. It can be obtained from Indian shops and will keep for several months when stored in a screw-top jar in a cool dark place. To use tamarind, break off about 25 g /1 oz, steep it in a little boiling water for about 30 minutes, then press it through a sieve and use the liquid. Added to fish dishes, curries and vegetables mixtures, tamarind imparts a pleasantly sour, citrus-like flavour. Use a little lemon juice as a substitute.

Turmeric is the dried root of a perennial plant, *Curcuma longa*, belonging to the ginger family. It is normally bought as a powder, which is bright mustard yellow and has a peppery smell and a warm, slightly bitter taste. Added to pickles, relishes, rice, egg and fish dishes, turmeric gives colour as

Left to right, top row: small chillies, dill seed (see page 85), dried chillies; second row: cinnamon powder (above), curry powder (below), paprika, saffron, fenugreek; third row: cinnamon bark (above), coriander seed (below), mace, celery seeds, ginger root; fourth row: mustard powder (see page 76), pickling spice, nutmegs, juniper berries; fifth row: cloves, cayenne pepper, cardamom, sesame seeds, turmeric, cloves, poppy seed

well as flavour; it can be used as a cheaper substitute for saffron.

Try blending a little turmeric with butter and lemon juice and serving it with plainly cooked vegetables. Or use turmeric for flavour as well as colour in an Anglo-Indian breakfast dish, Golden kedgeree (see recipe).

Sweet spices

Try these sweet spices to add a fragrant and aromatic touch to your recipes.

Allspice is the dried unripe berry of a small tree, *Pimenta officinalis*. It is also known as 'pimenta' or 'pimento' and 'Jamaican pepper', since it grows abundantly there. It tastes rather like a mixture of cloves, cinnamon and nutmeg. Buy it whole; as it is easily ground at home it makes a fresher substitute for bought mixed spice. Add crushed allspice to chutneys, spiced fruit and vegetable mixtures, or use marinades for meat. Powdered allspice is good in fruit cakes, and will pep up mashed vegetables or tomato soup.

Cinnamon is the bark of a small evergreen tree, *Cinnamon zeylanicum*, which belongs to the laurel family. It grows in Ceylon and South India. There is also a related spice called Cassia. Like cloves, cinnamon has been traded for thousands of years. Paper thin strips of the bark are peeled off, rolled into sticks and left to dry — stick cinnamon, as the result is called, is commonly available in shops, or the spice can be bought ready-ground as a powder. Do not try to grind cinnamon at home as the bark is very hard.

It is useful to have both forms of cinnamon in your store cupboard. Break off a piece of cinnamon and add it to milk puddings.

Stewed fruit, spiced rice, curries and mutton stews are enhanced by the addition of stick cinnamon. Powdered cinnamon is useful for sprinkling on top of milk puddings, for adding to cakes and biscuits or even cheese pastry for cheese straws. Sprinkle it on hot buttered toast to make that old favourite, cinnamon toast. It goes well with chocolate; try adding a pinch to a hot cocoa drink.

In eastern Mediterranean countries, including Greece, cinnamon is an essential ingredient of meat cookery. It is also contained in some curry powders.

Cloves are probably the best known of all spices — not just the sweet ones. They are the flower buds of *Eugenia caryophyllata*, a tree belonging to the myrtle family. It grows on tropical islands such as Zanzibar and the West Indies. Cloves have been imported into Europe for 2000 years. When freshly dried, they contain up to 18 per cent oil. They can be bought whole or powdered, for different uses, and it is worth buying both types as they are difficult to grind at home.

Whole cloves are pungent and should be used sparingly. Stick them into apples or onions before cooking, or into an orange for a mulled wine. They can be used generously in apple pie, bread sauce and in the topping for a glazed ham. Use one or two to add interest to a beef stew or a spicy rice dish, or to give a lift to dried pulse dishes, such as pease pudding or lentil soup. They can also be added to curries and pickles. Powdered cloves are used in making fruit cakes, puddings and buns.

Ginger is a root of a tropical plant which is indigenous to southern Asia but also grows in

China and Japan. The spice is sold in many forms: fresh, dried whole, powdered, crystallized or preserved. Fresh 'green' root ginger has a soft brown skin and is very knobbly — rather like a Jerusalem artichoke. Buy plump pieces with solid firm flesh and a smooth skin. Store closely wrapped in foil, in the lowest part of the refrigerator for up to three weeks or in the freezer for up to a year, and simply grate off some of the spice when you need it. In Chinese cookery, fresh ginger is peeled and very thinly sliced, then heated in the oil to flavour it before stir-frying. To give a subtle hint of ginger, rub a cut piece of the root around a salad bowl or over the skin of a duck or chicken. Try placing a couple of slices inside a whole fish before baking or steep one or two slices in oil for salad dressings.

Dried root ginger has a more concentrated flavour. Store it loosely wrapped or in a stoppered jar in a dark, cool place and use within three months. To extract the full flavour, peel the dried root if necessary, then lightly crush it. Bruised dried ginger is well suited to flavouring marinades — infuse it for several hours or even days. To make ground ginger, cut the root into small pieces and grind them in a coffee grinder. Whether home-made or bought, ground ginger is very

Spices are available whole or ground. Clockwise from the lidded jar are ground and whole cloves, ground mixed spice, vanilla pods, whole allspice, ground and whole nutmeg, whole mace in the sack, ground mace, cinnamon sticks and ground cinnamon. In the centre container is ground allspice.

versatile: use it to make gingerbread (see page 70) or ginger biscuits; to give a lift to crumble mixtures and for coatings such as oatmeal and ginger for belly of pork.

Crystallized and preserved ginger (sometimes known as 'stem' ginger) can be eaten on their own or added to fruit. Preserved ginger is also delicious in a glaze for baked ham or, for a change, try a ginger-glazed roast lamb. Ginger essence is also available but it must be used very sparingly if it is not to overwhelm a dish and is best saved for times when other forms of the spice are not available.

Mace is the husk around the nutmeg kernel, scarlet when fresh but orange-brown when dry. It is called blade mace and comes in spiky pieces too hard and brittle to grind at home. It was more commonly used in Britain between the 16th and 18th centuries than it is today. A blade of mace can be included in a bouquet garni for flavouring stews or in fish and chicken dishes. Ground mace is a traditional flavouring for potted shrimps and meat dishes. It is also good with eggs, and in ketchups and white sauces.

Mixed spice is a combination of ground spices, usually nutmeg, cinnamon, cloves and allspice. This is a useful way to buy spices when you want to add a small quantity of several spices to dishes. Use the mixture in fruit cakes, puddings and buns, or add a pinch to vanilla ice cream.

Nutmeg is the kernel of a yellow, plum-like fruit of an evergreen tree, *Myristica fragrans*. Whole nutmegs are dark brown, oval and about half the size of walnuts. They are extracted after a long and complicated drying process and are mainly exported from Indonesia and the West Indies.

Powdered nutmeg is available but the kernel is easy to grate and the flavour of freshly grated nutmeg is far superior. In many parts of Europe, nutmeg is used in much the same way as salt and pepper and, in the 18th century, British travellers carried their own nutmeg graters for flavouring food. Nowadays the fine holes of an ordinary grater are equally effective for grating.

Grated nutmeg is delicious with many vegetables: try a sprinkling over cauliflower, cabbage and all root vegetables. It is excellent with cheese and a pinch improves cream soups and sauces. Nutmeg also livens up mixtures containing sausage meat and is essential for 'proper' mashed potato.

Saffron is the world's most expensive spice. The best quality saffron is sold in strands, which are the stamens of the crocus. Beware of buying ground or powdered saffron as these products are rarely the genuine article, nor do they give a good flavour.

Saffron strands are generally soaked for at least 2 hours in a hot liquid which is then strained and the liquid used to add colour and taste to rice dishes, chicken, fish and soups or cakes.

Vanilla looks like a long black bean — and that is precisely what it is — the bean or pod of a climbing tropical orchid, *Vanilla plani-folia*. The pods are gathered before they are fully ripe and are then dried. Madagascar and Mexico are the main exporters.

To get the best, most delicate, flavouring you should use the whole vanilla pod, but the

Golden kedgeree

spice is also available in other forms. Vanilla liquid extract is genuine vanilla; vanilla essence contains some synthetic flavouring, and vanilla flavouring is totally synthetic in its make-up.

To use vanilla pods, steep them in hot liquid, for instance in the sugar syrup you intend to use to poach fruit, or in the milk needed to make custard. This is the classic way of flavouring an egg custard. After use, wash and dry the pod and store it for re-use. A vanilla pod stored buried in a jar of caster sugar will impregnate the sugar with a delicate vanilla flavour. Use this vanilla sugar to sprinkle over deep-fried, battered fruit (sweet beignets), or for making cakes and biscuits. Vanilla is also the classic flavouring for all sponge mixtures.

Buying and storing

Spices can be bought from most large supermarkets, or go to a specialist shop which has a rapid turnover, as spices lose their flavour if stored for a long time.

Avoid glass containers as the light can spoil them. Instead, choose small, airtight opaque drums. Spice racks filled with small glass bottles look decorative on a kitchen wall, but it is better to keep them in a cupboard out of the light, in a cool dry place. Although some spices will keep for several years, in general their flavour and fragrance deteriorate so it is a good thing to buy spices in small quantities and use them up within three months if possible.

Golden kedgeree

 1 hour 10 minutes

Serves 4
500 g /1 lb smoked haddock
1 bay leaf
50 g /2 oz butter
200 g /7 oz long-grain rice, washed and drained
5 ml /1 tsp turmeric
salt
freshly ground black pepper
10 ml /2 tsp lemon juice
3 hard-boiled eggs, coarsely chopped
30 ml /2 tbls chopped fresh parsley

1 Poach the haddock gently in 600 ml /1 pt water with the bay leaf for about 15 minutes, until it is tender. Drain the fish thoroughly, reserving the water, then skin, bone and flake the fish.

2 Melt half the butter in a medium-sized saucepan and add the rice and turmeric, stir for 1–2 minutes, then add the reserved water, making it up again, as necessary, to 600 ml / 1 pt. Add 2.5 ml /½ tsp salt and a grinding of pepper. Bring to the boil, cover and simmer over low heat for 20 minutes, until all the rice is tender.

3 Using a fork, add the flaked fish, lemon juice, hard-boiled egg and remaining butter to the rice. Check the seasoning, then re-heat gently, stirring so it doesn't stick to the bottom of the pan. Serve sprinkled with the chopped parsley.

Egg pâté

 15 minutes,
plus chilling

Serves 4
4 hard-boiled eggs
200 g /7 oz curd or cream cheese
2.5 ml /½ tsp powdered mace
5 ml /1 tsp finely grated onion
salt and freshly ground black pepper
a little extra powdered mace, to garnish

1 Purée the hard-boiled eggs in a blender
or food processor or through a vegetable mill.
Alternatively, chop, then mash them with a
fork until smooth.
2 Add the curd or cream cheese to the eggs
and mix well to make a creamy, fairly smooth
mixture. Beat in the mace, onion and salt and
pepper to taste.
3 Spoon the mixture into a pâté dish or
four individual ramekins; smooth the top and
sprinkle with a little more mace.
4 Chill the pâté in the refrigerator for at
least 30 minutes before serving.

Spicy red cabbage

 2 hours

Serves 4–6
700 g /1½ lb red cabbage, washed and
  shredded
2 large onions, chopped
2 large cooking apples, peeled, cored and
  chopped
45 ml /3 tbls oil
50 g /2 oz raisins
15 ml /1 tbls salt
25 mm /1 in cinnamon stick
1.5 ml /¼ tsp ground cloves
15 ml /1 tbls brown sugar
15–30 ml /1–2 tbls lemon juice

1 Put the cabbage into a large saucepan,
cover it with cold water and bring it to the
boil, then drain it in a colander.
2 Fry the onion and apple together in the
oil, in a large saucepan for 5–10 minutes.
Add the cabbage, raisins, salt, cinnamon,
ground cloves, sugar and 15 ml /1 tbls of the
lemon juice. Stir well, cover and cook over a
gentle heat for 1½ hours, until the cabbage is
tender, stirring occasionally.
3 To serve, remove the cinnamon stick,
taste the cabbage and add the rest of the
lemon juice if necessary.

Festive curried chicken salad

**This dish is a 20th century English classic. It
was served for the Jubilee of George V in
1935 and re-created for Queen Elizabeth II's
coronation. The curry powder reduces the
richness of the sauce.**

 1 hour 30 minutes

Serves 6
1.8 kg /4 lb roasting chicken
bouquet garni
1 carrot
1 onion
salt and freshly ground black pepper
15 ml /1 tbls cooking oil
1 small onion, chopped
1 garlic clove, crushed
10 ml /2 tsp curry powder
5 ml /1 tsp tomato purée
75 ml /3 fl oz red wine
15 ml /1 tbls apricot jam
300 ml /11 fl oz mayonnaise
50 ml /2 fl oz thick cream, whipped
5–10 ml /1–2 tsp lemon juice

To serve
cold boiled rice
a little paprika pepper

1 Put the chicken into a large saucepan,
with the bouquet garni, the carrot, onion, a
little salt and a good grinding of pepper.
Cover with water and simmer gently for
50–60 minutes, until tender. Leave to cool in
the liquid, then drain well, remove the skin
and slice off the meat.
2 Heat the oil and fry the onion and garlic
for 10 minutes until softened but not
browned. Add the curry powder and cook for
1–2 minutes, then stir in the tomato purée,
red wine and 50 ml /2 fl oz water and simmer

Festive curried chicken salad

gently for about 10 minutes. Add the apricot jam and cook for a further 2–3 minutes. Cool completely.
3 Put the mayonnaise into a bowl and sieve the curry mixture onto it. Add the whipped cream, mix well, and season to taste, adding enough lemon juice to pleasantly sharpen the flavour.
4 Place the chicken on a serving dish and spoon the mayonnaise mixture on top, so that it is covered. Surround the chicken with a border of cold boiled rice. Finally sprinkle a little red paprika pepper over the top of the mayonnaise and serve.

Sweet chilli tomato chutney

The mustard seeds can be omitted although they do give an interesting texture.

1 hour 20 minutes,
then 3 months

Makes about 1 kg /2¼ lb
500 g /1 lb cooking apples, weighed after
  peeling and coring
500 g /1 lb tomatoes, skinned
2 large onions
1 clove of garlic, peeled
10 ml /2 tsp salt
200 g /7 oz stoned pressed dates
100 g /4 oz brown sugar
300 ml /11 fl oz malt vinegar
30 ml /2 tbls black mustard seed
50 g /2 oz dried root ginger
5–10 ml /1–2 tsp chilli powder

1 Cut the apples and tomatoes into small pieces; peel and chop the onions. Crush the garlic cloves in the salt with the flat blade of a knife. Chop the dates.
2 Put the apples, tomatoes, onions, garlic and dates into a large saucepan and add the sugar, vinegar and mustard seed.
3 Bruise the ginger by banging it several times with a rolling pin, then tie it in a small piece of muslin and put it into the saucepan with the other ingredients.
4 Bring to the boil, then simmer gently for 45 minutes. Add the chilli powder, a little at a time, tasting after each addition, until the chutney is 'hot' enough.
5 Cook the mixture for a further 15 minutes, until it is fairly thick, stirring frequently towards the end. Remove the bag of ginger, pressing it against the side of the saucepan to extract all the juices.
6 Let the mixture cool a little, then put it into warmed, sterilized jars. Label and store in a cool, dark place.
7 Mature for 3 months, if possible, in a cool, dark, dry place before eating. The chutney will keep for 1 year or more.

Vanilla ice cream

30 minutes preparation,
plus cooling and freezing

Serves 4
200 ml /7 fl oz milk
a vanilla pod
3 large egg yolks or 4 smaller ones
50 g /2 oz vanilla sugar or caster sugar
200 ml /7 fl oz thick cream

1 Turn the refrigerator to its coldest setting (the highest number) if you are not using a domestic freezer.
2 Put the milk and vanilla pod into a medium-sized saucepan and bring it to the boil. Turn off the heat. Whisk the yolks in the top of a double boiler with the sugar.
3 Pour the hot milk (and the vanilla pod) onto the beaten yolks. Cook in the double boiler over very gently simmering water, stirring all the time with a wooden spoon, until the mixture thickens and your finger leaves a mark on the back of the coated spoon — about 15 minutes. Leave to cool completely, then remove the vanilla pod. (Wash, dry and store this, as the pod can be used for flavouring again.)
4 Whisk the cream until it has thickened slightly, then fold it into the cold custard.
5 Spoon the mixture into a metal container. Cover and place in a deep freeze or the ice-making compartment of your refrigerator. Leave for 30–45 minutes, or until the mixture is beginning to set around the edges. Tip the mixture into a bowl and whisk well, then return, covered, to the refrigerator and freeze until firm.
6 Allow the ice cream to stand for 30 minutes in the refrigerator before serving; this softens it and makes it easier to serve.

Honey bread

This enriched bread is from France, where it is called *pain d'épice* — spice bread.

2 hours,
then 2 days maturing

Makes 10 slices
butter, for greasing
300 g /11 oz honey, warmed to liquid
150 g /5 oz sugar
50 ml /2 fl oz boiling water
300 g /11 oz light rye flour
a pinch of salt
15 ml /1 tbls bicarbonate of soda
30 ml /2 tbls dark rum
15 ml /1 tbls ground aniseed
2.5 ml /½ tsp ground cinnamon
1.5 ml /¼ tsp ground mace
1.5 ml /¼ tsp almond essence
50 g /2 oz ground almonds
125 g /4 oz chopped crystallized peel

1 Heat the oven to 180C /350F /gas 4. Grease a 2 L /3½ pt loaf tin, line it with greaseproof paper and grease again.
2 Put the warmed liquid honey into a large bowl. Add the sugar and boiling water and beat until the sugar has dissolved.
3 Sift together the flour, the salt and the bicarbonate of soda. Add just enough flour mixture to the honey mixture to make a stiff, heavy dough-like consistency, which is still soft enough to be beaten. Beat hard for 5 minutes.
4 Beat in the remaining ingredients and any left-over flour mixture. Turn the dough into the prepared tin. Smooth the top with the back of a spoon dipped in water, doming it slightly in the middle.
5 Bake in the middle of the oven for 1½ hours. Do not open the oven door during this time, as the wet, heavy dough sinks easily if the temperature drops suddenly.
6 When the bread is cooked it will shrink away from the sides of the tin. Allow the bread to cool in the tin for 15 minutes, then unmould it onto a rack. Immediately peel off the paper and turn the bread right side up. When cold — after about 2 hours — wrap it tightly and keep for 48 hours before cutting, to allow it to mature.

Jewelled Danish loaf

Traditionally served at Christmas, this loaf is delicious with coffee at any time of year.

 3 hours, including 1½ hours rising, plus cooling

Makes 1 large loaf
100 ml /3 fl oz milk, lukewarm
25 g /1 oz fresh yeast
500 g /1 lb 2 oz strong flour
50 g /2 oz soft brown sugar
100 g /4 oz butter, plus extra for greasing
2.5 ml /½ tsp cardamom seeds, slightly crushed
10 ml /2 tsp vanilla essence
grated zest of ½ lemon
225 g /8 oz mixed candied fruit, chopped
2 medium-sized eggs, beaten
a little icing sugar, to dredge

1 Grease a 1.7 L /3 pt loaf tin with butter. Put the milk into a small bowl, crumble in the yeast and leave for 10 minutes until very frothy.
2 Meanwhile put the flour and sugar in a large bowl, dice the butter, and using your fingertips, rub it in. Mix in the cardamom seeds, vanilla, lemon zest, candied fruit and beaten eggs.
3 Make a well in the centre of the flour mixture and pour in the milk and yeast. Mix to a dough, adding a little more milk if necessary to make a medium-soft consistency. Knead the dough for 10 minutes.
4 Place the dough in a greased bowl which is large enough to allow it to double in size. Cover it with a piece of greased polythene and leave in a warm place for 45–60 minutes, or until it has doubled in bulk.
5 Punch down the mixture with your fist and knead the dough again for 2–3 minutes. Next, form it into a loaf shape to fit the prepared tin. Place the dough in the tin,

Jewelled Danish loaf

pressing it well into the corners. Cover the tin loosely with greased polythene and leave in a warm place to rise.
6 Heat the oven to 180C /350F /gas 4. When the loaf has risen to the top of the tin, bake in the centre of the oven for 1 hour, until golden and crisp. When turned out of its tin and rapped with the knuckles on its base, the loaf should sound hollow, like a drum. Cool on a wire rack.
7 Dust the loaf with a little icing sugar, or serve it ready sliced and lightly buttered.

● You can use chopped mixed peel in this cake, but for the most attractive colour effect use a selection of different coloured candied or glacé fruit, such as apricots, pineapple and red, yellow and green cherries. Wash them first to remove excess sugar (or they will sink in the cake), pat them dry with a clean cloth and chop coarsely.

Nuts

ALMONDS

Without doubt, this is one of the most popular and versatile nuts used in cooking. I have chosen a variety of enticing recipes where almonds feature equally successfully, whether the dish is sweet or savoury.

Almonds have been enjoyed for many centuries; there are references to them as far back as the Old Testament, and they were common in medieval cookery, even being salted and eaten before meals in the popular belief that this would prevent drunkenness! They were often ground and made into thick sauces, from which many different dishes were made.

Almonds are also used for making almond milk and almond butter, the latter being especially popular as a sweet until the 18th century. Cakes made from ground almonds were called marchpanes — eventually corrupted into the word marzipan. Today, marzipan is still widely used for covering fruit cakes and small sweets. Sugar-coated almonds, called dragées, are a popular sweet, and in some countries it is a traditional custom to distribute them to celebrate a birth or wedding.

Types of almonds

There are two types of almonds — bitter and sweet. The bitter almond (*Prunus dulcis amara*) is used very sparingly for flavouring and for making essences and oils for the skin. These should never be eaten in large quantities as they contain prussic acid which is poisonous. The sweet almond (*Prunus dulcis*) produces the edible nuts which are eaten whole and used in various forms for sweet and savoury recipes.

Almonds grow wherever the climate is hot and dry. Sicily is a big producer, also Spain, California, South Africa and Australia.

Buying almonds

If you are lucky enough to be in Spain or one of the other almond-producing countries at harvest time, you will be able to buy 'wet' almonds, which are preserved in sugar and eau-de-vie (a strong fruit brandy) and eaten as a dessert.

Almonds in their shells are in the shops in abundance around Christmas time. The shells should be bright and fresh looking — not wet. Although almonds that you shell yourself just before using are preferable, it is much more convenient to buy them already shelled; they should be crisp, moist and plump. Buy a month's supply at a time and store them in an airtight container in a cool, dry place.

Using almonds

Shelled almonds in their skins are often mixed with dried fruit and eaten as a dessert. You can also toss them in salads to add extra cruchiness. Whole blanched almonds can be added to savoury and fruit salads, and used in oriental stir-fried dishes, such as Stir-fried almonds and vegetables (see recipe).

You can also toast almonds, fry, salt and devil them. Toasted almonds can be used in salads, as a garnish, or eaten with drinks.

Both salted and devilled almonds are useful cocktail snacks. Halved almonds make pretty garnishes and can also be fried and sprinkled over fish or meat (trout with almonds is the classic example). They can also be used to garnish cakes, such as Dundee cake, or individual macaroons. Flaked almonds are excellent for garnishing sweet dishes and patisseries. Slivered almonds are usually added to rich, Christmas-type puddings, mincemeat and stuffings. Chopped almonds can be used to garnish mousses and soufflés, or added to salads and stuffings.

Combine ground almonds with sugar to make marzipan, macaroons or small sweetmeats, such as Cinnamon and almond sweets, and Italian-style soft nougat pudding (see recipes); the latter needs no cooking and can be made with great success by even the least experienced cook. Add ground almonds to cake mixtures or your crumble toppings. Make a melting almond pastry to use in the delicious Almond and strawberry tartlets (see recipe).

Ground almonds are still used to thicken savoury sauces, particularly in Spain and the Middle East. Try beating together ground almonds, oil and lemon juice for an unusual salad dressing. Mix ground almonds with flour to coat meat or fish before frying. Toasted ground almonds make an unusual coating for a roll of cream cheese.

Praline

Praline is a flavouring or garnish made by cooking together almonds and sugar.

For brown praline, which has a stronger flavour, use almonds in their skins. Spoon equal weights of almonds and caster sugar into a pan over a low heat and cook them until the sugar caramelizes. Turn the mixture

From left to right: coarsely chopped, flaked, devilled and blanched almonds

Preparing and serving almonds

Blanching: put the almonds in a shallow pan of cold water; bring it to the boil. Take it off the heat and drain the almonds. When they are cool enough to handle, you can gently squeeze them from their skins.
Toasting: put blanched almonds on a baking sheet in a single layer and bake at 180C / 350F /gas 4 for 10 minutes. Turn them once during cooking so they brown evenly.
Frying: heat 75 ml /3 fl oz olive or groundnut oil in a pan over a moderate heat. Add 225 g /8 oz blanched almonds; stir until they are browned. Remove the almonds from the pan; drain them on absorbent paper.
Salting and devilling: fry the almonds and coat them with fine sea salt; leave to cool. For devilled almonds, sprinkle lightly with cayenne pepper before the almonds cool.
Halving: for attractive, but thinner, almonds, split them in half when they are moist. Insert either a knife point or your thumb nail and ease the two halves apart.
Flaking: use almond flakes to garnish sweet dishes and patisseries. Cut parallel slivers off the nut from the flat side. You should get 4–5 flakes per almond.
Shredding: use blanched almonds. Cut slivers, as thinly as possible, from the side.
Nibbing: cut 4–6 large slivers from the side of each nut.
Chopping: the easiest way to chop blanched almonds is to use a curved knife, known as a mezzaluna, which fits into its own bowl or rocks to and fro across the nuts.
Grinding: use either a blender, food processor or a clean coffee mill. Put 50 g /2 oz dry almonds at a time into the machine. Grind finely, stopping occasionally to loosen nut pieces from the sides.

Blanching

Frying

Flaking

Chopping with a mezzaluna

---

onto oiled foil and leave it until the mixture has set. Next, crush the praline between sheets of greaseproof paper with a rolling pin, or put it through an electric grinder.

For praline ice cream, add 120–150 ml / 8–10 tbls praline to vanilla ice cream. For a cake filling, beat praline into butter cream. Store praline in an airtight jar or freeze it if you wish to keep it for longer than 1 month.

White praline is a coarse, white powder used to coat biscuits and small cakes. Make a sugar syrup by boiling 250 g /9 oz sugar with 250 ml /9 fl oz water. Remove it from the heat and stir in 125 g /4 oz ground almonds, and mix until the mixture looks like coarse sand. Sieve and store it.

Almond chicken with Marsala sauce

1¼ hours

Serves 4
1.5 kg /3–3½ lb roasting chicken
200 g /7 oz almonds, blanched
40 g /1½ oz seasoned flour
2 medium-sized eggs, beaten
oil, for deep frying

For the sauce
45 ml /3 tbls olive oil
1 large carrot, finely chopped
1 medium-sized onion, finely chopped
1 garlic clove, finely chopped
225 g /8 oz tomatoes
30 ml /2 tbls sherry or wine vinegar
100 ml /3½ fl oz Marsala

1 Take the meat from the bones and cut it into pieces about 15 mm × 5cm /½ × 2 in.
2 Grind the almonds and mix them with the flour in a large bowl.
3 Dip the chicken pieces in the beaten egg, then add them, a few at a time, to the bowl with the almonds. Mix the chicken pieces into the almonds, making sure they are well-coated. Repeat until all the pieces are coated. Refrigerate them until ready to cook.
4 Heat the oil for the sauce in a pan on a low heat. Add the carrot, onion and garlic, cover and cook for 10 minutes. Meanwhile pour boiling water over the tomatoes; let them stand for 10 seconds. Drain and pour cold water on them, then remove their skins and chop finely. Add the tomatoes, vinegar and Marsala to the sauce and cook gently for 15 minutes, until it thickens.
5 Heat the oil in a deep-fat frier to a high heat. Put in the chicken strips, about one third at a time, and deep-fry them until

golden. Drain them on absorbent paper and place them on a warm serving dish. Pour the sauce over the finished chicken pieces.

Curried almond and apple stuffing

30 minutes

Fills 1.5 kg /2½–3½ lb boned loin of pork
50 g /2 oz almonds, blanched
25 g /1 oz butter
2 large celery sticks, finely chopped
1 medium-sized onion, finely chopped
1 large cooking apple, peeled, cored and finely chopped
5 ml /1 tsp hot Madras curry powder
25 g /1 oz millet or burghul wheat

1 Sliver the almonds. Melt the butter in a frying-pan over a low heat. Mix in the celery and onion and cook until the onion is soft.
2 Mix in the apple, curry powder and millet or wheat and cook for 2 minutes. Take the pan from the heat and mix in the almonds. Cool the stuffing before filling the pork. Roll and tie it before roasting.

Stir-fried almonds and vegetables

 40 minutes

Serves 4
1 small cauliflower
2 medium-sized green peppers
1 medium-sized onion
200 g /7 oz bean sprouts
30 ml /2 tbls cornflour
30 ml /2 tbls soy sauce
60 ml /4 tbls sherry
30 ml /2 tbls tomato purée
300 ml /11 fl oz stock, home-made
  or from a cube
60 ml /4 tbls sunflower or groundnut oil
1 garlic clove, chopped
200 g /7 oz almonds, blanched
5 ml /1 tsp ground ginger

1 Break the cauliflower into small florets about 20 mm /¾ in long. Core and seed the peppers and cut them into pieces 25 × 5 mm / 1 × ¼ in. Finely chop the onion and pick over the bean sprouts, if necessary.
2 Put the cornflour into a bowl and gradually mix in the soy sauce, sherry and tomato purée so you have a smooth paste. Next, add the stock, mixing thoroughly.
3 Put the oil and garlic into a frying-pan or wok over a low heat. When the garlic begins to sizzle, add the almonds, cauliflower, peppers and onion and stir-fry for 2 minutes. Add the ground ginger and bean sprouts and cook for 1 minute more.
4 Give the cornflour mixture a stir and pour it into the pan. Cover and cook on a low heat for 10 minutes, stirring occasionally. Serve immediately.

Grilled lemon plaice with flaked almonds

The addition of flaked, browned almonds transforms this simple dish into an extra-special main course, suitable for a party.

30 minutes marinating,
then 10 minutes

Serves 4
500 g /1 lb plaice fillets
juice of 1 lemon
sea salt and freshly ground black pepper
75 g /3 oz almonds, blanched
50 g /2 oz butter
5 ml /1 tsp ground paprika
30 ml /2 tbls chopped fresh parsley

1 Cut the plaice fillets in half lengthways and arrange them on a large, flat, heatproof dish, overlapping them as little as possible. Sprinkle them with the lemon juice, season well with the sea salt and freshly ground black pepper and leave them to stand for 30 minutes at room temperature.
2 Heat the grill to high. Flake the almonds. Beat the butter until it is soft and gradually beat in the paprika and parsley.
3 Dot the plaice with the paprika butter and put it under the grill for about 7 minutes so that it is cooked through but not browned. Sprinkle the plaice with the almonds and return it to the grill for 1 minute, just long enough for the almonds to brown. Serve the plaice straight from the dish.

Almond pilaff and Stir-fried almonds and vegetables

Almond pilaff

Toasted almonds make a very tasty and attractive addition to a dish of spiced brown rice. Serve it with chicken, pork or lamb.

1¼ hours

Serves 4
50 g /2 oz almonds
25 g /1 oz butter
1 medium-sized onion, thinly sliced
225 g /8 oz long-grain brown rice
5 ml /1 tsp ground turmeric
5 ml /1 tsp ground cumin
600 ml /1 pt stock, home-made or from a cube
a pinch of sea salt
50 g /2 oz raisins

1 Heat the oven to 180C /350F /gas 4. Blanch and split the almonds. Melt the butter in a flameproof casserole on a high heat. Put in the almonds and brown them evenly. Remove them and reserve.
2 Lower the heat, put in the onion to soften. Stir in the rice, turmeric and cumin and cook them for 1½ minutes. Pour in the stock and bring it to the boil. Season.
3 Cover the casserole and put it into the oven for 45 minutes. Take the casserole out of the oven and mix in the almonds and raisins. Cover the casserole again and let it stand for 10 minutes before serving.

Italian-style soft nougat pudding

30 minutes,
plus 3 hours chilling

Serves 8–10
200 g /7 oz unsalted butter, softened
200 g /7 oz sugar
125 g /4 oz cocoa powder, sifted
1 medium-sized egg
1 medium-sized egg yolk
125 g /4 oz plain vanilla-flavoured biscuits,
  such as Petit beurre
125 g /4 oz almonds, blanched, peeled and
  chopped
30 ml /2 tbls brandy
oil, for greasing
To decorate
150 ml /5 fl oz thick cream, whipped
sugar flowers or cake decorations of your choice

1 Beat the butter and sugar together until creamy. Add the cocoa and mix well.
2 Beat the egg and the yolk together and beat them into the cocoa mixture.
3 Break and crush the biscuits with a rolling pin and add the crumbs to the mixture with the chopped almonds. Mix

well. Add the brandy and mix again very thoroughly.

4 Lightly oil a 22 cm /9 in sandwich tin and line it with greaseproof paper. Spoon the biscuit crumb mixture into the tin, then flatten it with a palette knife. Refrigerate the mixture for at least 3 hours.

5 Turn the nougat out onto a round or oval dish and cover the top of the pudding with whipped cream; then decorate it with sugar flowers or other edible cake decorations of your choice.

Almond and strawberry tartlets

Serve these melting almond pastry and strawberry tarts with whipped cream.

1½ hours for the pastry cases, plus cooling, 15 minutes to finish

Makes 10–12 tartlets
sifted icing sugar
50 g /2 oz redcurrant jelly
350 g /12 oz even-sized strawberries
25 g /1 oz almonds, blanched and split
For the pastry
50 g /2 oz almonds, blanched and ground ·
100 g /4 oz flour
25 g /1 oz caster sugar
a pinch of salt
50 g /2 oz cold butter, diced small, plus extra
*   for greasing*
15 ml /1 tbls clear honey
1 medium-sized egg yolk
2 drops almond essence

1 To make the pastry, mix the ground almonds, flour, sugar and salt in a large bowl. Make a well in the middle and put in the butter, honey, egg yolk and almond essence. Rub the mixture through your finger tips, flattening the butter and pulling in the dry ingredients to make a paste. Knead it until it is smooth. Wrap the pastry in cling film and rest it in the refrigerator for 1–1½ hours before rolling it out.

2 Heat the oven to 190C /375F /gas 5 and thoroughly grease a 12-hole tart tin. Sift a little icing sugar over the work surface and roll out the pastry 3 mm /⅛ in thick. Use a biscuit cutter a little larger than the tart moulds to cut 10–12 circles, re-rolling as necessary. Line the moulds and chill for 10 minutes. Prick the bases and line them with foil and beans. Bake them blind for 10 minutes, and for a further 10 minutes empty. Remove the tarts from the tin.

3 Make the glaze by whisking the redcurrant jelly until it is almost liquid. Melt it over a very low heat without letting it boil. Brush it over the warm pastry and leave the tarts to get completely cold.

4 Hull the strawberries; slice large ones or arrange small whole ones pointed end up in each tart case. Decorate the strawberries with the split almonds.

5 Warm the remaining redcurrant glaze. With a soft pastry brush, brush the glaze over the strawberries and almonds, working from the centre outwards. Leave them until the glaze is completely set, then serve.

Cassis and almond jelly

30 minutes, plus chilling

Serves 6
500 ml /18 fl oz milk
75 g /3 oz almonds, finely ground
100 g /4 oz sugar
15 g /½ oz (1 tbls) gelatine
2.5 ml /½ tsp almond essence
350 ml /12 fl oz thick cream
30 ml /2 tbls crème de cassis

1 Combine the milk, almonds and sugar in a saucepan and simmer over a low heat for 15 minutes. Strain through a sieve, pressing the almonds to extract all the flavour.

2 Sprinkle the gelatine onto 50 ml /2 fl oz water in a small bowl and let it soften for 5 minutes. Stir the softened gelatine into the hot almond-cream mixture and continue stirring until it is dissolved. Stir in the almond essence. Let the mixture cool.

3 Whisk 125 ml /4 fl oz thick cream until stiff peaks form and fold it gently into the cooled almond mixture.

4 Rinse a 1 L /1¾ pt ring mould in cold water. Pour in the almond mixture and refrigerate until it has become firmly set.

5 Whisk the remaining cream until stiff and fold in the crème de cassis in streaks.

6 Unmould the jelly and fill the centre with the cassis-flavoured cream.

● Strawberries or mixtures of soft fruit in season may also be added to the cream.

Cinnamon and almond sweets

Serve these cinnamon and ground almond sweetmeats with coffee after a meal, as a change from the usual mints. Rose water is obtainable from chemists.

50 minutes

Makes 20
butter, for greasing
200 g /7 oz almonds, blanched
200 g /7 oz Barbados sugar
10 ml /2 tsp ground cinnamon
30 ml /2 tbls rose water
½ medium-sized egg white, stiffly beaten
For decoration
10 almonds, blanched and halved

1 Heat the oven to 170C /325F /gas 3 and grease a baking sheet. Grind the almonds and mix them with the Barbados sugar and ground cinnamon. Mix in the rose water and egg white to make a stiff paste.

2 With your fingers, press the mixture into 20 small balls and put them onto the prepared baking sheet. Flatten them slightly and press an almond half onto each one. Bake them for 10 minutes.

3 Take them out of the oven and leave on the baking sheet for 1 minute to firm. Carefully lift them onto a flat plate and leave until they are completely cool. They should be firm on the outside and sticky inside.

Cassis and almond jelly

PEANUTS & CASHEWS

Here are two nuts with a deservedly wide appeal: they can be nibbled on their own as a tasty, nutritious snack, or incorporated into a huge variety of mouthwatering recipes like the ones on these pages.

A peanut is not a true nut, it is a legume and the 'nut' in the shell is a seed. Cashews are nuts but both peanuts and cashews are used for nibbles, nut butters and similar sorts of recipes.

Peanuts

Peanuts are also known as groundnuts and monkey nuts. They come from India, East and West Africa, the southern United States and parts of the Far East.

Peanuts consist of two oval-shaped kernels which grow in a soft, crinkly shell. The nuts are hard but smooth-textured.

Buying peanuts: sometimes peanuts are roasted in the shell and sold as snacks. They can also be shelled and roasted with salt and oil, or dry-roasted with a mixture of spices and flavourings. If you want your peanuts to be as versatile as possible in the kitchen, buy them shelled but unroasted.

Preparing peanuts: if a recipe calls for roasted peanuts, spread them out on a baking tray and place them in an oven heated to 200C /400F /gas 6 for 10 minutes. Tip them onto a clean tea towel to cool. To skin them, fold them in the towel and rub the skins off.

Using peanuts: peanuts can be mixed with raisins for a nourishing snack in place of sweets. They can be added to savoury salads, chopped and used in biscuits and cakes or ground and mixed with other nuts in vegetarian dishes. Try the Malaysian saté dish (see recipe) — succulent beef served with a piquant peanut sauce. Satisfy the sweet-toothed by making delicious confectionery such as chocolate-covered peanuts or Peanut brittle (see recipe). Spread Mixed nut butter (see recipe) on toast or bread for a tasty treat the family will love. For salads and stir-frying, peanut or groundnut oil is excellent.

Cashew nuts

These days most cashew nuts come from India, although they originated in Brazil. They are also grown in East Africa and Egypt.

Buying cashew nuts: cashew nuts are sold shelled and skinned, graded as whole, half or broken nuts. They should be white or just off white in colour, and they should not be twisted in shape. They should have a hard, almost crumbly texture and a light, slightly sweet flavour. You can also buy salted whole and halved cashew nuts.

Using cashew nuts: because they have such a delicate flavour, cashew nuts go well with the milder-flavoured meats such as chicken and pork, particularly in stir-fried dishes that include ginger (see recipe). They can also be stir-fried with an assortment of vegetables or mixed with fried rice. For something a little different, scatter them over a fruit salad.

In tropical countries they are served with soup, sprinkled on top as a garnish. Unsalted cashew nuts are added to curries and other savoury spiced dishes; as a dessert they can be eaten with palm sugar and coconut.

Beef saté with peanut sauce

Balachan is a pungent shrimp paste, used in very small quantities. It is available from most Oriental specialist food stores.

15 minutes, 2 hours marinating, then 20 minutes

Beef saté with peanut sauce

Serves 4
450 g /1 lb rump steak, 15 mm /¹/₂ in thick
2.5 ml /¹/₂ tsp chilli powder
juice of ¹/₂ lemon
10 ml /2 tsp brown sugar
5 ml /1 tsp salt
5 ml /1 tsp ground coriander or cumin
For the peanut sauce
30 ml /2 tbls vegetable oil
50 g /2 oz raw shelled peanuts
2 red chillies, seeded and chopped, or 5 ml /
* 1 tsp chilli powder*
2 shallots, chopped
1 garlic clove
1 slice balachan, about 10 mm /¹/₂ in long
5 ml /1 tsp brown sugar
juice of ¹/₂ lime
salt

1   Cut the steak into 15 mm /¹/₂ in cubes and put it into a large bowl with the chilli powder, lemon juice, brown sugar, salt and ground coriander or cumin. Mix thoroughly and leave the steak to marinate for at least 2 hours.
2   Meanwhile, make the peanut sauce. Put 15 ml / 1 tbls oil in a large frying-pan over a medium-high heat, add the peanuts and stir-fry for 2–3 minutes. Remove them from the pan and drain on absorbent paper.
3   With a pestle, pound the red chillies, the shallots, garlic and balachan in a mortar until they are a smooth paste.
4   Grind the peanuts to a fine powder. Put the remaining oil in a frying-pan over a medium-high heat, add the chilli paste and fry for 1–2 minutes, then add 175 ml /6 fl oz water. Bring the sauce to the boil, add the ground peanuts, brown sugar, lime juice and a pinch of salt, and stir over a medium heat until the sauce is thick (about 10 minutes).

Stir-fried chicken and cashew nuts

Put the sauce into a bowl and keep it warm.
5   Heat the grill to high.
6   Thread the beef cubes onto bamboo skewers, 5 cubes per skewer, and grill for 10 minutes or until the meat is cooked, turning the skewers several times. Serve with the peanut sauce handed separately.

Stir-fried chicken and cashew nuts

 45 minutes

Serves 4
1.2 kg /2³/₄ lb roasting chicken, skinned and
* jointed*
30 ml /2 tbls cornflour
150 ml /5 fl oz dry sherry
150 ml /5 fl oz chicken stock, home-made or
* from a cube*
30 ml /2 tbls soy sauce
60 ml /4 tbls sesame oil
1 garlic clove, finely chopped
15 ml /1 tbls ground ginger
2 medium-sized onions, finely chopped
¹/₄ Chinese cabbage, finely shredded
75 g /3 oz unsalted cashew nuts
boiled white rice, to serve

1   Cut the chicken meat from the bones and then into small, thin slivers. Put the cornflour in a bowl and gradually mix in the sherry, stock and soy sauce.
2   Place the oil and garlic in a wok or a large frying-pan and set it over a low heat until the garlic sizzles and begins to brown.

Add the chicken and stir until that is brown.
3   Lower the heat and add the ginger. Mix in the onions and cook for 2 minutes. Add the Chinese cabbage and cashew nuts and cook for 1 minute more.
4   Stir the cornflour mixture again and pour it into the frying-pan. Cook, stirring, until it becomes a thick, translucent sauce, and serve immediately with boiled white rice.

Peanut brittle

If you prefer, you can substitute shelled and skinned almonds, walnuts or even hazelnuts for the peanuts in this recipe.

 45 minutes,
plus 1 hour cooling

Makes about 750 g /1¹/₂ lb
oil, for greasing
500 g /18 oz sugar
juice of ¹/₂ lemon
250 g /9 oz roasted peanuts, shelled and
* skinned*

1   Cover a baking sheet with foil and oil it.
2   Put the sugar into a saucepan with the lemon juice and 150 ml /5 fl oz water. Set it over a low heat and stir until it dissolves. Boil the syrup until it takes on a light caramel colour; this will be about 160–170C / 320–338F on a sugar thermometer. Take the pan from the heat and dip the base of it in cold water to stop the cooking.
3   Stir the nuts into the caramel. Tip the mixture onto the prepared baking sheet and spread it out evenly with an oiled wooden spatula. Leave it to cool and harden (about 1 hour).
4   Break the brittle into pieces by holding it up and hitting it sharply with the handle of a heavy pair of scissors. Store the peanut brittle in an airtight tin.

Mixed nut butter

 1 hour

Makes about 350 g /12 oz
75 g /3 oz peanuts, shelled
75 g /3 oz cashew nuts
50 g /2 oz walnuts, shelled
50 g /2 oz almonds, shelled
50 g /2 oz hazelnuts, shelled
45 ml /3 tbls peanut oil
1.5 ml /¹/₄ tsp salt

1   Heat the oven to 200C /400F /gas 6. Spread the nuts on a baking sheet and place it in the oven for 10 minutes; then tip the nuts onto a flat dish to cool.
2   Rub the skins from the peanuts and hazelnuts. Place all the nuts in a blender and blend them for a few seconds. Stir nuts around and blend them again. Continue in the same way until all the nuts are very finely ground.
3   Add the oil and blend to a smooth paste. Add the salt and blend again. Pour into a jar and cover. Spread it on bread to serve. It will keep in the refrigerator for up to 1 month.

WALNUTS & CHESTNUTS

Walnuts and chestnuts make a valuable contribution in the kitchen. They are rich in protein so they feature prominently in vegetarian diets, but anyone with an interest in health — and taste — can enjoy them.

Walnuts are one of the best known nuts and are grown as far afield as France, Italy, California, Australia, New Zealand, South Africa, China and parts of Asia.

They are often eaten raw and unaccompanied, particularly around Christmas time, but they can also be prepared in a variety of ways. Walnuts can be sautéed whole in butter and scattered over casseroles, puréed to make a delicious Middle Eastern-style sauce, and are excellent in salads (see Tossed green salad with walnut dressing).

If you are lucky enough to have a walnut tree in your garden, you can make pickled walnuts to eat with cold meat or cheese. Pick them in early summer while they are still green; you should be able to stick a needle right through the outer husk to the inner fleshy casing, called the shuck.

The French make a cordial called *brou de noix* from green walnuts. Walnut oil, also made in France, has a buttery taste which gives a distinctive flavour to salad dressings.

Sweet chestnuts grow mainly in France, Italy, Spain, Portugal and Corsica. They can be roasted in the oven at 200C /400F /gas 6 for 20 minutes and are then easy to skin. Eat them immediately or use them to make soups (see my unusual Chestnut and celery soup), or delicious Chestnut purée (see recipe), the sweet version of which can be used in rich gateaux and creamy desserts. Chestnuts can also be skinned raw (see Peeling sweet chestnuts).

Dried chestnuts, which double in weight when reconstituted, are a very useful store cupboard item. Soak them in hot water for 30 minutes (or boil them for 3 minutes) and then use them as raw chestnuts. As a substitute for cooked chestnuts, boil them for 25 minutes. You can also buy canned whole (cooked) chestnuts and cans of sweetened and unsweetened purée.

Buying and storing nuts

Nuts in their shells are available from September until February in the Northern Hemisphere, with a peak in December. They are sold mainly in greengrocers, large supermarkets and health food shops.

Fresh nuts should be bright and fresh-looking, and the kernels should not rattle in the shells. Walnut shells will have a 'wet' look early in their season. Stored in a cool, dry place, hard-shelled nuts will keep fresh for up to three months.

Shelled nuts can be bought throughout the year, whole, halved, chopped, flaked or broken into larger pieces. They are usually sold separately, often packaged under brand names, but mixtures are available.

All shelled nuts should look moist and slightly oily. Avoid nuts that are dull or look a darker colour than usual. Because of the natural oils they contain, shelled nuts may easily develop a rancid flavour if kept for

longer than two months, so it is best not to buy in bulk. Keep them in air-tight jars.

Preparing nuts

If you buy nuts in their shells for a recipe, remember that they will lose about half their weight when they are shelled. Chestnuts will weigh about three-quarters of their unskinned weight once they are peeled. Most recipes for chestnuts specify unskinned weight.

Peeling sweet chestnuts: first slit the tops. Put them in a saucepan and cover with cold water. Bring the water to the boil, then remove from the heat. With a slotted spoon, take each nut out of the water separately. Hold it with folded absorbent paper while you peel off the thick outer and thin inner skins. If the water in the pan gets cold, boil it again but remove it from the heat immediately. The chestnuts must then be cooked, either as part of a savoury dish or in milk, with added vanilla and sugar, for a sweet one.

Tossed green salad with walnut dressing

 20 minutes, plus crisping

Serves 8
2–3 crisp lettuces
1 bunch of watercress
½ garlic clove
For the dressing
120–150 ml /8–10 tbls walnut oil
60 ml /4 tbls red wine
30 ml /2 tbls wine vinegar
½ garlic clove, finely chopped
salt and freshly ground black pepper
16 walnut halves, to garnish

1 Trim the lettuces, discarding any tough or wilting outer leaves and separate them into leaves. Trim the watercress stalks and discard any wilted or yellow leaves. Thoroughly wash the lettuce leaves and watercress sprigs in cold water, then spin or gently shake dry. Wrap the salad greens in a clean, dry tea-towel and place in the salad crisper drawer of the refrigerator until they are required.
2 Make the salad dressing. Pour the walnut oil into a small mixing bowl and add the red wine, wine vinegar and finely chopped garlic. Season to taste with salt and freshly ground black pepper and whisk well with a fork until the ingredients form an emulsion.
3 Just before serving, rub a large wooden salad bowl with the cut garlic clove. Put the lettuce and watercress in the bowl, pour over the dressing and toss the salad until each leaf glistens. Garnish with the walnut halves.

● Walnut oil has a distinctive, nutty flavour which adds a unique taste to this salad. The

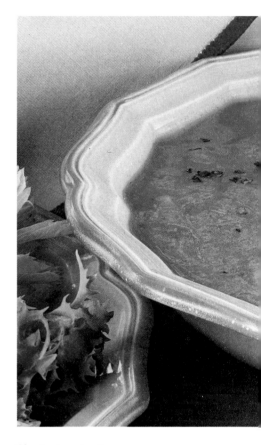

Chestnut and celery soup

walnut oil can usually be found in delicatessens, health food shops and some of the larger supermarkets; if it is unobtainable, use the best quality olive oil instead.

Chestnut and celery soup

The thick cream for this savoury soup can be omitted for family meals.

🍴🍴 1 hour

Serves 4
250 g /9 oz sweet chestnuts
25 g /1 oz butter
1 large onion, finely chopped
4 large celery sticks, finely chopped
850 ml /1½ pt chicken stock, home-made or from cubes
2.5 ml /½ tsp ground mace
bouquet garni
salt and freshly ground black pepper
60 ml /4 tbls thick cream
30 ml /2 tbls chopped fresh parsley

1 Bring the sweet chestnuts to the boil and skin them, then chop them finely.
2 Melt the butter in a saucepan over a low heat. Add the onion and the celery, cover and cook gently for 10 minutes.
3 Stir the chestnuts into the pan. Pour in the stock and bring to the boil. Add the mace and bouquet garni. Season with the salt and pepper. Simmer, uncovered, for 15 minutes.
4 Allow the soup to cool slightly then purée it in a blender until it is free of lumps and return it to the saucepan.

serving dish over the mould and reverse the two, giving a sharp shake. The palissade should slide out easily onto the dish.

7 Sprinkle the chocolate caraque over the top of the dessert and serve immediately.

● To make chocolate caraque, spread melted chocolate over greaseproof paper. Allow it to set, then shave it into chocolate filings using a sharp knife (see illustration, page 62).

Walnut and orange cake

 3 hours, including cooling

Makes a 20 cm /8 in cake
butter, for greasing
200 g /7 oz butter, softened
grated zest and juice of 1 large orange
200 g /7 oz caster sugar
300 g /11 oz flour
10 ml /2 tsp baking powder
3 eggs, beaten
100 g /4 oz shelled walnuts, chopped
For the butter cream
100 g /4 oz unsalted butter, softened
grated zest of 1 large orange
75 g /3 oz icing sugar, sifted
30 ml /2 tbls orange juice
75 g /3 oz shelled walnuts
For the decoration
30 ml /2 tbls icing sugar
4 walnut halves
4 pieces orange jelly cake decoration or
  4 canned mandarin orange segments

1 Line a deep 20 cm /8 in round cake tin with buttered greaseproof paper. Heat the oven to 170C /325F /gas 3.
2 Cream together the butter and the orange zest. Next, beat in the sugar until the mixture is light and fluffy.
3 Sift the flour with the baking powder and beat it into the creamed butter and sugar mixture alternately with the beaten eggs. Beat in the orange juice and finally mix in the chopped walnuts. Put the cake mixture into the tin and smooth the top.
4 Bake the cake for 1¼–1½ hours or until it has shrunk slightly from the sides of the tin and a skewer inserted in the centre comes out clean.
5 Cool the cake in the tin for 10 minutes, then turn it onto a wire rack to cool.
6 To make the butter cream, beat the butter with the orange zest until it is soft. Beat in the icing sugar and then the orange juice a few drops at a time.
7 Grind the walnuts in a blender and mix them into the butter cream.
8 Cut the cake in half horizontally and then sandwich the halves together with the butter cream, reserving 45 ml /3 tbls.
9 To decorate, sift icing sugar over the cake. Pipe 8 small whirls of butter cream evenly around the edge of the cake and decorate these alternately with walnut halves and orange jelly decorations or mandarin orange segments. If you are using mandarin orange segments, do not arrange them on the cake until just before serving.

5 Reheat the soup gently. Serve in heated individual soup bowls with a swirl of thick cream and a sprinkling of chopped fresh parsley on top of each serving.

Marinated chicken with walnuts

 24 hours marinating, then 1¼ hours

Serves 4
1.4–1.6 kg /3–3½ lb roasting chicken, dressed
  weight
juice of 1 lemon
100 ml /3½ fl oz olive oil
1 garlic clove, crushed with salt
freshly ground black pepper
75 g /3 oz shelled walnuts
45 ml /3 tbls chopped fresh parsley
8 walnut halves, to garnish

1 Cut the chicken into 8 pieces.
2 Mix together the lemon juice, the olive oil, the garlic and the freshly ground black pepper in a large, shallow bowl. Add the chicken pieces, turn them in the liquid and leave to marinate for 24 hours, turning the portions occasionally.
3 Heat the oven to 200C /400F /gas 6. Grind the shelled walnuts finely in a blender. Mix them with the chopped parsley and 30 ml /2 tbls of the marinade.
4 Put the chicken pieces in a single layer in a large ovenproof dish and bake them for 30 minutes.
5 Remove the chicken from the oven, then spread the walnut mixture over each piece. Return to the oven for a further 15 minutes. Serve straight from the dish, garnished with the walnut halves.

Palissade aux marrons

1 hour, plus at least 6 hours chilling

Serves 6–8
150 ml /5 fl oz milk
75 g /3 oz sugar
15 g /½ oz gelatine
50 g /2 oz dark (semi-sweet) cooking chocolate,
  melted
175 g /6 oz canned, unsweetened chestnut purée
275 ml /10 fl oz thick cream
150 g /5 oz canned glacé chestnuts (marrons
  glacés), drained and coarsely chopped
To decorate
25 g /1 oz chocolate caraque (see note below)

1 Line the base of a 1.1 L /2 pt charlotte mould with greaseproof or waxed paper.
2 In a medium-sized saucepan, heat the milk with the sugar, stirring until the sugar has dissolved. Remove from the heat.
3 Sprinkle the gelatine into 30 ml /2 tbls cold water in a cup and stand in a pan of gently simmering water until the gelatine has dissolved.
4 Add the gelatine to the milk (the mixture will look curdled at this point.) Add the melted chocolate and chestnut purée and beat until the ingredients are blended and smooth. Pour into a bowl and place in the refrigerator to chill for 10 minutes.
5 In another bowl, beat the cream until it is thick but not stiff. Then fold the cream and the coarsely chopped glacé chestnuts into the chestnut purée mixture. Spoon this into the mould and refrigerate for at least 6 hours.
6 When ready to serve this dessert, run a knife around the edge of the mould. Invert a

Chestnut purée

 1 hour

Makes about 425 ml /15 fl oz
500 g /1 lb raw chestnuts, skinned
200 ml /7 fl oz milk

1 Put the skinned chestnuts in a saucepan with the milk and 200 ml /7 fl oz water. Bring to the boil and simmer for 20 minutes or until the chestnuts are tender.

2 Drain the chestnuts. Mash them to a purée with a potato masher or rub them through the fine blade of a vegetable mill.

● For a savoury purée, season the simmering chestnuts with salt and pepper and add a bouquet garni or bay leaf.

● For a sweet purée, simmer with a vanilla pod or cinnamon stick and sweeten with a sugar syrup. For a purée made with 500 g / 1 lb chestnuts, dissolve 30 ml /2 tbls sugar in 60 ml /4 tbls water. Bring the syrup to the boil, then remove it from the heat and cool. Beat it, a little at a time, into the purée. This purée can be used as a cake filling or for a quick sweet if it is flavoured with cinnamon and chopped stem ginger.

Coffee morning nut ring

 3 hours

Serves 10
500 g /18 oz flour, plus extra for dusting
a pinch of salt
200 ml /7 fl oz milk
25 g /1 oz fresh yeast or 15 g /½ oz dried yeast
100 g /4 oz butter, cut in small dice, plus extra
  for greasing
100 g /4 oz caster sugar
2 eggs, beaten
For the filling
50 g /2 oz shelled walnuts
25 g /1 oz shelled hazelnuts
25 g /1 oz shelled Brazil nuts
25 g /1 oz butter
15 ml /1 tbls clear honey
10 ml /2 tsp ground cinnamon
For the decoration
100 g /4 oz icing sugar
10 glacé cherries
10 shelled walnut halves

1 Sift the flour with the salt into a bowl. Warm the milk gently and stir in the yeast, the butter and the sugar. When the butter has melted, pour the mixture into the flour, then add the beaten eggs.

2 Beat the mixture with a wooden spoon until it forms a moist dough. Next, knead the dough in the bowl, taking the sides to the centre, for at least 10 minutes, until it is smooth and comes easily away from the sides of the bowl.

3 Transfer the dough to a buttered bowl and cover it with a greased polythene bag. Leave it in a warm place for 45 minutes until it doubles in size.

4 Knock the dough down with the heel of your hand, and then knead it again for 2–3 minutes, taking the sides to the centre. Cover

Coffee morning nut ring

the dough again and leave it for a further 30 minutes. Heat the oven to 200C /400F / gas 6.

5 While the dough is rising, make the filling. Grind all the nuts finely in a blender or a coffee grinder. Gently melt the butter with the honey and then stir in the ground cinnamon and the nuts.

6 Roll the risen dough into a rectangle, roughly 45×30 cm /18×12 in. Spread the dough with the filling, taking it right to the edges of the short sides.

7 Roll up the dough from one of the long sides. Ease the rolled dough onto a floured baking sheet and bring the ends together, sealing them to make a ring.

8 Using a pair of sharp kitchen scissors, cut into the ring from the outside at intervals of about 25 mm /1 in, cutting about three-quarters through to make about 20 segments.

9 Cover the ring with a clean tea-cloth, and leave it in a warm place for about 20 minutes to prove.

10 Bake the ring for 35 minutes until it is golden brown and a skewer inserted into the centre comes out clean. Slide the ring onto a wire rack and leave it to cool.

11 To make the glacé icing: mix the icing sugar with enough warm water to form a coating consistency.

12 While the ring is still warm, brush it with about half the glacé icing. Arrange the cherries and the walnut halves alternatively on the inside edge of the segments. Brush the ring again with the rest of the icing and then leave it to become completely cool before serving it.

OTHER KINDS OF NUTS

Some of these six nuts will be familiar, others will perhaps not be quite as well known; all of them, however, bring their very distinctive flavours to these most attractive recipes.

These nuts are all useful in a variety of dishes — ranging from savoury to sweet. Try them for a change of taste.

Coconuts

Coconuts are one of the most important nuts of all, a staple food for thousands of people and an important source of oil for a range of products, including margarine and soap.

Many coconuts come from Sri Lanka and the islands of the Indian Ocean. Very high quality coconuts are either grated (coarse, medium or fine) or shredded into long, thin curls and then dried to produce desiccated coconut (three average-sized nuts are needed to yield 450 g /1 lb of desiccated coconut).

Buying and preparing coconuts: to make sure a coconut is fresh, hold it to your ear and shake it. You should hear the juice swishing around inside.

Before you open a coconut, this juice must be removed. Hold a thick skewer or a screwdriver against one of the 'eyes' at the top of the coconut and bang it with a hammer so that it goes right through the shell. Open one of the other eyes in the same way and hold the nut upside down over a receptacle to allow the juice to drain from it. The juice makes a healthy, thirst-quenching and unusual drink.

To open a coconut, first bake it in an oven heated to 200C /400F /gas 6 for 15 minutes. Remove the nut from the oven, place it on a hard, firm surface (concrete is ideal) and smash it open with a hammer. The baking process makes the shell split easily and also makes the nut fall away from the shell.

Cool the nut, then peel away the brown skin with a potato peeler. Grate the kernel with a hand grater or in a food processor.

Using coconuts: in India and the Far East grated coconut is often added to curries and hot, spicy dishes such as Minced pork saté (see recipe).

Try this idea for a refreshing salad: combine 100 g /4 oz freshly grated coconut with 225 g /8 oz coarsely grated carrot and 100 g /4 oz shredded white cabbage. Dress them with 30 ml /2 tbls salad oil and 15 ml / 1 tbls lemon juice. Add 50 g /2 oz plumped raisins and season with salt and black pepper. Serve the salad on a bed of crisp lettuce leaves, and garnish it with sprigs of fresh watercress.

In the United States, two favourite sweet dishes are a coconut cream pie and a pineapple ambrosia, which is a delightful combination of pineapple, oranges and coconut. Grated coconut can also be mixed with yoghurt or soured cream to make a delicious topping for fruit.

Desiccated coconut is delicious in cakes, in biscuits and puddings and it makes a useful quick garnish for fools, creams and gateaux. It can be placed under a hot grill for a few minutes for a pleasant golden brown colour

and delicious 'toasted' flavour. It can also be added to curries or used for making coconut milk (see below).

Coconut milk, cream and oil: coconut milk can easily be made at home. It is added to curries where the flavour but not the texture of coconut is required. To make it, soak the grated flesh of one fresh coconut or 75 g /3 oz desiccated coconut in 600 ml /1 pt boiling water for about 1 hour. Lay a piece of muslin over a bowl and pour in the mixture. Bring the edges of the muslin together and squeeze well. Discard the coconut.

An easier way to make coconut milk is to use coconut cream, which looks like soft white vegetable fat. Add 300 ml /11 fl oz boiling water to 25 g /1 oz coconut cream and stir.

Coconut oil gives a light coconut flavour to vegetables and meat that are stir-fried or sautéed in it. It solidifies to a white mass at room temperature so, before using it, stand the bottle in a bowl of warm water until the oil becomes a light amber liquid.

Brazil nuts

One of the most popular nuts, Brazil nuts grow on tall trees in the jungles of Brazil and Venezuela. They are contained inside a hard,

oval outer shell about the same size as a coconut, but more like an orange in shape. The Brazil nuts — as many as two dozen in their individual shells — are packed in the outer shell in much the same way as orange segments.

The kernels have a creamy flavour and their oily texture makes Brazils exceptionally good for vegetarian nut roasts, cutlets and rissoles; they are also good for stuffing dry meats such as turkey and chicken. Roasted and salted, they are a tasty, nutritious snack. Shave Brazils with a sharp knife into wafer-thin slices and use them to decorate mousses and trifles. Brazil nuts make delicious sweets when they are coated with dark chocolate or butter toffee.

Pistachio nuts

Pistachio nuts are cultivated all round the Mediterranean, in the southern United States and in India.

Buying and preparing pistachio nuts: the light-coloured, oval shells of pistachio nuts split when the nuts are ripe, making it easy to extract the kernel. The kernels are about 1 cm /⅓ in long and bright green in colour, covered by a red-tinged skin. You can buy the nuts in the shell, shelled but not skinned, or shelled and skinned. To get the best combination of convenience and freshness, buy them shelled and unskinned. You

Back row, left to right: unshelled hazelnuts, and Brazil nuts; below: shelled pistachio nuts, hazelnuts, pine kernels, Brazil nuts and peanuts

can also buy salted pistachio nuts, either shelled or in the shell, and these are good to nibble with drinks. Pistachio nuts are usually to be found in Oriental grocery shops or specialty food shops.

To skin pistachio nuts, put them into a shallow pan and cover them with cold water. Bring the water to the boil, drain the nuts and cover them again with cold water. Take them out of the water as you need them and skin them immediately.

Using pistachio nuts: in France and Italy pistachio nuts are added to pâtés, terrines and meat stuffings, as they give a delicate flavour and also enhance the appearance. Make Pork and pistachio pâté (see recipe) for a stylish light lunch or a rather different dinner party starter.

Pistachio nuts are a favourite ingredient in high-class confectionery such as nougat. In the United States pistachio ice cream is very popular. In Turkey pistachio nuts are made into a sweetmeat with almonds and rose-water called *rahat lokum* (Turkish delight). In India they are added to curries and spiced dishes, and are also made into all sorts of delicious sweetmeats.

Pine nuts

Pine nuts or pine kernels are also called Indian nuts, pignolias and pignoli. They are eaten a great deal in the Middle East and are exported mainly by Italy and Spain. They are rather expensive to buy (blanched almonds can be used as a cheaper substitute in some recipes).

Buying pine nuts: pine nuts are about 1 cm / ⅓ in long and shaped like grains of rice, but narrower at one end than the other. They are white or pale cream in colour and fairly soft-textured. As their dark, purplish brown shells have to be cracked by machinery, they are always sold shelled. You can usually find them either in Italian delicatessens or in health food shops.

Using pine nuts: they can be eaten as a snack, either raw or roasted and salted. They are delicious when added to vegetables or rice to make a main course or a side dish and are equally good when scattered over fruit before it is baked, or over raw fruit salads. They can sometimes be bought coated in chocolate.

Hazelnuts

Hazelnuts, cobs and filberts are all descended from the wild hazel, and are small and round with a deep brown skin and a slight point at one end. Cobs are grown commercially only on a small scale. Hazelnuts are much more common.

Chopped hazelnuts are a favourite ingredient in muesli-type breakfast cereals, and whole hazelnuts can be used instead of almonds to make praline (see page 98). Make Hazelnut crunchies (see recipe) for a rich, tea-time treat.

You can occasionally find ground hazelnuts in shops, but it is easy to grind your own in a coffee grinder or blender; mix them into biscuit and pastry doughs, or they can be used in a delicious savoury coating for fish, such as trout or plaice.

A very tasty hazelnut butter (*beurre de noisette*) for garnishing hors d'oeuvres can be

made by pounding lightly roasted hazelnuts and then beating them into twice their own weight of softened butter.

Pecans

Pecans grow in North America. They have a sweetish flavour and are used in cakes and pies, including the American speciality, pecan pie. Try Pecan ice cream (see the recipe overleaf).

Pork and pistachio pâté

2 hours, then overnight pressing

Serves 6–8
450 g /1 lb belly pork, without rind or bones
350 g /12 oz pig's liver
100 g /4 oz streaky bacon, without rind
1 small onion
2 garlic cloves
salt and freshly ground black pepper
50 ml /2 fl oz dry sherry
50 g /2 oz pistachio nuts, shelled
watercress sprigs, to garnish
fresh toast or green salad, to serve

1 Heat the oven to 160C /325F /gas 3. Mince the pork, liver and bacon and onion. Crush the garlic cloves and stir them into the meats. Season with salt and pepper to taste, then stir in the sherry.

Minced pork saté

2 Stir in the nuts then spoon the mixture into an 850 ml /1½ pt loaf tin.
3 Cover the top of the tin with foil and stand it in a roasting tin. Pour in boiling water to come halfway up the sides of the tin.
4 Bake in the oven for 1½ hours. Remove the loaf tin from the pan and loosen the foil. Place a board or plate inside the rim and weight it down. Leave the pâté overnight until it is completely cold. It will keep in the refrigerator for up to a week. Garnish it with sprigs of watercress and serve sliced, with toast or a salad.

Minced pork saté

30 minutes

Serves 4
3 garlic cloves, crushed
1 red chilli, crushed
2.5 ml /½ tsp powdered ginger
5 ml /1 tsp coriander seeds, lightly roasted
  and crushed
5 ml /1 tsp brown sugar
10 ml /2 tsp soy sauce
15 ml /1 tbls tamarind water (see note below)
500 g /1 lb boned leg or fillet of pork with a
  little fat, minced
30 ml /2 tbls grated fresh or desiccated coconut
1 medium-sized egg, beaten
salt

For the santen
60 g /2½ oz desiccated coconut or 25 g /1 oz
creamed coconut, grated

1 First make the santen. If you are using desiccated coconut, soak it in 60 ml /4 tbls hot water for three minutes, squeezing the coconut between the fingers. Strain the liquid through a piece of muslin placed inside a sieve. Twist the muslin to extract all the liquid and discard the coconut. If you are using grated creamed coconut, add 90 ml /6 tbls hot water and stir to dissolve it.
2 Mix the crushed garlic and chilli with the ginger, coriander, sugar, soy sauce and the tamarind water. Stir 2.5 ml /½ tsp of this into the santen. Keep the rest of the mixture cool until you are ready to grill the saté.
3 When ready to grill, mix the remaining spice mixture with the meat and add the fresh or desiccated coconut, the egg, and salt to taste. Shape the meat into small balls about the size of walnuts. Do not thread the balls onto the skewers until the last moment.
4 Heat the grill to medium. Thread the meatballs onto the bamboo or metal skewers and place them under the grill. Cook for 4–5 minutes, turning them from time to time, until the meat is firm. Take the satés from the grill and brush them lightly with the spiced santen. Continue grilling and turning the meat until the balls are golden brown.

● To make tamarind water: Soak 25 g /1 oz tamarind in 275 ml /10 fl oz warm water. Squeeze the tamarind until the water is flavoured and coloured. Strain it before using.

Savoury Brazil croquettes

 1 hour, including cooling

Serves 4
250 g /9 oz shelled Brazil nuts
75 ml /5 tbls sunflower oil
2 medium-sized onions, chopped
1 garlic clove, chopped
125 g /4 oz burghul (cracked) wheat
100 ml /3½ fl oz vegetable stock, home-made
or from a cube
30 ml /2 tbls tomato purée
30 ml /2 tbls chopped fresh parsley
15 ml /1 tbls chopped fresh thyme or 5 ml /
1 tsp dried thyme
15 ml /1 tbls chopped fresh marjoram or 5 ml /
1 tsp dried marjoram
10 ml /2 tsp chopped fresh rosemary or 2.5 ml /
½ tsp dried rosemary

1 Grind the nuts finely in a blender.
2 Heat the oil in a a frying-pan over a low heat. Add the onions and garlic and cook for 2 minutes. Add the wheat and cook, stirring, for 5 minutes. Pour in the stock and simmer, stirring frequently, for 10 minutes.
3 Remove the pan from the heat and mix in the ground nuts, tomato purée and herbs. Allow the mixture to cool for 10 minutes. Heat the oven to 200C /400F /gas 6.
4 Divide the mixture into 12 small balls and bake them for 20 minutes.

Carrot and pine nut tart

Carrots and pine nuts make a light spiced filling for this savoury tart. It is a perfect dish for a vegetarian lunch.

 1 hour 10 minutes

Serves 4–6
500 g /1 lb carrots, thinly sliced
6 medium-sized eggs
5 ml /1 tsp hot Madras curry powder
5 ml /1 tsp cumin seeds
400 g /14 oz made-weight shortcrust pastry
75 g /3 oz pine nuts

1 Heat the oven to 200C /400F /gas 6. Steam the carrots for 20 minutes or until they are tender. Cool them slightly.
2 Beat the eggs with the curry powder and cumin seeds and reserve. Line a 25 cm /10 in flan tin with the pastry.
3 Arrange the carrot slices in overlapping rings in the base of the flan. Scatter the pine nuts over the top and pour in the beaten egg mixture, making sure the pine nuts are evenly distributed.
4 Bake the tart for about 25 minutes or until the filling is set and looks a lovely golden brown.

● Serve it warm, with a crisp green salad and potatoes baked in their jackets.
● Chopped walnuts may be substituted for the pine nuts.

Pasta served with Basil, pine nut and Parmesan sauce

Basil, pine nut and Parmesan sauce

 10 minutes

Serves 4
100 g /4 oz fresh basil leaves
125 ml /4 fl oz olive oil
50 g /2 oz pine nuts
1 garlic clove
15 g /½ oz butter
15 g /½ tsp salt
15 ml /1 tbls fresh parsley leaves
100 g /4 oz freshly grated Parmesan cheese
15 ml /1 tbls yoghurt
freshly ground black pepper
225–275 g /8–10 oz pasta, freshly cooked,
to serve
50 g /2 oz butter, to serve

1 Discard any discoloured basil leaves. Wash the rest and dry them thoroughly with absorbent paper.
2 Combine the basil leaves, the olive oil, pine nuts, garlic, butter, salt and parsley in a blender or a food processor. Blend until the mixture is creamy. Fold in the Parmesan cheese and yoghurt, season with pepper to taste and mix thoroughly.
3 To serve, transfer the freshly cooked pasta to a warm bowl and add the sauce, 45–60 ml /3–4 tbls of the pasta cooking water and the butter. Mix thoroughly and serve at once.

● This sauce is known as pesto in Italy.
● Pesto freezes well if you omit the cheese and garlic and then add them when the sauce is thawed, just before serving.

Pecan ice cream

🍴 5½–6½ hours,
including freezing

Serves 6
700 ml /1¼ pt thick cream
1 vanilla pod
75 g /3 oz Barbados sugar
100 g /4 oz shelled pecan nuts, chopped
4 egg yolks

1 Put the cream into a saucepan with the vanilla pod, cover and set over a low heat. Simmer for 10 minutes but do not allow it to boil. Strain the cream into a bowl and cover it with dampened greaseproof paper to prevent a skin forming.
2 Put the sugar into a small, heavy-based saucepan with 125 ml /4 fl oz water. Stir over a low heat until the sugar has completely dissolved and then boil the syrup for 10 minutes. Remove it from the heat and stir in the pecans.
3 Beat the egg yolks until they are lightly coloured and frothy. Pour the syrup into the yolks, beating hard, with an electric beater if you have one. Continue beating until thick; mix in the cream.
4 Pour the mixture into a container and leave it until it is cold.
5 When it is cold, put the cream mixture

Decorated Brazil nut cake

into the coldest part of the freezer or the freezer compartment of the refrigerator at the coldest setting. Leave until it is frozen around the sides and slushy in the centre (this takes about 2 hours).
6 Transfer the mixture to a bowl and beat it until it is frothy. Return to the freezer and leave it until it is completely frozen.
7 Remove the ice cream and leave it at room temperature for 45 minutes; serve.

● This ice cream will keep for up to 2 months in the freezer or up to 2 weeks in the freezer compartment of the refrigerator.

Brazil nut cake

The Brazil nuts pulverize easily in an electric coffee mill, food processor or blender. In Brazil this cake is known as *Torta de castanhas-do-para*.

🍴 1 hour

Serves 8–10
100 g /4 oz self-raising flour
100 g /4 oz sugar
a pinch of salt
250 g /8 oz Brazil nuts, finely ground
250 g /8 oz stoned dates, finely chopped
15 ml /1 tbls fresh root ginger, finely chopped
4 medium-sized eggs, lightly beaten
butter, for greasing

1 Heat the oven to 180C /350F /gas 4. Sift the flour, sugar and salt into a large bowl. Add the nuts, dates and ginger and mix lightly. Fold in the eggs. Mix thoroughly.
2 Butter a 1½ L /2½ pt loaf tin and pour in the mixture. Bake on the middle shelf of the oven for 1½ hours or until the top is lightly browned. Cool slightly before turning onto a rack to finish cooling.
3 Serve sliced and buttered as a tea bread.

● This cake can also be used as the base for desserts. Mask it with whipped cream and garnish it with fruit such as strawberries and sliced peaches (see picture). The cake may also be halved and filled with cream, then masked with cream and garnished with fresh or canned fruit.

Hazelnut crunchies

These rich, nutty chocolate-coated biscuits can be served at tea-time or, alternatively, with coffee after dinner.

🍴 1 hour

Makes 20
75 g /3 oz butter
75 g /3 oz Demerara sugar
100 g /4 oz shelled hazelnuts, finely chopped
50 g /2 oz glacé cherries, quartered
25 g /1 oz candied peel, finely chopped
butter, for greasing
200 g /7 oz plain chocolate

1 Heat the oven to 180C /350F /gas 4. Melt the butter and sugar together in a saucepan and bring them gently to the boil, stirring constantly.
2 Remove the pan from the heat and stir in the hazelnuts, cherries and candied peel.
3 Cover 2 baking sheets with buttered greaseproof paper. Place 10 ml /2 tsp portions of the mixture, well apart, on the baking sheets and flatten them slightly.
4 Bake for 10 minutes. The mixture will spread considerably, so cut each biscuit into a perfect round with a 7.5 cm /3 in biscuit cutter while they are still warm and flexible. Cool the biscuits slightly, then, with a palette knife, lift them from the sheets and lay them, smooth side up, on a clean sheet of greaseproof paper.
5 Break up the chocolate and put it in the top part of a double boiler or a bowl set over a pan of hot, not boiling, water. Melt the chocolate over a low heat.
6 Using a pastry brush, brush a thin layer of melted chocolate over the smooth side of each biscuit. Leave to set, and keep the remaining chocolate warm.
7 Brush the remaining chocolate all over the chocolate side of the biscuits to make a thicker layer and leave until completely set.

● These crunchies are well worth the effort to make them. Since they look and taste so special they are ideal to wrap and pack in a decorative box in order to give as an unusual present.
● Almonds could be used instead of the hazelnuts in this recipe.

Index